Move to Greatness

*"**Move to Greatness** is a must-read! Its insight into the patterns of our energy represents a major breakthrough. This work is both original and immensely practical."*

—Jim Loehr, Ed.D., CEO Human Performance Institute, best-selling author of *The Power of Full Engagement*

"Finally, a tool and approach that makes intuitive, practical, and theoretical sense. The leadership and behavior patterns can be quickly grasped and easily applied, and as a result facilitate communication, self-acceptance, and the honoring of differences."

—David Dotlich, Ph.D., president, Oliver Wyman Executive Learning Center, author of *Why CEOs Fail, Unnatural Leadership,* and *Head, Heart, and Guts*

"Teams need more than wisdom about individual behaviors; they need the ability to act on those behavioral patterns to coalesce around unique individual strengths. Having followed—and professionally and personally benefited from—Ginny's practice for almost a decade, I can say unequivocally that the energy patterns are a most powerful concept: simply elegant, elegantly simple. And it works!"

—Rebecca S. Barna, former publisher, *Popular Science*

"Ginny Whitelaw's classes on the energy patterns are a vital component of our Columbia Senior Executive Program, where our objective is to create a learning community that harnesses the power of the 'whole leader.' "

—Schon Beechler, Ph.D., former faculty director, Columbia University's Senior Executive Program

"In her work as in her life, Ginny shows you how to find your way of practice."

—Dr. Gordon Hakuun Greene Roshi

"Ginny offers a much-needed bridge across the chasm between our wanting to change and our being able to make that change."

—Elizabeth Harper Neeld, Ph.D., author of *Seven Choices*

"In finding a balance that I cannot easily be swept from, Ginny's approach and coaching have helped me become dependably effective in the changes I face . . . with my team and with my family."

—Wil Wilhelm, Egon Zehnder International

"Ginny's work with the energy patterns is bringing a new dimension and depth to leadership programs."

—Stephen Rhinesmith, Ph.D.,
author of *A Manager's Guide to Globalization*

"Watching how easily, organically, and rapidly Ginny got 50 business coaches to each discover and fully express their individual ways of being was unforgettable. Ginny's workshop on the four patterns became the most talked about in the conference, as one that had most contributed to people's deeper understanding of self. Both spiritually and practically, Ginny is helping me vastly expand the depth and range of my work with global executives."

—Agnes Mura, director,
Professional Coaches and Mentors Association

Move to Greatness

*Focusing the Four Essential Energies
of a Whole and Balanced Leader*

Ginny Whitelaw

and

Betsy Wetzig

NICHOLAS BREALEY
INTERNATIONAL

BOSTON • LONDON

First published Nicholas Brealey International,
a division of Nicholas Brealey Publishing, in 2008.

Nicholas Brealey International, a division
  of Nicholas Brealey Publishing
20 Park Plaza, Suite 1115A
Boston, MA 02116, USA
Tel: + 617-523-3801
Fax: + 617-523-3708

Nicholas Brealey Publishing
3–5 Spafield Street, Clerkenwell
London, EC1R 4QB, UK
Tel: +44-(0)-207-239-0360
Fax: +44-(0)-207-239-0370

www.nicholasbrealey.com

Focus Energy Balance Indicator,™ FEBI™ & mini-FEBI™ are trademarks of Focus Leadership.

Coordination Patterns™ is a trademark of Besty Wetzig.

The mini-FEBI is © Focus Leadership, 2007. Used with permission.

Pattern landscape illustrations by Diane Chencharick, 2007

Printed in the United States of America

11 10 09 08   2 3 4 5

ISBN-13: 978-1-904838-20-3
ISBN-10: 1-904838-20-0

Library of Congress Cataloging-in-Publication Data

Whitelaw, Ginny.
  Move to greatness : focusing the four essential energies of a whole and balanced leader / Ginny Whitelaw and Betsy Wetzig.
    p. cm.
1. Leadership. I. Wetzig, Betsy. II. Title.

  HM1261.W485 2008
  158'.4—dc22

2007041495

To
Mark Kiefaber (a Collaborator putting up with a Driven Organizer)
and
John Wetzig (an Organizer putting up with a Driven Visionary)
Bless their hearts!

Contents

the driver

:-)

Drives for results
Challenges barriers
Loves to win
Gets to the point

:-(

Wins at all costs
Blows up
Gets impatient
Runs over people

**Leverage your
strengths, balance
your weaknesses –
Take a FREE pattern
test at:**

www.MoveToGreatness.com

the collaborator

:-)

Engages people
Has fun
Rolls with the punches
Sees both sides

:-(

Waffles on decisions
Gets too political
Not taken seriously

**Leverage your
strengths, balance
your weaknesses –
Take a FREE pattern
test at:**

www.MoveToGreatness.com

Acknowledgments

GINNY ACKNOWLEDGES . . .

I thank Mark Kiefaber, my terrific, Collaborator husband and partner, for being such a big part and promoter of this work, especially the FEBI research. Thanks to my muses: Holly Kerby and Libby Koponen for all the ways they "pushed without pushing" and helped me find my own expression of these patterns. And to my sister-muse, Diane Chencharick, for telling it like it was, especially when it got better, and for her wonderful, whimsical drawings of the pattern landscapes. My thanks to John, Betty, and Larry Whitelaw, Jean and Mike Lane, Mary Jane Kiefaber, and Julie Scher for their great support, humor and stories, some of which made it onto these pages.

My thanks to colleagues who were early supporters and beta testers of the patterns, who put up with my earliest efforts and encouraged all that followed: Virginia McLaughlin, Susan Dunn, Ron Meeks, Lars Cederholm, Carole France, Steffie Armontrout, Kathleen Hoogerhuis, Agnes Mura, John Heinritz, Cheryl Green, Anne Miller, Gyongyi Kallai, Schon Beechler, and Paul Connolly. Thanks to Bob Caron (and his dojo!) for being so much a part of the FEBI research and future. I'd especially like to thank David Dotlich, Steve Rhinesmith, and Peter Cairo of the Executive Learning Center for offering their considerable resourcefulness and launching the patterns to a level that would never have been possible without them.

My thanks to the terrific clients who have allowed me to step into their lives and from whom I've learned so much. (Don't worry; I haven't used your real names unless I asked you.) Special thanks to long-term supporters and early adopters of the patterns: Yolanda Hofer, Gigi Antoni, Melody Timinsky, and Lennart Rohlin.

Thanks to Everett Ogawa and Ximena Prudencio for teaching me new ways to work with the body. Finally, I thank my remarkable teachers: Fumio Toyoda, who was the greatest leader I ever followed, Hosokawa Roshi, the embodiment of Zen, and Tanouye Rotaishi—sliced by your Driver's sword; so grateful for the clean cut.

BETSY ACKNOWLEDGES . . .

A special thanks to Sally Fitt, who introduced me to the neuromuscular tension patterns and the work of Josephine Rathbone and Valerie Hunt. Thanks to all the dancers who worked with me and shared their expertise as I explored the patterns, especially Art Bauman, Judy Lasko, Evelyn Shepard, Meryl Green, Linda McAndrew, Kedzie Penfield, Peggy Hackney, and Carol Welton Kelly.

To Laban Movement analyzers Peter Madden and Carol Cassio, a special thanks for working with me on the correlation of the patterns to movement. Thanks, too, to Carroll Bouman, Joyce P. Dohaney, Carl Michaelson, Dick Barnett, and Sarah Lavelle, who supported my earliest investigations of the patterns.

A great thanks is due to Alex Lotas and Elsie Ritzenheim, who worked with me on how the patterns function in learning and creativity. I also thank Patricia Pinciotti, who worked with me developing Full Potential Learning, and Joyce Mumford, who has supported my work in education and beyond.

I thank the many psychologists who have also given me important insights into the patterns, especially James Stohl, Laurel Leland, Nancy Miller, and Marylyn Mussomeli. And finally, thanks to the many body workers and movement trainers who have helped me further develop exercises for the patterns: Gene Miller, Mark Stahley, Jean Hopkins, Tracey Epting, and especially Carole Amend.

Betsy and I would like to thank our publisher, Patricia O'Hare, for believing in this project, and the great staff at Nicholas Brealey Publishing for bringing it to light. And thanks to the most persevering of agents, Michael and Pat Snell, for seeing this project to a happy ending.

INTRODUCTION

Your Guide to the Patterns

In these pages you'll discover your patterns of personality and how to move yourself toward the greatness of a whole and balanced life. Are you already wondering if you have time for it? If so, this book is for you. The patterns you learn about in this book will give you your time, indeed your life, back. I, too, have spent many a day caught in the hamster wheel of an endless to-do list, feeling relentless pressure to get a program designed, follow up with clients, race to the airport, return calls on a cutting-out mobile phone, hit the ground running to deliver a program, and catch up on e-mail, as I'm interrupted by a pop-up window reminding me that I forgot to block pop-ups. It's easy to blame the world for speeding up. But the truth of the hamster wheel is that it's ultimately driven by the hamster. In this book, you'll learn that the patterns of drive and discipline are only half your story. In uncovering the other half, you'll become wholly effective.

Perhaps you recoil from all that drive and discipline, or wish you had more of it. Maybe people and relationships are what you're about, or your leaping imagination is always taking you in new directions. In these patterns of engagement and ideas, it can be a struggle to simply take care of the practicalities of everyday life. Imagine the possibilities if you could balance dreaming things up with nailing things down.

The fact is that most of us have barriers of one sort or another. They show up in the ineffective "buts" in leadership style ("She's great at making the numbers, *but* hard on people") and in deeply felt personal needs ("He's successful at work, *but* he lacks balance"). These barriers originate in our use (and misuse) of four fundamental patterns in the nervous system. Once we know these patterns, we can learn to use them appropriately. Taken together, these patterns create wholly effective leaders; used appropriately, they engender unshakable balance. Leaders today need both. And by "leaders" I mean not only those at the top of an organization, but people at any level with active intention and influence. Kevin Cashman offers a suitably broad definition of leadership as: "authentic self expression that adds value."

Authenticity is key. While this book shows you how you can move to a greater wholeness and balance in your life and work, at no point will it suggest you do anything that is not 100 percent You. This book is about reclaiming your whole self, not trying to be all things to all people. You'll find that you already have everything you need to be whole and balanced. Some of it may be buried treasure, but you've got it. Once you understand what it can do for you—and how to uncover it—you won't have to keep struggling without it, which allows you to add your greatest value. Knowing and using the patterns, you'll be able to do excellent things the easiest way, to clear barriers and get things done.

Running through your nervous system are four essential energy patterns that manifest in every movement, thought, feeling, and action—from how you get out of bed in the morning to how you interact with colleagues. These patterns function mentally, physically, and through your whole behavior as they're based in the primary neuromuscular link of mind and body

The Driver pushes into every barrier with speed, directness, and intensity.

The Organizer does the right thing, putting every thought and action into its proper place, with discipline and order.

The Collaborator swings into playful engagement with life and the people in it.

The Visionary goes with the flow, hangs out in the chaos, and leaps to new possibilities.

Each pattern has its own way of moving, talking, playing, and even getting into trouble. Activate the movement of a particular pattern and you access the feelings, thoughts, and behaviors that go with it. For example, if you sit forward in your chair and jab a finger at someone to make your point, you engage the pattern of the Driver. You might notice that you start talking faster and more emphatically as you feel a greater sense of urgency to make your point! By contrast, if you lean back in your chair and gaze out the window, you'll enter the drifting expansiveness of the Visionary where you might chill a bit. Here you sense a bigger picture and ideas may pop in from left field.

While you have access to all four of these patterns, some will be more comfortable for you than others. Those that have become the dominant patterns of your personality (and in this book, you'll discover which ones those are) will be easier for you to use. But keep in mind that you fully own all four patterns. You're able to move to greatness by not only winning with your strengths but also being able to call up any pattern—if only as a bit player—when you need it. Once you learn this for yourself, your life and leadership rises to a new level of ease and effectiveness, and your whole and balanced acts will be positively contagious to those around you.

Peter Drucker once said, "Your first and foremost job as a leader is to take charge of your own energy, and then to orchestrate the energy of those around you." But how? If we're good at details but miss the big picture, how do we access the energy of a strategic thinker? How, if we're great on ideas, but can't manage a plan to save our soul, do we find the Organizing energy of a skilled project manager? If we're exhausted by the endless treadmill, how do we renew ourselves and find energy for our people, our families, and our*selves*? The key is this: you can *move* there. This book will show you how.

My Journey to the Patterns

These patterns have been intuited for ages and have been scientifically known since the 1930s. But it was coauthor Betsy Wetzig, after decades of developing ways to work with these patterns, who brought that knowledge to me. While you'll be hearing my voice throughout the book, since I work with leaders every day using these patterns, Betsy's research and wisdom inform every one of these pages.

I had always been intrigued by body-mind connections, first as a biophysicist studying energy and development in the nervous system and later as an aikido and Zen practitioner. As a senior manager at NASA I was exposed to excellent leadership training, yet it dealt with leadership only from the neck up, as if leadership style and effectiveness were simply a matter of putting one's mind to it. Even the personality tests that we took as part of the training failed to consider the body. Yet I knew from years of teaching aikido and Zen that training the body was key to training the mind. I would watch my aikido students progress from stiff and brittle beginnings to learning (quite literally) to roll with the punches and become more resilient, traits they took back to their life and work. I knew there had to be a more integrated view of personality and a more holistic way of developing leaders.

There was and there is. Betsy called them Coordination Patterns™ because they describe how opposing muscle groups are coordinated in motion and also how motion, emotion, thoughts, and actions function together. Learning about the patterns was like finding a missing map that connected movement, mindset, and behavior. Suddenly, I understood why people like my conscientious aikido student Tom, a strong Organizer, had such perfect form but struggled with speed. He was too slow not only on the mat, but also in running his business. Suddenly, I understood why a leader like Dan Goldin, a Visionary, never stopped moving or dreaming up new ideas but struggled to get NASA's Organized engineers moving with him.

Using the patterns as a map, you too will come to understand people more easily and more deeply, and will see how to lead them more effectively. Moreover, you'll learn how to move yourself to your greatest potential—not just struggle to put your mind to it, but *move* there. In mapping the vital links between inner condition and outward behaviors, the patterns go beyond providing simply another four-square model and instead provide a view into the whole leader. The four fundamental energy patterns give you a way to reclaim your whole self.

Your Journey through the Patterns

Learning the patterns is a journey of several stages. The first stage is **recognition**, seeing the patterns in yourself and others. In chapter 1 you'll become more familiar with the patterns and start to recognize them in yourself, in others, and in work situations you face every day. You might even guess which patterns are your favorite, though in chapter 2 you can move beyond guesswork. By taking an abbreviated version of the Focus Energy Balance Indicator (FEBI™), included in this chapter, you'll get a sense of which patterns are your favorites and which might be your "bit players."

Most people hang out in this "Aha!" stage of recognizing the patterns for some time—from a few hours to a few months. Take your time. If you learn nothing more from this book than simply to recognize these patterns in yourself and others, you'll find it richly rewarding and validating.

As you venture onward, you'll enter the second stage, seeing the **limitations** of overdoing favorite patterns or under-using weaker ones. You'll discover both strengths and limitations as chapters 3 through 6 dive deeper into each of the patterns, providing stories of leaders, teams, and companies that exemplify the patterns at their best and worst. You will likely recognize yourself in some of the stories and come to appreciate the strengths of patterns used well and the limitations of patterns misapplied. These chapters will also give you countless ideas on how to focus these pattern energies in you.

Chapter 7 gives you the opportunity to enter the third stage, finding **freedom** to move toward any pattern you'd like. Just as with working the biceps, exercising the "muscles" of patience, influence, or lateral thinking makes them stronger and easier to use. You'll learn how to design an on-the-job practice to uncover any pattern you'd like to develop. You'll also learn how to support it from inside out—using the body—either through movement (the best!) or by engaging your senses (the easiest!). You'll see how to tailor your practice so that it doesn't rely on extra time (for those of you who have none) or relentless discipline (for those of you who have little). Moreover, you'll learn how to use your strongest patterns to develop weaker ones.

To welcome you to this new freedom of movement, we'll also show you several ways to apply it to your leadership. Chapter 8 explores whole and balanced approaches to communicating effectively, influencing others, and handling conflict. Chapter 9 gives you ideas for expanding your freedom of movement to the teams and organizations you're a part of. Finally, chapter 10 shows you how to continue your move to greatness in both your inner journey and your outward life.

In your own journey to find your patterns, I hope that the promises of this book become your own genuine experience, that you do, in fact, uncover and appropriately focus the four essential energies of your whole and balanced team. You'll find that it awakens your full energy, inspires peak performance in yourself and others, and lets you enjoy the wholeness and balance that is your work at its best, your life at its fullest!

CHAPTER ONE

Enter the Patterns

AN OPENING TOUR

Charge first into the Driver pattern—full speed ahead! Sit forward in your chair and bore your eyes into this page as though, like lasers, they could burn a hole through it. You might notice a sense of urgency (and blood pressure!) rising as your reading voice CLIMBS TO THE SHOUT OF A BATTLE CRY!

Too hot? Take a deep, slow breath and sit back, still straight in your chair with your feet flat on the floor, and place yourself squarely in the Organizer pattern. Hold this book for a moment at chest level, as if it were a choir book, and invite a moment of order and composure.

> *"Nothing happens until something moves."*
> —*Albert Einstein*

Too slow? Swing into the pattern of the Collaborator, which you can roll into by rocking in your chair—side to side, back and forth—letting your head go as well. Perhaps you notice a loosening feeling from the belly up, a great starting point for playing with the give and take of relationships or rolling with the punches.

Too silly? Let go and lean back in your chair, letting your eyes drift up to the ceiling; allow your peripheral vision to engage, seeing the whole room at once and nothing in particular. You're hanging out in the pattern of the Visionary.

Too pointless? Go back to the Driver, and already you might notice a complementary relationship among these four distinct patterns. Taken together and used appropriately, they allow us to be whole and balanced. While they start as inner movements in our nervous system, they show up as outer movements in the world: in how we communicate, organize our time, make decisions, handle conflict, lead teams, manage our lives, and run companies. Those who learn to recognize and skillfully use these

> *We are moved to greatness by knowing and skillfully using all four essential patterns.*

The move to greatness is a journey of three stages:

- *Recognition Seeing the patterns in ourselves and others*
- *Limitations Seeing how suboptimal use of the patterns hurts us*
- *Freedom Moving into a pattern we want easier access to; using any pattern as it's appropriate*

patterns move themselves to greatness—that is, to their greatest capacity and sustaining renewal.

THE WAY TO BALANCE

Even if they don't all mean the same thing by "balance," virtually every leader I talk to hungers for more of it. When I teach people about the energy patterns, I often start by asking them to reflect on how balanced their lives are. I read off a list of 10 symptoms of imbalance—frenetic energy, difficulty sleeping, health problems, and so on—and have them mark which symptoms apply. "By show of hands, how many have 10 tick marks?" I ask at the end. A few hands go up. "Nine? Eight?" By "five" every hand in the room has been raised. Numerous studies confirm this growing sense of imbalance and the desire for greater balance. In a recent Fortune 500 survey, 84 percent of the executives said they would like a greater balance in their life and work, and nearly all (98 percent) are sympathetic to such requests from their employees.[1]

Most of these leaders feel caught up in the familiar bind of having to do more with less. They can't keep up the way they used to, but the demands on them—especially if they've been successful and given more responsibility—continue to increase. "No matter how well you did last year, do more this year," they're told. As the pace gets faster, they find themselves juggling more meetings, more e-mail, more travel, more people to support, serve, or report to, more competing demands, more uncertainty, more, more, more. What driven people tend to do when work speeds up is to speed up with it, which keeps them stuck in the Driver pattern until they're driving themselves and everyone around them toward exhaustion.

This book provides the map to four essential energies that, used appropriately, provide balance and, taken together, create whole leaders.

The Pitfalls of Balancing Time

When I ask people what they could do to bring better balance into their lives, they generally talk about leaving work at a certain time or keeping weekends free for family. In other words, they start with their calendar and ways of allocating their time. This approach doesn't work too well for a couple of reasons. First, it's hard to stick to, especially for people who are caught up in Drive and are ambitiously, urgently filling their lives trying to meet more demands. The way we run our day on the outside is characteristic of the patterns we most commonly use on the inside. Trying to find balance by making changes only to our schedule is, in a sense, working too far upstream.

I came across a great example of this in an article that contrasted the daily schedules of several CEOs.[2] At one extreme was "The Overtime Guy," Brett Yorkmark, CEO of the Nets basketball team. He's up before 4:00 A.M., drives a fast car to work, races through e-mail, works out, makes deals ("Everything is a chance to drive revenue," he tells his staff)—meets, greets, schmoozes all the way to and through a Nets game (victory!), driving himself through another 19-hour day.

Jim Buckmaster, the CEO of Craigslist.org, anchored the other end of the spectrum with his eight-hour-or-so workday spent mostly on the Web, a Blackberry beneath his thumbs and a keen intuition working away; his day is bracketed by chill time. Jim's schedule would be inconceivable to a Driver like "Overtime" Brett. The pacing, appointments, surprises (are we even open to them?), and stresses of our day already contain so many conscious and less-than-conscious choices about Things That Matter. Trying to change our day on the outside without changing our internal patterns is deeply disquieting. People like Brett feel like they're slacking when they cut back their hours, and without accessing counterbalancing patterns on the inside—the playful Collaborator or chill-time Visionary in Brett's case—they don't stick with it for long.

That's not to say Jim has balance and Brett doesn't, for balance is more subtle than hours in a workday, which is the second reason that a time-managed approach to balance doesn't work very well: appropriating hours is not really the point. The point, rather, is to have the energy to perform at our best without burning out, to engage our lives fully, give of our gifts, and renew ourselves as we go. Balance is a matter of managing energy rather than time. We can allocate hours to our family, for example, but if we're anxious about work and not really present, the time neither balances nor renews us— and our family picks up on our anxiety as well. Time is wasted or wisely spent depending on our energy. Energy is what matters and energy turns into things that matter. This is as true in our own life as in our impact on others; as Drucker reminds us, managing energy *is* our fundamental job as leaders.

Spotlights: Brett Yorkmark and Jim Buckmaster

Spotlight #1: Brett Yorkmark, CEO, Nets Basketball

Quotes: *"Everything is a chance to drive revenue." "I just love what I do. If you want to get everything in, it takes time."*

Workday: *19 hours.*

Expressed Profile: highly charged Driver, with an Organizer assist

versus

Spotlight #2: Jim Buckmaster, CEO, Craigslist

Quote: *"I'm very fortunate. Managing Craigslist is a job that's full of the unexpected, very colorful and almost always fun."*

Workday: *Around eight hours, though hard to say when it starts and stops.*

Expressed Profile: A Visionary–Collaborator, open to surprises and fun.

"Balance mastery . . . is a dynamic reconciliation of extremes . . . a centered fluidity that lets us go in any direction with ease and agility."

—*Kevin Cashman*

Yerkes–Dodson Curve (1909)

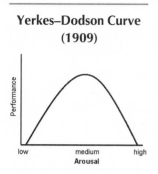

Research on the relationship between stress (arousal) and performance shows an optimal midpoint.

Energy Is Best Managed with a Pulse

Fortunately, a good deal is known about how to take charge of our energy and manage it well. More than 100 years of research tells us that, up to a point, energy rises to a challenge.[3] Too little challenge or stress and we rust out: we never reach all that we're capable of. But too much stress and we burn out. In between lies an optimal balance of our best sustainable performance. Moreover, this balance is not achieved by working our guts out for 50 weeks a year and then expecting a two-week blowout vacation to renew us. That's the absolute worst way to manage our energy, as it allows all the stress-induced hormones our body manufactures to wreak their internal havoc most of the time.

Rather, energy is best managed in bite-sized chunks. Jim Loehr and Tony Schwartz, in their terrific book, *The Power of Full Engagement*, show that optimal, sustainable performance "requires cultivating a dynamic balance between expenditure of energy (stress) and renewal of energy (recovery)." It calls for alternating drive and recovery. Pushing and then renewing. Stretching to our limits and then resting. Finding this rhythm between pushing ourselves and then recovering is also the way we grow. As Loehr and Schwartz continue, "The key to expanding capacity is to both push beyond one's ordinary limits and to regularly seek recovery, which is when growth actually occurs."

So the real question of balance for Brett or Jim or you or me is not "How many hours do you work?" but "Are you performing at your best and can you keep up this pace?" Sustainable growth, peak performance, and ongoing renewal are possible only when we manage our energy with a pulse, only when we're able to move in and out of drive. In the most physical, practical sense, this calls for moving between the Driver pattern (pushing) and the other patterns that allow recovery by quieting down (Organizer), playing (Collaborator), or letting go (Visionary). Stretching to our limits could also involve moving into a pattern that's uncomfortable for us—which takes a good deal of energy—and then renewing ourselves by returning to our most comfortable, or Home, pattern.

From waking and sleeping to inhaling and exhaling to our very heartbeat, we run on a pulse. Likewise, managing our energy with a rhythm of drive and recovery is the key to performance and balance.

As for Overtime Brett, maybe he's doing just fine; maybe he's finding small ways to recover during his day and his pace is a perfectly matched pulse of drive and renewal. But the breathless evidence would suggest otherwise; we might guess that Brett is in over-Drive and eventually will either learn balance or pay a price for the lack of it.

The stakes for balance are high; the alternatives are suboptimal performance, lack of growth, exhaustion, even illness and injury. The way to balance is to dynamically manage our energy. And the way to manage our energy is, fundamentally, at the source, using the four essential energies.

THE WAY TO WHOLENESS

The way to wholeness through the patterns is the process of discovering and reclaiming the depth and breadth of who we are. Depth is connecting what we do with who we are, making our actions on the outside an authentic expression of who we are on the inside. Breadth is the versatility to handle whatever life throws at us and still add our value.

Leading with Authentic Depth

Let's consider depth first. Kevin Cashman, founder and president of Leader-Source, who studied what it takes for good athletes to reach greatness, came to two conclusions that apply more generally to moving to greatness. First, the athletes had to be in the right game. It had to be *their* game, a game for which they had abundant talent and passion. Second, they had to practice, practice, practice. The best basketball players were first to the court in the morning and the last to leave at night, practicing 2,500 jump shots a day, so strong was their passion and so high were their standards.

Being great in our own game—whether it's sports or leadership—is only possible when outside matches inside, that is, when our actions are an authentic expression of who we are and what we're feeling on the inside. We may be able to perform acceptably well when we're motoring through on the surface, such as making social chitchat with our colleagues when we'd rather be analyzing sales figures. But if we want to become great at engaging people so deeply that we can get them moving with us, we have to feel it on the inside. A perfunctory surface act might get us to good, but only when our whole being shows up do we move to greatness.

The four energy patterns show us exactly how to make this inside-out connection. To picture this more easily, we can think of our inner condition as a pyramid of levels, borrowing a model from Loehr and Schwartz.[4] At the base is our physical condition. Riding on top of that is an emotional state, a mental state, and finally what we might call a spiritual orientation, in other words, a sense of purpose or connectedness beyond our ego. Our greatest actions—the equivalent of "our game"—arises from a deep alignment through all of these

The Four Levels of Being

Our most purposeful and powerful actions arise from alignment through all of these levels.

levels. And the patterns connect the dots; they show us exactly where we need to move on the inside to act in specific ways on the outside with excellence and ease.

I've come to think of these patterns as energy that manifests in different but related ways at every level within us, in accordance with the nature of each level. For example, physical muscle mass is different from the electricity of mental thought, but the same energy can infuse both. As an analogy, imagine a sandy-bottom lake. The energy of the lake manifests in the water as waves and in the sandy bottom as ripples. The ripples and waves aren't identical because sand is different from water but they are linked by common energy.

Similarly, the four essential energies in us show up in the different levels or aspects of who we are. Driver energy, for example, shows up physically as pushing or thrusting. Emotionally it emerges as a sense of urgency and intensity. Mentally it manifests as sharply focused, challenging thoughts. Its spiritual dimension is based around accomplishing a mission. Driver actions are typically fast and focused on winning. Leaders who want to be excellent at winning on the outside need to be able to find the Driver's push on the inside.

Likewise, all of the patterns link through all of these levels. Physical endurance—brought to you by Organizer energy—feeds emotional stability, which ties to rigorous mental discipline and doing the right thing in the largest sense of "rightness." Physical resilience—courtesy of the Collaborator—is connected to optimism and the ability to bounce back emotionally, which ties to the mental ability to find another way or see both sides, and ultimately to be happy and spread happiness to others. Visionary energy reveals itself physically as extended, flexible movements, which feed emotional openness and mental curiosity and tie to a broad sense of purposefulness. Table 1-1 traces all of the patterns through these levels of being and doing, and further into ways they manifest in the world of work. While we may be able to perform the leadership behaviors associated with any of the patterns with surface-level goodness, we are moved to greatness through the inward integration of body, mind, and spirit when all of these levels line up and passion and purpose infuse our actions.

Philanthropist John Wood, known for "leaving Microsoft to change the world,"[5] wonderfully exemplifies this integrated quality of leading on purpose. Founder of Room to Read, he was consumed with the mission to build libraries and schools, first in Nepal and eventually throughout Asia. He brought unstoppable drive and singular focus to this mission, built on a passion for books and a mountain of empathy for children without access to them. Indeed,

TABLE 1-1. Examples of the Energy Patterns at Every Level

	Driver	*Organizer*	*Collaborator*	*Visionary*
Coordination Pattern Name	Thrust	Shape	Swing	Hang
Physical	Pushing, thrusting	Holding form, posture perfect	Swinging, rocking	Hanging, drifting, extending
Emotional	Urgent, abrupt, assertive, quick to anger	Composed, calm, placid, tendency to worry	Optimistic, warm, interactive, resilient	Open, detached, spontaneous, being one with
Mental	Sharply focused, calculating, competitive	Linear, logical, step-by-step, do the right thing	One thing leads to another, stories, humor, sees both sides	Leaps to new insight, gets to essence
Spiritual	Accomplish the mission	Serve a greater good beyond oneself	Spread happiness to others	Manifest essence and purpose in the world
Leadership behaviors	Focus on priorities, action, outcomes, bottom line	Establish orderly processes, clear roles, responsibility	Oriented to customers, employees, loyalty, fun	Create the future, think outside the box
Workplace	Bold, no-frills architecture, cubicles	Orderly; quiet spaces to think. A place for everything	Colorful, common places to gather, exchange ideas	Places to move in, be with others or alone, commune with nature
Work Processes	Minimal, focused on outcomes	Step-by-step, orderly and unambiguous	Practical, oriented toward how people really work	Loose, adjustable to circumstances
Corporate Culture	Winning, competitive, fast, no-nonsense, goal oriented; e.g., "Just Do It"	Stable, dependable, ethical, process oriented; e.g., "Solid as a Rock"	Fun, zany, family oriented, customer oriented; e.g., "the LUV Airline"	Creative, paradigm breaking, problem-solving oriented; e.g., "Invent . . ."

it was through mountain climbing that he was first catalyzed to this mission. An avid marathoner, his considerable physical energy was also evident (and sustained) by his running. Putting this all together in the span of only a few years, Wood's integrated intensity and contagious enthusiasm brought learning opportunities to millions of children.

Conversely, we've all experienced the opposite: the confusion of warring feelings ("On the one hand I want this promotion, on the other hand I don't want the job to eat my life") or failed good intentions ("I try to keep my cool, but I keep losing it!"). As an example, say we're highly focused on results and the bottom line and that's been our winning way as a leader. We may have good intentions to be more supportive of our people, yet somehow find day after day disappearing with one emergency after another, this meeting to race to, that call to make, and no time for career discussions or even to find out what's going on with our people. We tell ourselves that we just don't have time, but if we look more deeply, we'd see there's a pattern to what we never have time for, in this case, developing our people. Our original intention gets vetoed daily because it's not part of the pattern we keep moving in. If we sincerely want to change our outward actions, we have to create alignment on the inside.

Train the Body, Train the Mind

The patterns give us the map and tools to create this deep alignment and become whole in our intention. By physically moving in the pattern that matches the behaviors we want to excel at, we gain easier access to that pattern through all of our levels. The fact that movement can change us on the inside is how habits develop, why rituals matter, why practice makes perfect, and how training in general works. Training the body also trains the mind. Yoga, for example, has been a great spiritual path for more than 5,000 years, as countless people have experienced that flexibility in the body *does* relate to the ability to let go emotionally, to agility of thought, and to openness to transformation, all wonderful Visionary qualities.[6] Yoga comes in many styles and can exercise any of the patterns, but the principle is always the same: changing the body changes the mind, which results in a deeper quality to our actions.

Leading with Essential Breadth

As much as we need the depth of whole leadership to be effective, we need its breadth as well. As Loehr and Schwartz observe, our best sustainable performance "requires strength, endurance, flexibility, and resilience" at every level of being. These four qualities are none other than the four patterns expressed through every level of our being: Driver (strength), Organizer (endurance), Visionary (flexibility), and Collaborator (resilience). We need all of them to be both inwardly at our best and outwardly versatile. We need all of them to be whole.

Just consider the incredibly complex demands placed on leaders today: be firm yet flexible, have a vision of the future yet also execute in the present, hit targets yet also develop people, honor traditions yet also embrace innovation, see multiple sides of an issue and still be able to make a decision, do more with less, and do all of this amidst the constant drubbing of dozens of e-mails and other assorted interruptions.

Not everyone can do this. It requires a great deal of energy. And it calls for a broad, mature mindset that we're all theoretically capable of (and we work mightily in leadership programs to develop!) but not everyone achieves. A recent study done by Mercer Delta and *The Economist* Intelligence Unit interviewed hundreds of senior executives of Global 1000 companies and found that they saw critical leadership shortages in their organizations, with the greatest one being the lack of "whole leaders."

Whole Leaders, Partial Leaders

For individuals, the lack of whole leadership leaves a trail of "buts" that follow them through their career. As in: "Susan is great with the details, *but* she doesn't see the bigger picture." Or "Jim makes war on his numbers, *but* he's killing his people." These comments surface in water cooler conversations, performance reviews, and, if the leaders are fortunate, reach their ears in some form of feedback. While helping leaders make sense of the feedback they've received in leadership programs, I've read hundreds of comments like these. They sound a similar theme: the leader's strengths invariably come out of a different pattern than the weaknesses described in the "but." Being great with details, for example, is the hallmark of the Organizer, but seeing the big picture comes out of the Visionary pattern. Reliably making the numbers is the strength of the Driver and Organizer, but it's the Collaborator pattern that knows how to engage people. A weak pattern becomes our "but."

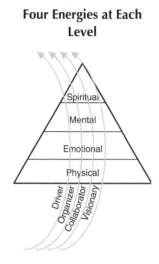

Four Energies at Each Level

Running through each level are four qualities of energy. Each energy pattern characterizes how the levels are interlinked and connected to action; taken together, the four patterns create essential breadth.

Every pattern is essential to a whole leader:

- **Driver:** Focusing attention, hitting targets, breaking down barriers

- **Organizer:** Managing disciplined execution, doing the right thing

- **Collaborator:** Enlisting support, reconciling competing perspectives, developing people

- **Visionary:** Thinking outside the box, being agile and open

While we are wise to leverage our natural preferences in the way we lead, the absence or repeated misuse of any of these four essential energies creates gaps in our leadership. These gaps are quickly exposed under the pressures of leading today. You might recognize some of these:

Not Enough Driver These leaders fail to set clear priorities, maintain focus or a sense or urgency, hit goals, get to the point, or tell it like it is; they're often perceived as lacking clear direction, ambition, or edge.

Not Enough Organizer These Un-Organized leaders have trouble simply getting stuff done. They're unable to break large jobs into executable tasks, deliver on time, do things right, or do the right (e.g., ethical) things; they're often perceived as sloppy and undependable.

Not Enough Collaborator These leaders show an inability to engage with people, see others' points of view, or care about and influence their colleagues. They have trouble seeing both sides of an issue, lightening up, or making work fun; they're often perceived as rigid, insular, and poor team players.

Not Enough Visionary These leaders are often criticized for lacking imagination, failing to see the big picture, or not being strategic. They have trouble thinking outside the box, leaping to novel insights, scanning the horizon for what to pay attention to, or simply letting go and sensing the flow.

Knowing and using patterns, we don't have to be saddled with any of these limitations. Integrating our whole self, we are able to lead at a whole new level.

PATTERNS FROM THE INSIDE OUT

Since nothing happens until something moves, as Einstein once observed, and our movements happen in these patterns, these same four energies are manifest in all that we do and create in the world around us. We can see examples of them at every level of human endeavor from teams and families to art and architecture to work processes and corporate cultures. Buckle your seatbelt—let's start with the Driver.

The Driver

Stab the air with your index finger over and over, like a politician making a point or an angry coach challenging an umpire's decision. Or take your pen and jab a bunch of rapid dots onto a piece of paper. These sharp, thrusting movements bring out the Driver. Direct and aggressive, this is the pathway of people who love to win. Picture a military drill sergeant jabbing his finger at a recruit, "YOU'RE OUT OF LINE!" "DO. YOU. HEAR. ME?!"

The physical foundation of the Driver pattern is to thrust or push.[7] Emotionally, it emerges as a sense of urgency, intensity, impatience, and quickness to anger. Mentally, it manifests in sharply focused, challenging thoughts. Spiritually, the Driver focuses on accomplishing a mission. Driver leaders think and talk fast, as they're constantly pushing against time itself. Often the thoughts of Drivers are critical of others or suspicious of their motives. "Only the paranoid survive," leaders in this mindset might say, as Andy Grove once did. Sports analogies are big with Drivers: "Winning isn't everything, it's the only thing!" as Vince Lombardi summarized this mindset in its extreme. The Driver loves to win, so much so that someone in this pattern may see challenges or pick a fight just for the sake of having something to push against.

Out of this mountain of Driver being, you can well imagine that Driver actions come hard and fast. Driver leaders are great at setting clear priorities, cutting through red tape, keeping a sense of urgency, hitting their targets, keeping score, breaking down barriers, and, of course, winning. Leaders in this pattern—and I'm intentionally describing an extreme—prefer working fast and alone, but will bark out enough orders to give structure to the situation around them.

Relationships between Drivers tend to have a one-upmanship quality to them, although Drivers who respect each other can get on quite well. Teams driven out of this pattern tend to focus on task, set clear goals, divide the work for each to do on his or her own, and measure progress; they generally dismiss team-building activities as "too touchy-feely."

Glance into the office of a Driver. No frills here, as we find her desk clear except for the one thing she wants to focus on. A dashboard of key performance indicators is on the screen of her computer. A few plaques, mounted on the wall, announce past victories.

Driver work processes similarly follow this minimalist theme, and focus on essential outcomes. A Driver-dominated corporate culture pushes itself toward (or others away from) dominant market positions, as in GE's push to be number one or number two in every market it served. Driver companies

The Driver (Thrust)

Gets to the point—fast!

Leadership Strengths:
Maintains speed and sense of urgency, sets clear goals and direction, is sharply focused, competitive, and bottom-line oriented; keeps score and loves to win

The Driver: On the move—straight to the goal

The Organizer (Shape)

Does the right thing step by step

Leadership Strengths:
Breaks big tasks into small ones, systematizes processes, builds quality in, plans the work and works the plan, does things right, stays on task, is efficient, orderly, and rational

tend to be aggressive and acquisitive (think: Mittal Steel). They measure everything, keep score (think: Dell), and cut through the crap to "Just Do It!"

Phew! The Driver pattern is, without a doubt, the accelerator pedal of business. But all engine, all the time is a surefire formula for collision, not to mention exhaustion. Let's take a breath, slow down, and enter our next pattern.

The Organizer

Put your feet together, knees touching, sit up straight, and fold your hands neatly in your lap. Take a couple of quiet breaths and feel the composure settle in. Like Queen Elizabeth II, the Organizer holds perfect form, with "a place for everything, and everything in its place." Taking things one step at a time, the Organizer is great at breaking large tasks into small ones, ticking through a project list, doing the right thing and doing things right.

The physical foundation of the Organizer is to hold shape or form and move, in posture-perfect ways, one step at a time.[8] Picture a wedding party stepping to a wedding march or a graduation ceremony dignified by "Pomp and Circumstance" and you've got the correct regal feel. The emotions of the Organizer are similarly contained, composed, and calm. Mentally, the Organizer manifests as logical, stepwise thought that adds numbers well, follows directions, keeps lists, and knows that if A implies B and B implies C, well then A implies C. As you can imagine, this is a great mind for puzzle solving of a certain type: the Organizer loves a good Sudoku or crossword, or the challenge of balancing a budget or finding the dependencies in a project plan.

Anne Lamott tells the heartwarming story behind the title of her book *Bird by Bird*. Her 10-year-old brother had been given three months to write a paper on birds. The night before it was due, he sat at the kitchen table, surrounded by paper and unopened books on birds, completely overwhelmed by the enormity of his task. How could he do a three-month project in one night?

"Bird by bird, buddy," their father said. "Just take it bird by bird." That quiet, systematic way is the gift of the Organizer.

Spiritually, Organizers want to get it right in the greatest sense of the word, whether that's being ethically right by the highest standards, showing corporate responsibility in the world, or living right by the standards of their religion or spirituality, (e.g., being good in the eyes of God).

In action, Organizers are the relatively predictable and do what they say they will do. They are conscientious and responsible, even to a fault. With their sense of propriety and high standards for what's right, they're a generally self-critical bunch who work hard to get it right, worry about getting it wrong, and will often avoid risk if they aren't sure what the rules are.

Organizers prefer to take their relationships like Anne Lamott's birds: person by person, one at a time. They like one-on-one meetings with direct reports, for example, rather than meeting with a whole group. Teams organized out of this pattern tend to be great at planning their work, tracking their actions, and starting and stopping their meetings on time.

The Organizer: Stays composed and constantly dependable

Step into the office of an Organizer and you'll find a place for everything; it could be featured in an ad for the Container Store. Paper is neatly stacked, files are alphabetical, bookshelves are symmetric, and pencils are in holders. A to-do list with several items carefully checked off is on a sticky note next to the computer.

The Organized leader finds it easy to plan the work of others. In making assignments, she's clear about roles and responsibilities, due dates, and what has to be done in what order. She's a natural at systematizing processes and improving their quality step by step.

Corporate cultures dominated by Organizers tend to get it right. They care deeply about being good corporate citizens, enforcing high standards of quality, working to impeccable ethics, and stating their earnings correctly. They are in the game for the long haul. Organizer companies build their brand around trust and dependability; Johnson & Johnson ("Everything we do must be of high quality . . .") and Merck ("Where patients come first") are two such examples. Merck's legal battles over Vioxx deeply shook the company, but its strategy to tackle each one—lawsuit by lawsuit—reflected its ethical foundation. As CEO Richard Clark was quoted, "We know what we did was right and we're going to be able to defend that."[9]

After stepping carefully among all this order and responsibility, maybe you're ready to break loose and play? Let's roll into the next pattern.

The Collaborator

Move your head or your hips from side to side and let your whole body follow. Feel the loosening in all your joints. You're getting into the swing of the Collaborator, who knows how to roll with the punches and have a good time. When Oprah tilts her head, smiles, and draws people into the discussion, she's using this pattern that loves to engage others.

The Collaborator (Swing)

Plays in the give and take of relationships

Leadership Strengths:
Influencing, networking, team-building, understanding customers, devising pragmatic solutions, working around obstacles, seeing both sides of an issue, using humor, making work fun

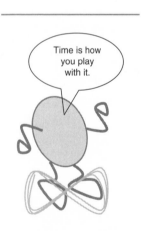

Time is how you play with it.

The Collaborator: Rolls with the punches, finds a way around obstacles

The physical foundation of the Collaborator is back-and-forth, swinging, or what would be more formally called, perceveration.[10] Emotionally, the Collaborator tends to be upbeat and positive, though prone to mood swings. This is a pattern of resilience and bouncing back. Mentally, Collaborators love to think and talk in stories, metaphors, jokes, and tales with a twist, where one thing leads to another and—oh, did you hear the one about? . . .

Why stick to one subject when weaving in and out is so much fun? Fun most certainly catches the attention of the Collaborator. Collaborators can become so engrossed in what they're doing that even work turns into play. In contrast to the well-structured Driver and Organizer, this pattern tends to be messier, if more creative. Collaborators tend to be especially creative around improvising solutions to problems; like water sloshing, they find their way around obstacles. If this doesn't work, try that. If you can't go this way, go that way. Spiritually, Collaborators can become deeply dedicated to others, not so much out of a sense of duty as from their compassion and desire to spread happiness.

The Collaborator's swinging nature also shows up in how they make decisions—and unmake them, and after another conversation, make them again. They similarly engage relationships with a certain ease. They generally read other people well, empathize with their concerns and perspectives, engage them with their contagious optimism, and are often humorous to boot. They can be so people-oriented that they commit to more than they can deliver.

Indeed the Collaborator's life can become as overstuffed and cluttered as his office. We don't find much empty space in the office of a Collaborator. Brightly colored Mylar balloons are still hovering against the ceiling, left over from a celebration last week. Paper, files, CDs, gadgets, half a headset, fast food containers, and his daughter's artwork are strewn across the credenza.

In ways of working, Collaborators are practical and pragmatic; they want to know what really works. They will lay a diagonal sidewalk through a park, knowing that people will cut across the grass if the only sidewalks are square and linear. They have a good sense about what's important to customers and employees, in part because they're constantly engaging people to find out. And they care; they are drawn to the human story.

Corporate cultures owned by Collaborators are relatively under-represented, but stand out for the fun and loyalty they generate among customers and employees alike. Southwest Airlines—ticker symbol LUV—is a great example. From brightly colored planes to joke-cracking, Hawaiian-shirt-wearing cabin crew to practical ways to get people aboard planes to family friendly policies, Southwest has built a fun-loving brand from the Collaborator spirit.

As our tour nears its completion, we're ready to move on to the last essential energy. It's time to drift into the pattern of no-pattern.

The Visionary

Soften your eyes, letting your vision blur ever so slightly as your sense of seeing expands to the very edges of your eyes. Let your arm rise effortlessly, as though it's buoyed by air, and allow your hand to move randomly through space. Feel the movement come from a line running along the back of your arm, spontaneously extending, drifting, changing direction in ways that surprise even you. These extending, drifting motions bring out the Visionary, like a Tai Chi master, open to anything and sensing the flow. The Visionary is the pattern of chaos, of unfolding possibility, imagination, and breakthrough.

The physical foundation of the Visionary is to extend, with a sense of hanging in midair.[11] Picture Michael Jordan in a gravity-defying leap into hang-time before letting the ball just drop in. That sense of effortless extension is the hallmark of the Visionary. But because it's effortless, it may seem uncontrolled and chaotic. At its best, Visionary movement comes from a flow state, a sense of oneness with and functioning within the Way of the Universe.

The Visionary (Hang)
Goes with the flow, is open to new possibility

Emotionally, the Visionary is open and inquisitive. He drifts in and out of emotional contact with others, at times seeming quite detached and other times deeply connected. Mentally, Visionaries think in leaps, as in paradigm-breaking, blue-ocean strategies.[12] They connect the dots—often in novel ways—and discern underlying patterns. Sometimes the leaps in thought happen so quickly we mistakenly label it an attention deficit. And sometimes Visionary thinking is so wildly creative, few can follow it.

Leadership Strengths:
Envisioning the future, setting strategy, imagining new solutions, products, services, and opportunities; scanning for possibilities and knowing what really matters; letting go and sensing the flow

Visionaries yearn to get to the essence of things. The spiritual dimension of this pattern asks in the largest sense, "What *really* matters?" or in the deepest sense, "Who am I?" It seeks or senses connectedness to God, the universe, or a greater purpose that it can manifest in everyday life.

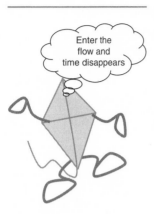

The Visionary: Extends
beyond convention, hangs
in the eternal Now

Visionary leaders are long on, well, vision. Their strength is finding the future and putting that into a vision and strategy. They also have a knack for seeing with fresh eyes and coming up with original ways to approach problems big and little, from doing an IPO as an auction (think Google) to seeing a use for ineffective glue that doesn't dry (think 3M and Post-It® notes).

Relationships among Visionaries give plenty of room for everyone to do their own thing. Or just Be. Visionaries rejoice in surfacing others' talents, especially as it opens new possibilities. Visionary teams are long on ideas, brainstorming sessions, original solutions, and big-picture thinking. But did anyone hear them commit to a deadline?

Well-defined work processes, to a Visionary, are an invitation to innovation. Visionaries work in ways that are emergent and generative—what wants to happen here? Corporate cultures dominated by Visionaries—and they rapidly are on the rise—are flexible, innovative, and often turn on a dime. Their speed comes not from rapid-fire movements like those executed by Drivers, but primarily from leaping freely into the unknown and landing on the Next Big Thing (think Apple).

Having now toured these four energies, do you have a favorite? Most of us do, and in the next chapter, you'll have a chance to discover what yours is. But can you imagine leading effectively without any of them? It's truly impossible, and fortunately, you don't have to. You already possess all four, even if you don't use them all. The beauty in recognizing these wonderful patterns is knowing that we already have everything we need for wholeness and balance. We don't need to do more, work faster, become something we're not, or follow someone else's formula. We can rise to every opportunity and challenge, not by speeding up but by opening up to the fullness of who we are.

CHAPTER TWO

Discover Your Winning Way

PATTERNS WE LOVE TO HATE

"I hated that one!" said one of the more direct participants in a program where I had people on their feet, moving through each of the patterns. Okay, so I played music, which was a risk with this group of leaders who mostly preferred the Driver and Organizer patterns. They hadn't objected when I had them doing sharp martial arts jabs for the Driver pattern or tidying up their space for the Organizer. But when we moved into rocking and swaying for the Collaborator—dangerously close to dancing!—we were over the edge for at least one of them.

"What does *that* have to do with work?" he challenged in his typical Driver way. I had to laugh because that was exactly how I used to feel about this exuberant, playful pattern.

You may already have a sense from learning about the patterns that one or two of them feel less comfortable than the others. Pay attention to that. The signs may be subtle—a slight awkwardness, a tad of embarrassment, a dismissive sense that this pattern is less valuable than the others. These reactions are indicators that these patterns run up against some internal resistance. They require more energy. They're almost certainly at the tail end of our preference order, the highest steps of our pattern staircase.

It came as no surprise that this Collaborator-hating participant found that Collaborator was his most under-used pattern. Neither was it a surprise that his boss and coworkers had told him that he was too abrupt, lacked social skills, and didn't listen to others' points of view, exactly the ills most ably treated by the Collaborator pattern. As I told him, the pattern we like least—or in the extreme, the pattern we hate, not only in ourselves, but also in others—may well be the one we need to cultivate for greater wholeness and balance.

"Everything that irritates us about others can lead us to an understanding about ourselves."   —Carl Jung

At the other extreme, we may hate a pattern we overuse and sometimes get stuck in. I had an aversion to the Organizer when I was first learning about the patterns. It wasn't awkward or foreign to me, I simply *resented* this pattern. I resented people who always had to be so proper and right and—yikes—just like me! The more I dug, the more I saw that the Organizer had been behind so much of the worry, self-consciousness, and cautiousness that had haunted me through the years. *"This* pattern gets me in trouble," I knew.

If you've been feeling any emotional stirrings—even the most minute—as you read about the various patterns, pay attention to them. They signal that this pattern has created some issues for you in the past. You don't simply put this pattern on like a jacket in the spring and take it off in the summer when you no longer need it. No, patterns that we love or hate, we generally "wear" too long or can't find when we need them.

Fortunately, once you understand your reactions to the patterns, those reactions don't get all of you anymore. Recognizing the patterns in yourself—and all of their good, bad, and ugly little footprints—leads to greater self awareness and freedom. The awkward feelings, resentments, judgments, and other pattern prejudices can initially cloud one's view and slow recognition. So as you explore which patterns make up your winning way and which ones you use less, stay tuned in to your emotions and attend to what they're telling you.

Before we go on to more formal ways of assessing your pattern preferences, you might take a few minutes to reflect on some of the trends in your life and leadership, and whether you've got even a little bit of an attitude about any of the patterns.

- What are a few of your strengths? What do others consistently say you do well?
- Which patterns would you guess are most closely associated with those strengths?
- What gets in your way? When others have told you about your weaknesses, what do they consistently say you need to work on?
- Which patterns would you guess are most closely associated with those weaknesses, either by being underused or overused?
- In touring the patterns in the previous chapter, did any of them seem more or less valuable than the rest? If so, why?
- Did any of the patterns trigger other attitudes or feelings? Jot down any that come to mind.

Using the example of the top pie chart in the sidebar, which depicts equal use of all four patterns, depict yourself as you are today, from your most used pattern (biggest slice) to your smallest sliver. In the bottom circle, make a pie chart of you as you'd like to be, which may be identical to how you see yourself now or may include a bigger slice of one pattern and a smaller piece of another. As important as anything you draw are the thoughts and emotions that surface for you in deciding *what* to draw. What do you notice?

Driver	Visionary
Organizer	Collaborator

**Equal parts of
each pattern**

THE BASIS OF BIAS

"As soon as you had us move in the Driver pattern," confided Tomiko, one of the Japanese women in a patterns session I was teaching recently, "I reflexively held back, flashing back to being a young girl in Japan when any sign of that kind of aggression was punished. We were told we could not show that!" My compassion and admiration for Tomiko swelled as I imagined all the obstacles she must have cleared in her own surreptitious-Driver way to be sitting in this high-level leadership program. I was so consumed thinking about the wonderful Driver energy that refuses to be kept down that it took me a while to notice how invested my own values were in this analysis, how much my own nature and nurture has led me to admire Drive, and my hair-trigger indignation when anyone is discouraged from winning.

Actual You
as you see
yourself today

Our pattern biases don't just come from society or business cultures, though they can be reinforced at any level from the inside (e.g., physical, emotional, mental or spiritual) to the outside (e.g., individual behaviors, team or family climates, corporate cultures, national cultures). Like the patterns themselves, these biases start in the body, with our intrinsic preference for a Home pattern followed by the other three patterns at increasing levels of effort.

Desired You
as you'd be more
effective or happier

The Science behind the Patterns

Every culture has had intuitive classification schemes for human personality that go back centuries, from Indian elements of fire, earth, water, and air to Carl Jung's four temperaments. But it's fair to say that the science of these four patterns as connected to movement in the body traces back to the work

If we could learn how to balance rest against effort, calmness against striving, quiet against turmoil, we could assure ourselves of joy in living and psychological health for life.

—Josephine Rathbone

of Josephine Rathbone in the 1930s.[13] By this time it was known that muscles only shorten when they tense, and that movement is coordinated by opposing muscle groups acting like an engine and brake. Rathbone found four distinct ways in which the engine and brake could be fired, which give rise to four distinct qualities of movement.[14] For example, in the Driver pattern, the brake is applied first and then the engine is gunned, resulting in a pushing-against movement. At the other extreme, the Visionary fires the engine first, seeming to "go with" the motion, and then brings in the brake as necessary. This results in the hanging, extended movements characteristic of the Visionary. In between these two extremes, the Organizer applies both engine and brake from the start—more brake than engine, proceeding with caution—and meters its way through Organized movement. The Collaborator also starts with both engine and brake, but in an alternating rhythm, with more engine than brake, giving rise to the back-and-forth, swinging motion characteristic of the Collaborator.

Thirty years later, with the benefit of electrophysiological recording, Dr. Valerie Hunt, working with Rathbone and other colleagues, further validated that these patterns represented different firing orders of nerves acting on muscles.[15] She also found that when one part of the body went into a particular pattern, the rest of the body tended to follow. You can experience this for yourself if you try clenching the bottom half of your body while keeping the top half completely relaxed; you'll feel the collision of internal signals as the bottom-half tension keeps trying to spread upward.

Links between Temperament and the Movement Patterns

Rathbone and Hunt speculated on the connection between these movement patterns and temperament, but it was not until Betsy's work starting in the 1970s that the links to temperament and style were mapped more clearly. These early researchers, however, did establish some basics around the patterns: everyone they tested, for example, was capable of using all four patterns, but in a characteristic order (of tension level) that was stable over time, barring massive trauma. Characteristic pattern differences were found in people of all ages, including babies, suggesting that even before nurture has much chance to take effect, nature has made some choices.

Even slight differences at birth can show up as big differences in pattern preferences over time, given the way the nervous system functions. It's not too much of a simplification to say, as neuroscientist Gerald Edelman puts it, "neurons that fire together, wire together." The connections between nerves and the connections that nerves make to muscles get stronger as they're used, making them more likely to be used again.[16] To picture how this works, imagine yourself crossing a field of tall grass that has a number of footpaths through it; some are pretty clear and others are heavily overgrown and hard to make out. If given the choice, you'd probably cross the field using one of the easier footpaths, but even as you're using it, you're trampling down grass and making it a still easier path to use again. If you took one of the more overgrown paths, the first time you went through it, you'd have to cut and clear your way and it would be pretty slow going. You might even give up or think, "I'm never going to do this again" (similar to what a strong Driver might feel on the Visionary pathway). But if you persevered, the second time would be easier, and so on. So in some sense, our preferred patterns have become paths of least resistance through the very process of preferring them! And from years of relative disuse, one or two of our patterns could be the equivalent of heavily overgrown and hard to find.

Pattern Biases in Childhood

In addition to nature and habit playing into our pattern preferences, just the process of growing up seems to play a role. Judith Kestenberg did some research mapping the patterns and the role of movement to early stages of child development.[17] For example, around the time the ego develops, a stage sometimes referred to as "the terrible twos," the Driver pattern emerges. We learn important words like *no!* and *mine!* as we starting pushing for our way. This is followed by a more sociable stage in three-year-olds[18] where kids figure out how to get along in the sandbox, calling on the Collaborator pattern. Typical four-year-olds enter a stage of ritualistic, Organizer behavior where the teddy bear has to be placed *here* not *there*, the sandwich has to be cut straight, not on the diagonal, and to everything there is a question: Why this? Why that? This opens into a Visionary stage typical of five-year-olds, where new possibilities and open-ended inquisitiveness emerge. Now it's not just about rules, but about new ways of being in which children mimic a favorite cartoon character, for example, or their mother's way of talking.

As these different patterns emerge, they don't supplant the Home pattern, but rather are modulated and integrated by it into a style that our young selves try on for size. It is as if our early development encourages us to try out all the patterns—after all, we will need every one of them later on. What happens

Driver—Brake (i.e., Antagonist) fires first and then the engine fires with something to push against.

Visionary—Engine (i.e., Agonist) fires first, and brake comes in as needed.

Organizer—Both engine and brake fire at the same time, but with more brake.

Collaborator—Both engine and brake fire in alternating sequence with more engine.

Four Ways to Flex an Arm

when we do venture down one of our roads less traveled has a good deal to do with whether we want to return.

Which brings us to the final factor in our pattern biases: the environment that nurtured us, starting with our family, but extending to our neighborhood, society, culture, and all the situations we faced. Tomiko's Driver, for example, was punished in her family, whereas her polite, Organizer pattern was greatly encouraged. Many children encounter this kind of reprimand or reward as their patterns run up against those of their parents and siblings. When these nurturing biases match our natural biases, our natural preferences get even stronger. But when the opposite happens and we're discouraged from using our natural strengths, we can become more accustomed to using weaker patterns as well as more conflicted about what we're really good at. That's one reason that leaders like Tomiko are often surprised when they learn about the patterns to discover strengths they didn't know they had.

Pattern Preferences Meet Corporate Cultures

So if we now take you with all your natural and nurtured pattern biases and drop you into a particular role, in a particular corporate culture, some patterns in you will resonate and be called out in that situation, while some aspects of you may feel deprived or under-nourished. You may have found yourself flourishing in certain contexts and floundering in others, satisfied at one point, and then needing to move on at another. Recognizing the patterns in you and in those around you can give you endless new insights into why this is so. Even if you don't change a thing, simply recognizing your Home pattern can help you see more clearly where your natural strengths lie and what you're likely to find fulfilling.

While no energy pattern is any better or worse than the others, we as individuals tend to value them differently, and so do families, cultures, professions, life stages, industries, and corporate cultures. The basis for our bias starts inside out and is reflected in a pattern sequence that has most likely been with us from birth. An assessment called the Focus Energy Balance Indicator™[19]—FEBI™ ("fee-bee") for short—can tell you about your own pattern sequence.

WHICH PATTERNS DO YOU FAVOR?

Even if you already have a pretty good idea of which patterns you favor, take the mini-FEBI below; the answers may surprise you. For a more detailed report and the full version of the FEBI (which has to be scored online), go to our online assessment center at www.movetogreatness.com and sign up to take it. Answering the questions below will give you a fairly reliable read of your pattern sequence. It's best to answer the questions without too much deliberation or second guessing and to answer them all before looking at the scoring.

Directions: On a scale of 1 (never) to 10 (always), indicate how true the following statements are for you. Use as much of the 10-point scale as you can; see if you can tease out differences in how often you do these things or how true they are for you so that you're not giving everything the same number. A "5" means average; in other words, this statement is about as true for you as it is for other people you know.[20]

When facing a big task, I break it down, and take it one step at a time.	1.
I am direct and to the point.	2.
My moods go up and down.	3.
I love to win.	4.
I'm conscientious about commitments.	5.
I enjoy the energy of networking.	6.
I have many stacks of papers, articles, etc. around my office and home.	7.
When faced with obstacles, I push harder.	8.
I have a hard time finding where I put things.	9.
I make work fun.	10.
I know how to work the system and get cooperation.	11.
When people are upset, I remain calm and rational.	12.
I do things in a hurry.	13.
I used to daydream in school.	14.
I think life is flux, nothing is fixed.	15.
I can get stuck and not know which way to move under pressure.	16.
I like to let go and see where events will lead.	17.
In conflict, I fire back.	18.
I'm an optimistic person.	19.
I'm steady and dependable.	20.
I often go back and forth on tough decisions.	21.
I come up with highly unusual ideas.	22.
It's important to me to do what's expected of me.	23.
If something isn't getting done fast enough, I'll just do it myself.	24.

To calculate your totals for each pattern, add:

2, 4, 8, 13, 18, and 24 for **Driver**: _____

1, 5, 12, 16, 20, and 23 for **Organizer**: _____

3, 6, 10, 11, 19, and 21 for **Collaborator**: _____

7, 9, 14, 15, 17, and 22 for **Visionary**: _____

Scoring the FEBI

< 32 Low

These are weakly expressed patterns that are more difficult for you to access; you may not use them when they're called for.

32–44 Moderate

With moderate ease you can access these patterns when you need to.

> 44 High

These are strongly expressed patterns that are easy for you to access and are likely connected to your natural strengths; you may have a tendency to overuse these patterns.

You can score your answers as shown below. Add your total for each pattern; the higher the number, the easier this pattern is for you to access. Your highest number, barring a tie, is likely to be your Home pattern (a tie is considered to be scores within two points of one another). Even if you have a tie, you still have a Home pattern, but we can't tell what it is from your results. If you have a tie, you might want to come back to the mini-FEBI later (or go to our website and take the full instrument). As you get to know the patterns better and watch your life, your Home pattern will eventually become clear.

Scores in the range of 32–44 are considered moderate, suggesting that with moderate ease you can use this pattern when you need it. Scores above 44 are high, suggesting these patterns make up your winning way; you may even try to use them when they're not appropriate, or get stuck in them unknowingly. Scores below 32 are considered low; these are patterns you don't see yourself using often, and you may not be using them even when they're called for.

Many people are surprised by their FEBI results, sometimes in the strength of their preferences. "No wonder I struggle with endless to-do lists and trying to stay out of the weeds," said one leader whose results showed high use of the Organizer and Driver, and low use of the Collaborator and Visionary. "I could have guessed what I'm strong in, but I'm surprised that I seem to be using only half of myself!"

Other times, people can guess one of their strong suits, but miss another. You might take a few minutes to reflect on insights or surprises from your results.

- What is your pattern order from the mini-FEBI?
- What stands out or surprises you in this pattern order?
- What connections can you make between this pattern order and any attitudes you identified earlier about the patterns?
- What connections can you make between this pattern order and any feedback you've received on strengths and weaknesses?
- What connection can you make between this pattern order and how you depicted your actual and desired self in the pie chart earlier?

LEADING IN STYLE

Some leaders—few in number, but they're out there—are so strong in one pattern and so weak in the others that they operate out of their Home pattern in the extreme. You'll meet some examples of these fairly vulnerable leaders in the coming chapters. But most leaders have high or moderate access to more than one pattern and are able to lead in what we call "style." Style is the combination of two patterns. It reflects the fact that our Home pattern is foundational to how we function in the world, and even as we move into our second, third, or fourth patterns, we do so in a way that's modulated by our Home pattern. I have an Organizer Home pattern, for example and, as my Collaborator husband is fond of ribbing me, even when I move into the Collaborator, it still looks sort of Organized. "Fun isn't something you do after your homework is done," he says laughingly (it isn't?). "Fun is blowing off your homework."

Most leaders combine their Home pattern and second pattern into a primary style that they use most of the time. Unless your second pattern is already down in the low range, chances are good that you have a primary leadership style described by your Home + second pattern. The four patterns give rise to 12 style combinations, and some of the most characteristic leadership traits of each are summarized in the style table (Table 2-1) that follows. If you have a tie for Home pattern (or for second and third pattern), you can read the couple of style descriptions that might apply and see which one seems most like you.

If you read opposite pairings in the style table, you will get a better idea of how Home pattern dominates and shines through even when we move into another pattern. For example, both a Visionary–Driver and a Driver–Visionary combine the big picture with a sense of urgency. But they differ in what's fundamental to each of them. To the Driver–Visionary (i.e., where Driver is the Home pattern), winning or more broadly, accomplishing a mission, is the point. The Visionary's ability to sense the flow is put in service of finding ways to win. Conversely, for the Visionary–Driver (i.e., where Visionary is the Home pattern), the essence of life or leadership has to do with manifesting purpose, and the Driver is put in service of super-charging that purpose.

In addition to a primary style, whole and balanced leaders also have backup styles that they can move into when their first approach doesn't work. If your third or fourth patterns are still in the moderate range or higher, these, in combination with your Home pattern (i.e., Home + third pattern, Home + fourth pattern), represent backup styles that you're moderately comfortable using. If your third or fourth patterns are in

Style = Combination of two patterns

Primary Style: Home + second pattern*

Backup Styles: Home + third pattern, Home + fourth pattern*

* for patterns scoring moderate or higher

TABLE 2-1. Style Table

Two patterns combine to form a style. Read down the column of your Home pattern to find your primary style and possible backup styles. A whole and balanced leader is able to use all three of the styles associated with the Home pattern.

Home or 1st Pattern ⇒ / 2nd or supporting Pattern ⇓	Driver	Organizer	Collaborator	Visionary
Driver		*Organizer–Driver* — Hard, sharply discerning, correct and responsible—a solid leader of action. This style plans the work and works the plan, and the to-do list is endless. This style is analytically minded and first with a question.	*Collaborator–Driver* — Bold, fun and enthusiastic, this style gets noticed; it engages and challenges others, with ambitious goals, winning for and through people. This style brings both fun and focus to work.	*Visionary–Driver* — A self-starter who senses openings in the big picture, this style thinks big and acts quickly. It brings a sense of urgency to serving a larger purpose; it wins for a cause.
Organizer	*Driver–Organizer* — Crisp, pinpointed, often highly critical of self and others, this is the style of a make-it-happen leader who sets goals, structures processes, and does the right thing with a strong sense of urgency.		*Collaborator–Organizer* — The consummate team player or coach, this style combines can-do energy with planful ways of getting things done. It is oriented toward doing the right thing by people.	*Visionary–Organizer* — Both flexible and dependable, this style brings order to chaos, giving form to imagination or aesthetics. Dedicated to principles or a larger sense of purpose, it does the right thing for the bigger picture.

26

	Driver	Organizer	Visionary / Collaborator
Collaborator	**Driver–Collaborator** A "there," make-it-happen leader who works easily through people, this style is challenging, solid, but also fun, bringing a human touch to an often-ambitious agenda. Can be a political animal.	**Organizer–Collaborator** Responsible and loyal—a "teddy bear"—often driven by the need to serve people. This style does what's right in human, practical terms, working more one-on-one than with society in general. Can be a gracious diplomat.	**Visionary–Collaborator** Spontaneous and quirky, this style engages people, and leads with vision. It serves a bigger picture in human-oriented ways. This style tends to be loose and friendly and wanders about.
Visionary	**Driver–Visionary** Scans for opportunities to turn into new wins. This style is mission driven, and can inspire with vision as well as set well-defined goals. Alternately forceful and laid back, this style leaps to action when it senses the timing is right.	**Organizer–Visionary** Open and conscientious, this style lives and leads on purpose, and can also go let go and sense the flow. Highly introspective, this style can see the big picture and parse it into plans, processes, and task lists.	**Collaborator–Visionary** A natural networker who loves to play and can go with the flow, this style can be highly imaginative and humorous. It often plays well to an audience, and brings together unusual combinations of ideas and people.

the low range, you probably don't use these styles readily or particularly well. If you were to develop easier access to these patterns, you'd gain the agility and balance of these additional backup styles. You wouldn't be mistaken for a native using your fourth pattern in a backup style—my planned fun still looks more Organized than my husband's spontaneous play—but at least you'll have enough to get by.

Before moving on, you might take a moment to reflect on your own leadership style and its implications for your current role.

- Write down your primary style if you have one, which is Home + second pattern (provided the second pattern scored moderate or higher). If you have a tie or aren't sure, jot down the couple that might apply.
- How much do you leverage this style in your current role? How much does your current role call upon the strengths of this style?
- Write down any backup styles that you have moderately easy access to; i.e., your Home pattern plus any others that scored moderate or higher.
- If you do have backup styles, how do you see yourself making use of them in your current role?
- If you could use more backup styles, which one would you most like to have access to?
- What insights do you have regarding the fit of your leadership style and current role?

DÉJÀ VU?

Maybe this is all sounding strangely familiar to you. "Haven't we been here before?" you may be asking. Isn't this like situational leadership, or DISC, or the Myers Briggs Type Indicator (MBTI)? Indeed, as a coordinate system for personality, these four energy patterns do show similarities to other models. For example, the Driver pattern aligns with the Dominance factor in DISC and the Directive style in situational leadership.

What makes the patterns groundbreaking is that by linking body, mind, and behavior, and showing the common energies that run through all of our levels, they give us a much deeper way to understand and work with ourselves. So, to continue the Directive/Driver example, say you face a leadership situation where that style is simply not appropriate. If the situation calls for a participative style, what do you do? Do you say, "I prefer Directive style so I'll just fail in this situation?" Probably not. Most likely you'd want to try to be Participative, but how do you pull it off? Maybe you've read a behavioral description of what Participative looks like and you try it on for size, but if you're still Driving underneath, you'll find you don't make a very convincing Participative leader. If you really want a whole-leader approach to becoming more Participative (or whatever the situation calls for), the patterns will show you how to *move* there through and through.

> *Learning is movement from moment to moment.*
> —*J. Krishnamurti*

Numerous models of personality (or temperament[21]) have been developed over the years. I don't know them all, but I do know the most popular ones; I've used them in leadership programs for years, and have found them to be incredibly useful. Yet every one of them has the same limitation: they treat personality as an "I" separate from the body. While the interconnectedness of mind and body has been established by an enormous body of research,[22] none of these instruments, or the models on which they're based, make a behavioral link to the body. In this sense, the energy patterns represent a new paradigm that I think advances the whole field of "personality tests" by getting underneath these models to their physical basis, and adding the body back into a more integrated view of the whole person. The patterns don't stop at the neck!

Even though the unique feature of the pattern model is its linkage through the whole person, many leaders who have taken other instruments are interested to know how the FEBI relates to other models. If you're curious about this too, or interested in some of the research we've done with the FEBI, see Appendix I for a summary.

GOING DEEPER

At this point in our journey, I hope you're getting a sense about the patterns that make up your winning way. Maybe you're also getting some insight into why you don't like or use some of the patterns as much as others. Before we venture more deeply into the patterns and how to use or strengthen them, let me offer a few tips on how you can use what you've learned about yourself in this chapter as you read the next four.

Your Winning Way

As you read the chapters on your favorite patterns and learn of leaders who model them—especially at their extremes—see if any of them remind you of yourself. And ask yourself if you might at times get stuck in that pattern and use it too much. As one leader said when he learned about his winning way, "My groove has become my rut."

Your Weak Pattern

If you have a pattern that scored low on the FEBI or is at the bottom of your pattern stack by some margin (say five points or more), pay particular attention to that chapter, and the possible benefits of that pattern. You may have a hard time seeing the value at first. For example, my super-Organizer father has trouble seeing any value in the Visionary. "A waste of time," he says. "I don't see what it's good for in bottom-line business." Someone like my Dad might want to read the Visionary chapter twice. I read the Collaborator chapter once a month (you think I'm kidding?).

What's Missing in the Middle

Even if you have moderately easy access to a pattern or it scored in the middle of the pack among your preferences, that doesn't mean you use it when you need to, or enjoy all of what it offers. A colleague of mine, Steve, is a world-class leader who is nearing retirement. He has moderately easy access to the Visionary—it's one of his middle patterns—and he's a wonderful big-picture thinker who readily connects the dots. But he recognized that he didn't enjoy easy access to the letting go part of the Visionary, that go-with-the-flow part that could serve him so well in his transition to retirement.

As you spend time in the coming chapters learning more about the patterns in your middle range, ask which aspects of them you readily use and which could serve you better if you used them more.

If you start seeing that the way you use the patterns creates some gaps, quirks, or downright dangers in how you lead your life or lead others, don't despair! You're entering the second stage of seeing the limitations in how you use the patterns today. If your life and leadership are largely working, don't change a thing. But if some of these limitations are getting in your way, and you want to kick the "buts" that have been holding you back, use that dissatisfaction to blast off to the third stage: gaining freedom. We'll get there in due course. First, let's review the four patterns so that you can experience them more fully and see them in action more clearly. And since we're starting with the Driver, better get a move on it.

CHAPTER THREE

Push into the Driver

HEY! I'M TALKING TO YOU!

If that seems a little in your face—well, that's the Driver for you. Open one hand and "cut" the palm with the blade of your other hand, punctuating each point,

> each
> urgent
> word
> of
> this
> sentence,

The Driver

and you'll quickly get a feel for the pressure and pushiness that drives the Driver.

Push yourself into Driver territory and immediately you start speeding up: you talk faster, walk faster, and get right to the point. Here you might run into the likes of Donald Trump, calculating the angles on a new business or jabbing his finger in the face of a disappointed apprentice with an abrupt, "You're fired!" You'd find Madonna in your face with a pointy-sharp outfit and brilliant, attention-grabbing antics. You'd meet leaders like Michael Dell, who responded to an ad for taking a test to get a high school diploma when he was only eight years old. "I liked third grade," he said, "But being impatient and curious, if there was a direct, quick way to get something done, I wanted to try it." Michael Dell went on to champion a direct model for build-to-order computers, growing a company that is renowned for its velocity.

Get on it. The Driver is the accelerator pedal, making things happen. Set a goal, cut the crap, hit the target: that's how the Driver works.

Measure what matters and keep score. The space around a Driver is free of clutter. With stark lines, high contrast, and edginess, the Driver pattern is visually striking whether in attire, art, or architecture. If the Driver were a city, it would look

> *The speed of the boss is the speed of the team.*
> *—Lee Iacocca*

something like Manhattan, with its jutting skyscrapers outdoing one another in their push to new heights. It has a rapid pulse: the light changes and honking begins; taxis and pedestrians challenge each other for crosswalk supremacy.

Driver Territory—pushing to new heights

Driver teams stay focused on their task. Ready, aim, fire! If it's not done fast enough the Driver says, "I'll do it myself!" Driver companies are fast places with no frills; the point is the bottom line and beating the competition—and don't forget it!

Phew! In the right dose, the Driver's energy, like adrenaline itself, is incredibly energizing. The Driver's pushiness is indispensable to maintaining a sense of urgency, raising the performance bar, setting clear direction, and focusing on the vital few priorities. But if we have too much Drive we become exhausted, impatient, abrasive, hotheaded, or worse. Driving to win at all costs can cost everything—ask Enron's Jeff Skilling. As with each of the patterns, the Driver is an essential part, but not the entirety, of a whole a balanced leader and a whole and balanced life.

THE DRIVER IN YOU

How much Driver energy do you have? Whether you love it or hate it, you've got it. And it doesn't take much pushing to bring it out. Indeed pushing or thrusting movements are the ticket to entering the Driver, which you can experience sitting right there reading this book. Just set it down for a moment so you can try this.

Clasp your hands in front of you, close to your chest, with elbows bent. Push your hands together as hard as you can, then—hanging on tight—try to pull them apart as hard as you can. Do this a few times, and you'll notice your eyes have focused to a pinpoint and your mind feels scrunched behind your furrowed brow.

This "scrunched" feeling and piercing eyes are visible signs of the Driver's extraordinary, single-point focus. That focus is what makes the Driver so effective at setting and hitting goals, but it also raises the risk of being blindsided ("never saw it coming") or aiming at the wrong target. As you push and pull your hands, you might notice a certain tightness or muscle contraction at the base of the abdomen; this is the center organizing the Driver pattern in your physical body.

To get a better feel for this center, try this experiment: push down on the floor through your feet, and notice the same tension in the lower abdomen that you felt when pressing your hands together. Clench your jaw for a moment and note—same thing! I think this is one reason that people often clench their jaw when they're trying to focus: it activates the Driver center. Notice whenever you push—arms, legs, jaw, whatever—this tension comes into the lower abdomen; you can't push without it. If you're not used to feeling for tension in your body, the first time you look for it, you may not see much. It's an acquired skill, something like wine tasting. But if you keep looking as you push your hands or press your feet, you'll find a point of tightness at the bottom of the abdomen that every form of pushing has in common. This is the Driver center, that is, the center from which Driver movements are coordinated. It corresponds with the lowest "root"

The Voice of the Driver

"What's the bottom line?"

What the Driver Does Best

Gets to the point, makes the goal

What Motivates the Driver

Power, winning

Too Much Drive

Impatient and too aggressive, sharp, cutting edge, no room for people

Not Enough Drive

Lacking sense of urgency, focus, not assertive enough

Move from the Driver center and you move into the Driver pattern

Understanding the center of a pattern is the fastest way to access it. Having felt the Driver center through pushing, try moving from this center as you walk across the room. You'll feel yourself move in the Driver pattern immediately. You can use this technique to access the pattern at will. You can also try this with any of the patterns as you learn about their centers in coming chapters.

chakra in the Indian energetic system. It's more than a metaphor to say people with a lot of Driver energy have "guts"!

The Driver's fundamental posture to the world is pushing[23]: challenging barriers, raising the bar, pushing against the clock, beating the odds, knocking competitors out of the way and above all: winning, Winning, WINNING!

THE DRIVER IN DELL: WHEN DRIVING SUPERCHARGES PERFORMANCE

The book, *Direct from Dell* (a rather direct title), which Michael Dell describes as "a guide to developing and honing your competitive edge," opens with a telling tale of Dell's own third-grade experience.[24] Clad in a red terrycloth bathrobe, Michael entered the living room after a bath to explain to his mother and the woman who had arrived from the testing company that he really was serious about getting his high school diploma in one quick test. Michael Dell: Driver exemplar!

Despite his precocious attempt at graduation, Michael ended up attending high school and, when he was 16, took a summer job selling subscriptions to *The Houston Post*. He was given a list of phone numbers to call, but quickly figured out that such a random approach was inefficient. He could beat the odds by finding a pattern to the people who most frequently subscribed and focusing on them. Newlyweds and new homeowners became his target market; he found he could obtain courthouse records of marriage licensees and listings of new mortgages and he was off and running. In his first experience of segmenting a market—the targeted calculus of the Driver's mind—"subscriptions came in by the thousands." He made more money that year than did his high school teacher!

Dell's Driver-Sharp Mind for Business

Drivers tend to be good with numbers; they keep score. They get a clear picture of the goal and then figure out the shortest distance to get there. Although Michael Dell never went to business school, he quickly figured out the essential equation for making money:

$$\text{Profit} = \text{Margin} \times \text{Velocity}$$

Spotlight: Michael Dell

CEO, chairman of Dell

Expressed Profile: Driver and Visionary, in that order. Driver dominates Dell's style, with a focus on directness ("Cut out the middle"), speed, and raising the bar. His Visionary strength in seeing patterns (for example, most likely subscribers to the newspaper), works in service of a keen competitive edge.

Dell as a Company: Driver and Visionary in that order. Driver dominates from the austere, utilitarian offices to the relentless rigor around the business model. Visionary innovation in areas like supply chain are put in service of the Driver's push to enhance the bottom line.

---

where margin is how much money you make per unit and velocity is how fast you can crank out the units (also called "inventory turns" for people who did go to business school). Dell's Driver mind was able to key in to a few priorities that became the hallmark of his business model: focus on customer needs, manage expenses, and move fast—and do these things better than the competitors.

Dell's Driving nature also shows up in his relentless raising of the performance bar, both for himself and his company. "'Pleased but never satisfied' has been our mantra for more than 20 years," says Dell. "One of the ways I try to motivate the team is to set our goals very, very high."[25] He drives that point home relentlessly, as when he toured a manufacturing plant in Austin that had just increased its processing rate from 300 to 350 computers per hour. No sooner had he congratulated the team—high fives all around—than he threw down a challenge: "How can we improve to 400?"[26]

Balancing Dell's Drive

That's not to say Michael Dell is all Driver. His leadership style also has a healthy balance of the other patterns. Visionary energy comes through in his remarkable ability to connect the dots, see patterns, and leap to what's most essential. His focus on execution gets strong support from the Organizer, with its ability to manage projects and set up processes that scale with growth. The Collaborator Dell comes out in his connection to customers and his caring for employees. But this is an area that he has particularly focused on and it's a good bet that Collaborator is his weakest pattern. When he learned that he came across as something of a cold technocrat, he worked with an executive coach to temper his abruptness and warm up his style.[27] He also instituted a policy of regular feedback from subordinates to target areas for improvement. This is a great example of a basic principle for working with the patterns: use a strength to approach a weakness. Being a highly Driven, data-based guy, he basically kept score on himself for how well he addressed issues that were important to his people, strengthening the Collaborator in a Driver's way.

Dell's Driving Corporate Culture

In many respects, the company, Dell, resembles the man. Even though it now employs more than 80,000 people, every one of them gets steeped in the business model and learns how customer focus, expense management, and speed apply in their jobs. The principle of segmentation that Michael Dell knew instinctively in his subscription-selling days is used throughout Dell to focus efforts on the best market niche in the fastest growing province of China or the most significant time contributor to the 23 seconds it takes to assemble part of a computer. Segment, focus, and fix it fast—the Driver at work.

The emphasis on speed is everywhere at Dell, and is even woven into the dialogue. "Answer First" is Dell's version of a particular way of communicating that is fast, efficient, and gets to the point right up front. E-mails are written that way. Presentations are organized that way. Make your point, make your case, and be done! In its corporate culture, Dell combines the Driver's focus on making the numbers with the Visionary's expansive view of what's possible. It focuses relentlessly on the essentials: adding value, subtracting cost, and maintaining speed. "If you're working on something that does not add value to a customer or cut costs, you should rethink what you're doing," was the blunt advice of a seasoned pro to an orientation session for new Dell executives. As technology firms go, Dell is not the most innovative in new products. "We're not about building a better video chip," Michael Dell told the same audience. "But we'll watch the other eight companies doing it and see what's best. That's what we'll bring to our customers." And Dell will roll it out faster and better than anyone, applying its great Visionary strength to transforming the supply chain and its Organizer strength to executing processes. Dick Hunter, then the head of supply chain and a remarkable leader and mentor in the organization, describes how, in effect, he gets his people thinking like Visionaries and operating like Organizers: "I've learned you've got to throw down a big goal to get people out of incremental thinking. My rule of thumb is 50 percent. What would it take to do 50 percent more? How could we take out 50 percent of the cost?" Dick's highly creative team was able to cut assembly time for a computer in the Austin plant by—you guessed it—50 percent.

Bringing Dell's Culture into Balance

Much as Drive is good for performance, balancing Drive is what makes that performance sustainable. Not only does Michael Dell know and live this personally, but the company he founded also recognizes it. Of the four energies, Collaborator is the weakest at Dell, and it receives a good deal of conscious attention. "Tell Dell" surveys from employees, similar to the program Michael put in place for himself, are now the norm for all managers in the organization, and the results are taken seriously. Managers who consistently score poorly are asked to move on. According to Dick Hunter, those who get the best Tell Dell results on the "soft" items also get the best performance in "hard" numbers. "It's all about the people," Dick says. "Leaders have the responsibility to create vitality in their organization. And when they do, they get better results."

Recognizing that the pace of the organization was burning people out or discouraging them from staying if they wanted to have families, Dell put the matter of work–life balance to its management team. They came up with a number of ways to enable better balance for their employees, not unlike other companies. But what was unique to Dell—again using the Driver to strengthen the Collaborator—was that it collected statistics on how well managers created a climate of balance for their employees and published the numbers. Managers who did well were not only rewarded financially, but everyone wanted to come work for them!

This attention to balance is part of the strength of Dell as a person and Dell as a company. That's not to say that either is flawless; indeed, even as I write this, the company is going through another rough patch of restated earnings and shuffling at the top. Being whole and balanced does not make one immune to difficulties or forever perfect in the public eye. But what I've noticed about both leaders and companies that attend to wholeness is that they're more resourceful in facing difficulties. They have more freedom of movement and are less likely to completely derail. The Driver is most assuredly Dell's winning way, supported by a sense of Visionary expansiveness. But if the leader and the company can bring in enough do-the-right-thing Organizer and connected Collaborator, both will be able to weather this and other storms most successfully.

A CEO WHO DROVE TOO MUCH

I haven't been Michael Dell's coach, but I did coach another Driver, Ron, who was the CEO of a $2 billion digital imaging business. Ron was an absolute go-getter and an incredibly likeable guy. He had high energy, a ready smile, a firm handshake; it was easy to see why he'd risen so successfully through the sales ranks to head the company. But with every area now reporting to him, not just the sales area he knew well, he had to listen in new ways to his senior leaders in engineering, finance, and other divisions where he had no technical expertise. An extreme extrovert, listening was not his strong suit.

But that was not his biggest problem. His biggest problem was that important conversations weren't even happening because of his temper. "When I start getting upset in a meeting," he told me, "the vein on my forehead starts to pulse. I mean, it gets really large and people notice it. Guys who know me well make a joke of it. 'Oh, he's going to blow,' they used to chide me in the sales meetings: 'Contain the vein!' But now I'm leading all kinds of people, and I really DO need to contain the vein if we're going to work well together."

Recognizing the Patterns and the Problem

Ron didn't even have to see his FEBI report when I was sitting in his office ready to go over it with him. No sooner had I introduced the patterns, he cut

To manage your temper, manage your breath . . .

Try this simple exercise now and the next time you want to calm down in a hurry.

Start with a **sigh of relief**, exhaling through your mouth, letting as much tension fall away as possible.

Open your palms and place them palms up on your thighs. Imagine a stream of energy running along the **backs** of your hands, out the ends of your fingertips.

Breathing in and out through your nose, make your breath as **slow, quiet**, and **invisible** as you can, almost as if it isn't happening at all.

At first this feels impossible, but if you take **three breaths** this way, you'll notice the third one is quieter than the first.

Use your Driver strength to focus entirely on your breath and nothing else. The more you focus on the breath, the more you can quiet it down, and with it, your emotions.

me off with an Aha! flash of recognition. "No question, I'm a Driver," he pronounced. "And you're right, I don't listen, I get impatient, I cut people off—like I just did you," he said laughingly. At least he was a self-aware Driver! With the more emotional, mood-swinging Collaborator as his second pattern, it was easy to see how Ron's leadership style could be so determinedly gregarious and also temperamental. Ron wasted no time in digging into the patterns to analyze his own behavior and started analyzing the patterns in everyone around him. Ron reveled in this stage of recognizing the patterns because suddenly so many relationships—both the productive and the awkward—made sense to him. He had everyone on his executive team take the FEBI and the patterns became part of their shared lingo.

Moving to a Solution

But Ron didn't stop at the stage of recognition. He was serious about "containing the vein" and dealing with the limitations of Driver impatience and super-charged emotion. "If I can access my weaker patterns," he said, referring to the Organizer's quiet composure and the Visionary's sense of flow, "I can achieve so much more as a leader." Ron professed an interest in meditation, which is an ideal practice for bringing out the Visionary and Organizer, "but I don't know if I can sit still that long," he admitted. He had a background and interest in the martial arts—and a son who shared that interest—so I suggested he try the more meditative martial art of aikido. Aikido would use Ron's strengths as a Driver and Collaborator with its speed, focus, and emphasis on (literally) rolling with the punches. But it would also teach him how to manage his breath, which is the key to managing temper (try the exercise in the sidebar if this would also be useful to you). He would learn how to quiet himself and listen to others with every pore in his body, and open up to chaotic activity without becoming anxious. Quick to close on a deal, he was sold.

I know these sorts of stories have a predictable rhythm to them; this is where I tell you that some time later, Ron was a new and improved guy. And actually, he did improve. But you can already tell that someone of Ron's determination (that's the Driver energy for you!) and self-awareness can improve just about any way he or she wants. The patterns just gave him a practical way of working with himself. But it was still fun to watch. Ron would come into a meeting with me and start out with some report of how he'd been something besides a Driver during the previous month. "We were in a big negotiation last week and I needed to be more of a Collaborator. I made sure I went in loose and relaxed and ready to engage the other people." Later in the meeting when the going got tough, he remembered to breathe. "No vein!" he laughed triumphantly. "We had a great meeting."

Ron was moving into what we call the third stage of working with the patterns: new freedom of movement where he could access any of the patterns and choose what he needed in the moment. He was still going to win in his Driving way. But now he could listen, not explode, and not derail as a Driver.

DO YOU HAVE DRIVING AMBITION?

Another way to recognize the Driver in you—and others—is by its ambition. A good many famous leaders display a good deal of Driver, which is one reason they're famous. While a leader can be successful in any Home pattern—and all of us have some Driver—this is the most ambitious of patterns. Drivers are driven to succeed, they're up for a good fight, and the more they win, the bigger their agenda (and ego!) grows. Some people are attracted to driving ambition; others are repulsed by it. Check out your own reactions to the following examples: they'll tell you something about the Driver in you.

Eliot Spitzer: Driving Large

As Attorney General of New York, Eliot Spitzer took on Wall Street analysts, mutual fund traders, and insurance brokers, thrusting himself into the national spotlight as an unprecedented activist, "an alpha male willing and able to rattle biggest, toughest CEOs."[28] As described in a *Fortune* magazine article, he's the very picture of the Driver: "If ever a man had that lean and hungry look, it is Spitzer. At six feet and 180 pounds, he is taut, with angular features and that famously jutting jaw. (Not to mention notoriously sharp elbows)." He rises early and runs three miles or pumps iron. "He even has a thing for NASCAR. 'There's an adrenaline to it,' he says."

Moving to Greatness: Balancing Driver

Ron, president, digital imaging company

Situation: Bright, new leader of areas where he had no expertise, Ron needed to listen better and not blow up at people.

Expressed Profile: Strong in Driver with Collaborator as his second pattern; weakest in Visionary and Organizer.

Great Moves: Ron took up the meditative martial art of Aikido with his son, and learned to physically listen and use his breath to settle his temper. He practiced listening and patience in work meetings and solicited feedback from others on his progress.

Spotlight: Eliot Spitzer

Governor of New York

Quote: [When asked if he'd overstepped as Attorney General] *"Let me be very clear about this point. We don't believe in covering up for those who commit a crime."*

Others Say: *"The way he practices law is a kind of physical sport,"* says supporter, Lloyd Constantine. *"He enjoys power and he likes to win."*

Expressed Profile: Driver, with enough support from the other patterns to keep winning.

Of course he would be drawn to adrenaline, for that is the recyclable fuel of the Driver. Drivers love to get pumped up for the game. Indeed, *up* is the overall trajectory of the Driver, both in the yogic sense of energy rising from the Driver center (i.e., base of the abdomen) and in the conventional sense of driving ambition. Many Drivers are active in sports—or were active and still find a sports analogy for every business angle, from moving the ball forward to avoiding the end run. Whether the Driver is one of your favorite patterns or not, you'll find that Driver-like movement—pushing, stomping, hard and fast motions—physically charges the body with adrenaline.

While Driver may be the defining trait of Spitzer, even he has learned that Driver alone won't get him where he wants to go. He lost his first political race because he didn't connect effectively with voters or with others in the Democratic Party. Hating to lose, as any Driver does, Spitzer didn't make the same mistake twice. In his second race, he brought out his Collaborator side, attending dozens of county fairs and shaking countless hands. He also engaged other members of his party, making contributions to candidates in local races. By his second, successful run at office, Spitzer had become a more rounded politician. From Attorney General, he pushed to the New York Governor's mansion, and his driving ambition is unlikely to stop there. His father was once asked whether Eliot would like to be president one day. "It's his very nature," he replied.

Intimidating Drivers

Like Eliot Spitzer, Drivers may be intimidating leaders, people who take a tough stance, stare down their opponents, and often get their way. In the extreme, their ability to bully others can cause huge damage. Consider Enron's Jeff Skilling, whose love of winning turned into winning at all costs. Skilling was known and feared as a great intimidator, driving over whoever got in his way. Even during his trial he was filmed mouthing insults at his accusers. His driving ambition cost Enron more than $66 billion, and the entire business world has borne the cost of the Sarbanes–Oxley legislation that followed to curb extreme Drivers run amuck.

Short of the extremes, some intimidation can lead to good results. There's something to be said for the Driver energy that isn't afraid to use power, take a stand, and push hard on people. When I think back to one of my Zen teachers, Tanouye Roshi, he was absolutely an intimidating leader; I spent years terrified of the man. But Tanouye was acting fundamentally in my interest, not in his own interest. His no-nonsense severity pushed me beyond any place I could have found without him.

Rod Kramer, who's made a study of hard-Driving, intimidating leaders, would agree that their high-pressure tactics are sometimes useful, especially if they're harnessed in service of a greater good. Hard pushing is sometimes necessary to propel people through uncertainty or to a greatness they didn't think they had in them. Of the often-intimidating Martha Stewart, he relays the positive experience of an executive who once worked with her:[29] "She could be incredibly impatient and brusque if you were slow on the uptake—but if you could keep up with her, and perform to her standard, it was tremendously satisfying."

Martha Stewart could grasp things instantly and showed the Driver's characteristic impatience for people who were slower. But she could also focus attention like a laser, both her own and others'. "She had the ability," this executive continued, "to direct your attention to the single most important thing you should be thinking about or doing at that particular moment." Sometimes even intimidating levels of Driver are what's needed to move to greatness.

Watch Out, Women Drivers

But Drivers pay a price for their intimidating ways. When they fail, they fail spectacularly, and often to the applause of other competitive Drivers and anyone who has felt run over by them. Martha Stewart's Driving energy contributed to her vast success, to be sure, but it also made her something of a bull's-eye for an insider-trading charge that was probably not the most egregious of its kind. Driving leaders themselves become easy targets in the game of win and lose.

Hillary Clinton—the Democrat that Republicans most like to hate—is another example. Although she has learned the smoothness of her political profession, and earned high marks as a U.S. senator, people sense—and many want to fight with—the fierce competitor underneath. "I know how Washington Republicans think," reads a Clinton fundraising letter, "how they operate, and how to defeat them. I'm not afraid to fight for the things I believe in . . ." She is a worthy opponent for every conservative talk show host who wants to take a shot because she has some edge, something to push against. The rewards are high for highly Driven people, but so are the risks.

The Unsuccessful Habits of the Over-Driven

- Works endlessly
- Overly aggressive
- Close minded
- Wears blinders
- Overuses authority
- Rejects what doesn't fit his or her structure
- Keeps score of favors and expects payback
- Sees things only one way
- Sees a fight everywhere

Not unlike Martha Stewart and Hillary Clinton, strong Driving women, in particular, can draw ire for being too bold, even abrasive. Men can fall prey to this too, no question, but most cultures—both business and national cultures—give men more room to operate in this pattern. The energy of the Driver is stereotypically masculine, and men can get away with using more of it. At comparable levels of Drive, men are hard-charging go-getters while women are pushy broads.

Mary Minnick, the high-flying former head of marketing at Coca-Cola, knows well the difficulty of crossing this line and being labeled abrasive. It's the one thing that could hold her back from a coveted CEO role. "Intensity has been a big contributor to my success," she said in a business magazine interview.[30] But she also knows, "A lot of times your greatest strength can be your weakness." She's been coached around how to bring more balance into her leadership style. "It's not so much about softening as it is about being less intense and more balanced in my sense of urgency." How can she find that balance that brings her tremendous Driver energy to sustainable greatness? How can you?

BALANCING YOUR DRIVER ENERGY

Few people know more about balancing Drive than does Jim Loehr. Jim, the sports psychologist you met in chapter 1, is the consummate Driver. Taut, toned, and with less than 15 percent body fat, he motors into a leadership program. "I'm over 60 years old," he opens with a challenge, "and I could take on any one of you." Pure Drive. Over the next 89 minutes, he drills into the group the way to eat, work, and work out to "complete the mission." Jim has done terrific work moving premier sports athletes and corporate athletes to greatness. And as you might imagine, he's learned a thing or two about balancing Drive.

The Driver is always raising the bar—*up*, remember? But as Jim knows, you don't keep going up by relentlessly pushing up; in fact, that's a surefire recipe for wearing yourself (and others) down. Instead, as Jim says, "We must balance energy expenditure with intermittent energy renewal."[31] Drive and recover is the key. Stretch and renew. This powerful pulse is not only key to our best sustainable performance, it is particularly key to balancing the Driver.

Focus More on the Other Patterns, Not Less on the Driver

The challenge for Drivers, however, and Mary Minnick is a good example, is that they're so action-oriented that doing anything other than Driving makes them feel like they're doing *less*. The patterns can be an especially helpful framework for Drivers by giving them something to do *more*, as in move into another pattern. Rather than focusing on doing *less* Driver, they can focus on doing *more* of the Organizer, Collaborator, or Visionary. It shows them where to go in order to modulate their strong Driver, that it's balanced by renewal in a powerful pulse.

If you find yourself getting stuck in the Driver gear and need some modulation, here are some things you can do. First, use your strength, which is your ability to focus, set goals, and hit them. Set a goal for your recovery time. How many breaks will you take in a day? How long will they be? Write down your intention and keep score on yourself. (For you strong Collaborators and Visionaries, this probably sounds like a lot of hard work, and it wouldn't be your way. But it is a way for Drivers!)

What do you do in your recovery time? A lot of Drivers like to do Driving exercise—running, weightlifting, some kind of aerobic workout. It's a great break, energizing, and mind freshening. But let's not kid ourselves that this is going to modulate our Driver. It's just going to keep upping our intensity. That's not to say don't do it, but also do other activities. Something quiet. Something fun. Something creative.

> *If you need to balance your over-Drive, figure out what you need to do more.*
>
> Chances are good it's associated with your weakest pattern.
>
> *If you need to . . .*
>
> **Shape Up**—get organized or calm down: draw on more of the Organizer's steady ways. Plan for some orderly, Organizer breaks in your day.
>
> **Warm Up**—and engage people: add some fun, social, Collaborator activities to your day or week.
>
> **Open Up**—explore new possibility or let go: take a creative, Visionary break in your day.

Calm Down, Have Fun, Let Go

If more of the composure and discipline of the Organizer is what you need, plan a break in your day to do something quietly, orderly, and step-by-step. It can be sitting silently for a few moments, counting your breaths. It can be walking step-by-mindful-step through a nearby park. It can be a Sudoku puzzle or a game of solitaire.

If more of the optimism and engagement of the Collaborator is what you need, put a fun break in your day. It could be lunch with colleagues, playtime with your kids, or laughter with a good friend as you stumble your way through a six-week salsa dance class. Ideally, this kind of break involves other people and is genuinely fun.

If more of the expansive, letting-go-ness of the Visionary is what you need, put a creative break in your day. This could be a time when you paint, play piano, or let your imagination play out in wood, metal, paper, clay, glass, fabric, or landscaping. It could be what Julia Cameron calls an "artist's date," a time to fill yourself with varied inputs and ideas: taking in a museum, hanging out in nature, even walking through a mall—as long as you don't have a point. I know it's hard as a Driver not to have a point, but the point of this sort of break is to let go of having a point!

Any of these breaks can also be a good time for reflection. Maybe you'd share thoughts in conversation while taking the Collaborator break, maybe you'd write them in a journal or on the back of a museum map in the Organizer or Visionary breaks. But reflection is a key for balancing the action-oriented Driver. And we know that in the powerful pulse of stretch and renewal, the growth actually occurs during the rest part of the cycle, when we're renewing, not driving. So rather than racing through your break time and selling it short, give yourself a chance to *notice* it, and notice anything it wants to tell you.

All you über-Drivers out there, are you listening?

OVERCOMING UNDERDRIVE

Perhaps you don't identify with the Mary Minnicks of the world, or with the great intimidators and Drivingly ambitious. Too much Driver is not your problem; you may instead have a problem with Driving too little. Many leaders who are strong in other respects are perceived as weak overall, too nice, or lacking edge if they're not strong in the Driver pattern. In the leadership program that Rod Kramer runs at Stanford University,[32] most of the participants already consider themselves strong in people skills, but held back by not being sufficiently tough or having a commanding presence. "I would love to have Carly [Fiorina]'s ability to stare down her opponents," one of the participants said in reference to another famously high-Driving and fast-falling leader who nevertheless had admirable presence.

I've also worked with many leaders like those who come through the Stanford program who are nice people; in fact they're so nice that they have trouble doing not-nice things like pushing others. Some people Drive so little they have trouble pushing themselves. But most of the leaders I work with have gotten down the pushing themselves part or they wouldn't be where they are. It's pushing other people—getting into conflict, taking a tough stance, staring down the opposition—that vexes them.

A Nice Guy Who Didn't Finish Last

Todd was the sort of leader who didn't like to push. A wonderful guy, he was promoted to president of a large insurance company. At first people breathed a sigh of relief. His predecessor had been notoriously mercurial, and Todd's easy-going, steady nature was a welcome change. But this was an organization with a number of strong personalities, a euphemism for opinionated Drivers. In an insurance company, opinions are always divided on whether to underwrite a deal. Brokers who sell the deal want it to go through; the credit department wants better terms or less risk. When those opinions get supercharged by the Driver's strong will and single-point focus (which only sees one point of view) it's easy for fireworks to erupt. Todd couldn't put an end to the in-fighting; in a sense he wasn't enough of a fighter himself to keep the fighters in line. Moreover, when people pushed Todd and he didn't push back, he lost respect in their eyes. He was never going to be successful in this role without drawing on his inner Driver.

"Not someone else's Driver," I answered his concern that all this fighting was just not him. "You don't have to be a Jack Welch sort of Driver. Or even the kind of Drivers you have in your brokers and credit shop. You have this pattern. You have to let it come out as a Todd kind of Driver." Todd's strength—in his Organizer Home pattern—was his maturity and steadiness. He acted like a grown-up. And since so many people in his department were acting like rebellious teenagers, if he could bring in enough edge to have a voice of true authority, he'd be able to raise them to a more civilized level.

Todd's Practice in Edge

Todd already had some good habits to build on. He worked out regularly (strong Organizers, if you haven't figured this out, do everything regularly), so it wasn't hard to bring more of the Driver's edge into his daily exercise. For example, sprints on the treadmill, instead of the steady pace he normally jogged at, pushed him more into the Driver pattern.

Using that same intensity, he sharpened his communication at staff meetings, setting a standard for fact-based decisions and a "zero tolerance for backbiting bullshit." He gave private warning to the worst offender to cut it out within 90 days or find a new job, and Todd would be asking around. And while it wasn't a pleasant day for Todd, three months later, armed with evidence that this offender hadn't changed his ways, Todd gave him formal notice.

At no point did Todd himself become abrasive, cruel, or intimidating. He simply did what he said he was going to do and put some edge in it. Todd's version of Driver was still more measured than we might find in an Eliot Spitzer. But

---

**Moving to Greatness:
Overcoming Underdrive**

Todd, president,
insurance company

Situation: Recently promoted, likeable guy, Todd struggled with in-fighting among his people and a loss of respect when he didn't fight back.

Expressed Profile: Strong in Organizer, Driver was his second pattern. But he still needed to use more of it in this conflict situation.

Great Moves: Todd added some intensity to his regular, treadmill workouts and consciously applied more intensity in setting out clearer ground rules with his staff. He gave warning to the worst offender in the conflicts and eventually followed through with action.

Net Net: He may not be a native Driver, but he's found enough for the job.

here is the moral of the story: *it was enough to do the job.* Todd and his insurance company are doing just fine.

DO YOU NEED MORE DRIVE?

What might be some of the signs you'd look for in your own leadership to assess whether you could use more Driver energy? Even if Driver is one of your favorite patterns, you may not be calling on it at times when it would be useful. And certainly if it's the least of your pattern preferences, some of these limitations of "underdrive" will resonate. How many are true for you?

- You lack a sense of urgency; everything can be done later.
- You have a hard time staying focused.
- You don't measure performance accurately or hold yourself or others accountable.
- You're not setting a clear enough direction for yourself or others to follow.
- You don't get to the point quickly enough.
- You're not clear on your priorities.
- It's easy for other people to run over you or take advantage of you.
- You get anxious in conflict and want to exit as quickly as possible.
- You miss deadlines.
- In a stare-down—literal or metaphorical—you blink first.
- You don't know what you want to accomplish in life.
- You don't challenge people, even when it's appropriate.
- You have a hard time setting or hitting goals.
- You don't pay enough attention to the bottom line.
- You hate competition.

If a number of these sound familiar and you've had enough of these limitations, what do you do to unleash your inner Driver?

How to Get More Driver Energy

It's simple. Start pushing. The exercise in the sidebar is a quick one you can do in your office when you need to bring up your Driver energy and focus. Even sitting in a meeting, you can call up more Driver energy by making your hands into fists (I'd recommend under the table) and pressing into the floor with your feet. Exhale through your nose as if you could send the breath right through your feet. If you do this even for one breath—one breath!—you'll notice a change in your focus and sense of determination. *This* is the mindset you need when you have to stare someone down!

There are countless other ways you can call up the Driver. Physical activities are the best, since this is the pattern of adrenaline, and short of fear and shock, nothing gets the adrenaline going like hard and fast movement: jabbing, hitting, stomping, striking, punching, kicking, jumping, sprinting. Almost anything done hard and fast or with some amount of force will put you into the Driver's seat, both in body and in mind. But here's the safety warning: check with your doctor before undertaking any hard or fast activities—they may not be right for you and there are plenty of other ways to access the Driver. This is the pattern most prone to injury, so know your limits. If you're determined to push yourself, work with a good trainer or teacher so you don't break yourself.

Some good Driver activities to try include tennis, running (especially sprinting), weightlifting, most martial arts, Pilates, or any sort of aerobic workout; see also the table of Driver activities at the end of this chapter. If the activity is not already competitive, you can add more Driver's edge to it by keeping score on yourself, beating your best time in a sprint or your heaviest weight in a bench press. Better yet, challenge a friend or make a bet to give your activity a sharper edge. If aerobic activities or competitions are not for you, you can build Driver determination simply pushing on a wall.

Start with Your Strengths

As always, it's best to use your strengths to address a weakness. If you're starting from a strong Organizer Home pattern and want to increase your Driver, use your sense of discipline and order. Set aside scheduled time for your Driver breaks; once you've organized around them, they'll be appointments you keep. Also keep a table of your progress over time. As an activity for practice, you might start with something quiet like yoga, but do it in a more Driven way, as in power yoga or hot yoga.

If you're a fun-loving Collaborator wanting more of the Driver, make a game of it. Choose activities you can do with other people. Aikido is a great example; it's great fun, powerfully engaging with other people, and will make good use of your swing-like Collaborator energy. But it will also give you focus, split-second timing, and a more commanding presence. If the activity

---

To strengthen the Driver, start with your known strengths.

If your Home Pattern is . . .

Organizer—Plan it. Schedule Driver breaks in your day and keep them as you would any other appointment. Keep track of your progress.

Collaborator—Play with it. Engage in Driver activities with friends or family, or wrap social time around your Driver breaks. Keep it fun and varied.

Visionary—Experiment with it. Make a study of how you can engage the Driver center in different activities and notice the effects.

Instant focus . . .

You can call up more Driver energy in an instant by making your hands into fists and pressing your feet into the floor. Exhale through your nose as if you could send the breath right through your feet.

you want to do doesn't already include other people, do it with a friend. And maybe mix some social time around the edges. Don't get discouraged if you can't stick with the same program for long—Collaborators like to swing from one thing to another. Just keep starting up again, mixing it up, changing it up, and playing with it.

If the Visionary is your Home and you want to open up more to the Driver, make a study of it. Get *really* curious about how this pattern unfolds in you. Experiment with different activities and ways of using the senses and notice their effect. Some of the meditative approaches to bringing out the Driver might appeal to you more than the wildly aerobic. For example Chi Kung—which is energy development work—has many techniques for developing Driver energy ("Fire breath" as it's called in Taoist terminology). The breathing exercise we did earlier for pushing into the Driver is an example. Several times a day—spontaneously, when you feel like it—bring your attention to the Driver center in your lower abdomen and feel how you can engage this center in whatever activity you're doing in that moment. Notice that if you do engage that center, whatever you're doing—writing an e-mail, walking down the hall, cutting vegetables—comes out with greater intensity.

Enter the Driver through Action

Regardless of where you're starting from, you can use any of these approaches to push into the Driver. You don't necessarily have to add anything new to your day: you can bring more of the Driver's edge to something you're already doing by breathing differently, making it a competition, keeping score, giving yourself a deadline (and beating it!) or simply doing it *faster*.

No kidding, it works! I've done this myself with e-mail. Sometimes I spend enormous amounts of time writing or replying to e-mail, and when I don't have that kind of time, I give myself a firm deadline: 10 minutes. That's it. And automatically my mind starts prioritizing the messages in my inbox and determining the crucial few that need attention. My responses are brief and to the point, sort of like Dell's "Answer First." (Of course, this is not the way to have a deep or emotional conversation, but for simple messages it works, and is probably preferred by my Blackberry-viewing recipients squinting at two-inch screens.) In 10 minutes I've done enough. Some notes didn't get an answer but they didn't absolutely need one. This contrasts with the instances when I take all the time in the world for e-mail and even acknowledge acknowledgements (you know what I'm talking about!).

Your inner Driver,
an action figure

What's the Point?

At work you can sharpen your Driver by having a point to every meeting you go to, every conversation you have. What's the most important point you need to make in this meeting (conversation, e-mail, etc.)? What's the most important thing you need to take away? Simply priming yourself with crisp answers to these questions before going into a conversation can help keep it on point.

"Always know your top three priorities" was the advice from Steve, one of Dell's high-Driving, highly successful leaders. "When I first got into this job," he told a group of colleagues, "my schedule was already booked with meetings. 'How could this be?!' I asked incredulously. Nobody even knew me yet. But I agreed to follow the schedule for two weeks. And at every meeting I decided if this one fit my priorities. Could I make a difference here? Did I really need to be here? More than half the meetings came off my calendar." This kind of Driving clarity is an absolute blessing for today's busy leader. It cuts through the morass of all the things you *could* do to focus you on the vital few. Always knowing your top three priorities and getting low-priority work off your plate are great ways to both develop the Driver pattern and benefit from it.

Enter the Driver through Your Senses

As oriented as the Driver is to action, not all ways of bringing out the Driver have to be things you do. You can also use your senses and plant cues in your environment that help you keep this edge. In your office, for example, clear your desk or workspace of all clutter except for the one thing you want to focus on. Use bold, high-contrast colors like black, white, and red to bring out the Driver's energy, or use sharp angles, metal surfaces, and stay away from frills. When it comes to art, think Andy Warhol or Picasso. You might hang some Driver posters or artwork on your office walls, maybe a sharply focused samurai or a sprinter crossing the finish line—*success*!

Driver music is thrusting, pounding, and stomping music and makes you want to do the same. It conjures up images of legendary dancer Martha Graham or Latin dances like the tango. Heavy metal, hip-hop, Japanese drumming music, the rock part of rock-and-roll (the roll part moves us into the Collaborator, as you might imagine), and anything with a driving beat will bring out the intensity of this pattern. You can add intensity-building music to those moments in your day when you need the lift.

Self-Talk: Wake Up!

Even the voice in your own head—what coaches refer to as "self talk"—can be trained in the Driver. "Get on point!," "Wake up!," "Cut to the chase!," "Don't worry about perfection; just do it!" These might be just the things you need to hear at crucial moments. But notice that they all end with an exclamation point, as if we're shouting to ourselves. And that's often what this voice is doing inside our heads. Take notice of this voice inside you. If Driver is a weak pattern for you, it may be that you find this a thoroughly irritating voice, even when it's your own. You've perhaps felt beaten up by this voice much of your life. Your Driver self-talk may be a remnant from a screaming parent, a school bully, or your worst critic. The Driver voice is a critical voice, in both senses of the word: it finds fault and it's crucial that we listen. You make a subtle but radical, shift when you turn this voice into one that you know is fundamentally *for* you; when you make this voice truly your own. I'm thinking again of my harsh but benevolent Zen teacher. This is the kind of voice you want to select for your Driver. Or that of someone like Dr. Phil, one of the United States' most popular talk show psychologists, who cuts through the story with a penetrating, "Is it workin' for you?" No nonsense. No slack. But fundamentally for you, fundamentally *you*.

REFLECTING ON THE DRIVER IN YOU

The Driver can be developed in so many ways: through exercises, activities, work behaviors with an edge, using any of your senses, self-talk, and even breathing. The tables in the next section capture all of these ideas and more; you can read them now or come back to them later. But before leaving the Driver, take a moment to take stock of the Driver in you. In true Driver fashion, answer first, fast, and be done with it!

- Would you say that you're more of a Driver or less of a Driver than the people you work with, or are you about in the middle? And what does this mean for your work and leadership?
- If there's one aspect of the Driver that you overuse, what is it?
- If there were one aspect of the Driver you could use more of, what would it be?

DRIVER MINI-BREAKS AND BEST PRACTICES

The next few pages summarize numerous ways to push into the Driver using breath, body, background, and everyday leadership behaviors. The **breath** exercises get you focused in the moment and they take but a moment to do. The **body** activities not only thrust you into the Driver in the moment, but give you easier access over time. These exercises, and all of the exercises in this book, should be done pain-free. (If you feel any pain, stop and get it checked out.) The **background** suggestions will help you keep your Driver's edge through various senses and don't require extra "doing" at all. And finally, the **behavior** ideas will show you how to Up the Driver in the way you work and lead.

This section is intended as a reference for when you design a practice (which we'll get to in chapter 7) or need a Driver reminder weeks or months from now. You can use some of the exercises to create a mini, two-minute break in your day (shown with the ❷ icon). Other activities are more suited to longer practice (indicated by ☯). All the two-minute exercises are good warm-ups to the longer practices—and get you focused fast!

Push into the Driver (❷)

1. Stand or sit forward in your chair in a way that you can press your feet into the floor.
2. Focus your eyes like a laser on a pinpoint in front of you.
3. Picture your torso as a thermometer with a huge bulb at the bottom. Open your mouth and inhale deeply, filling the thermometer bulb.
4. Close your mouth and exhale fairly intensely through your nose (don't overdo it!), as if you're pushing the breath further down into the bulb of the thermometer (i.e., lower abdomen). As you exhale, press your hands down like a piston in front of you (from the level of your heart to the lower abdomen) and press your feet into the floor.
5. At the end of your exhale, quit pressing with your hands and feet, open your mouth and inhale deeply again. Repeat three times, each time more slowly and with greater concentration. Relax and breathe normally if you get light-headed.

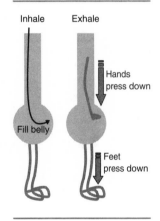

Connect to the Driver (❷)

1. Stand relaxed with feet hip-width apart. Let out a sigh of relief to drop tension out of your upper body.
2. Imagining your torso like a thermometer, start with your hands in front of the bulb at the base, fingers touching, palms up.
3. Breathing in through the nose, draw your hands up over your head, turning palms to the ceiling, and stretch onto your toes.

Breath Exercises for focusing fast.

2   3

4, 5

4. Drop down on your heels, and let out a little air through your mouth. Bend your wrists sharply, and press your palms toward the ceiling. Notice as you press a sense of "thereness" in the lower abdomen, where you've connected to the Driver center.

5. Continuing to push out with your palms and breathing out through your mouth, let each hand carve a semicircle back to your center.

6. Relax on the inhale, releasing slight tension in the Driver center. Repeat five times, making each breath slower and more deliberate.

Pushing Arms (❷)

1. Sit or stand with hands grasped in front of you

2. Push your hands together as hard as you can, and then try to pull them apart as hard as you can (without letting go).

3. Feel the firing of muscles in the very base of the abdomen, the Driver Center. Also notice how your eyes go into pinpointed focus.

Driving Elbow Jabs (❷)

1. Stand with your feet shoulder-width apart. Make your left hand into a fist and cup it with your right hand.

2. Drive the left elbow down diagonally behind you, pushed by the right hand, as you exhale sharply. Don't overdo it!

3. As your hands come back up in front of you, make the fist with your right hand, cupped by your left hand.

4. Drive the right elbow down behind you, as in #2. Feel the motion come from the base of your abdomen.

Driving Elbow and Heel Jabs (❷)

1. Stand with your feet shoulder-width apart, hands in a doubled-handed fist as above.

2. Lifting your left leg slightly from the base of your abdomen, thrust out the heel in a low side kick, no more than a foot off the floor. Exhale sharply.

3. As foot comes down, follow with a left elbow jab, exhaling sharply.

4. Repeat on other side. Notice the firing of the Driver Center and the intensity that develops.

Driving Seated Walk (❷)

1. Sit on floor with your legs straight in front of you, hands forming fists.
2. Keeping both "sits" bones on the floor (i.e., don't lift up), drive one heel forward, exhaling sharply.
3. Repeat on other side, letting your arms move. Repeat several more times. Feel the drive come from the Driver Center. Try to move forward. If you don't move at first, be patient with yourself; it will come.
4. To go backward, drive the elbow down diagonally behind you to pull the hip back along the floor (don't lift up or you'll start rocking in the Collaborator pattern).

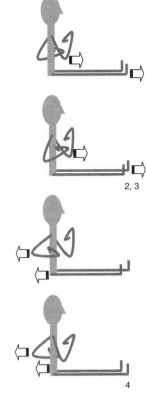

2, 3

4

Add these elements to your office or home . . .

By adding these elements to your office, or making time to work in places that have these elements, your senses will focus with the Driver.

Driver offices are sparse and clear of clutter. Clear your desk of everything except the one thing you need to focus on. Driver spaces use high-contrast colors and provide places to work alone.

Driver furnishings are simple, clean, with sharp lines and bold but basic colors (e.g., red, black, and white). Metal, marble, or metallic-looking surfaces figure prominently.

Driver art is bold and in your face—it focuses your attention on a point. Driver energy shows up in motivational posters with themes around winning, raising the bar, and success. Or line your walls with sports pictures and quotes that foster a competitive spirit ("Winning isn't everything, it's the only thing").

Driver music thrusts on the beat, as in hip-hop and hard rock. You can also listen to bold, edgy classical music, as in parts of Beethoven, Mussorgsky, Stravinsky, or Philip Glass.

Background

Add some edge to your surrounds.

Things you might say to yourself . . .

- "Be here now." (or "Hey! You, here, now!")
- "What's most important?"
- "What are you trying to achieve?"
- "Cut through the crap."
- "Wake up!"
- "Get on point."

- "Cut to the chase!"
- "Wrap it up."
- "Is it working for you?"
- "It doesn't have to be perfect; just do it!"
- "Focus!"

Cultivate your own inner Driver.

Driver Activities (☯)

Weightlifting, weight-resistance training

Running—especially sprinting and alternating with brief periods of recovery; running hard using sharp elbow movements to add momentum

Tennis, racquetball—even hitting a soft surface (like a cushion or mattress) with a tennis racquet or paddle brings out Driver energy

Bicycling—hard and fast, alternating Drive with recovery

Kayaking, rowing—hard and fast, again alternating with recovery time

Racing, driving with rapid acceleration, deceleration (on a track, please!), boat racing—any kind of competition to finish something first brings out the Driver

Pilates, Coordination Pattern training

Many martial arts, especially, karate, kendo, fencing, and arts involving sword work

Competitive sports—especially those that using Driving, thrusting movements, as in football, soccer, or hockey; any sport where a score is kept brings out some competitive edge

Many kinds of aerobic workouts, including aerobic dance

Most cardiovascular machines used with vigor (and recovery!)

Downhill skiing, cross-country skiing—hard and fast, with time for recovery

Creating visual art using Driver energy—with bold elements, high contrast, sharp angles, and no nonsense; Driver art is direct and in-your-face, often challenging or disturbing, always clear

Playing or singing Driver music, especially playing percussion—Driver music has a pounding beat, a staccato edge, and a repeating intensity; it can be high energy, or darkly disturbing (e.g., Stravinsky, punk rock)

Body

Nothing develops the Driver pattern more than moving in it. These activities can be built into a 20- or 30-minute-a-day practice.

Dancing to Driver music or in a Driver style—with movements that are sharp, angular, or thrusting (e.g., tango or African dance)

Landscaping—using bold, high-contrast materials such as sharp, angular rocks, or a single, jutting cactus surrounded by lines of stone

Cooking in a Driver way—using sharp knives, making crisp cuts, as would a Japanese sushi chef; cooking with simple ingredients, clear, contrasting flavors, and with visually pleasing presentation

Driver Work Behaviors

Behaviors

Bring intensity, focus, and simplicity to your leadership.

Focus for meetings. Before going into a meeting, write down the most important point you want to make at the meeting and the most important objective you want to take from the meeting. After the meeting, check yourself: did you say and get what you needed?

Know your top priorities. Write down the three most important things you need to accomplish, and keep refreshing your list as things get done or new things come up. Always know your Top 3. Take a few minutes at the beginning of each week to orient yourself to this week's Top 3; at the end of the week check yourself as to whether you were able to focus the bulk of your time on these priorities. If not, identify one way you'll focus more effectively on your Top 3 the next week.

Measure how and what you're doing. If you can measure it, you can manage it. Pick something you want to improve, measure where it's at now, set your goal for improvement, and track your progress. For example: set a goal to cut the time you spend on e-mail by 50 percent. For one week, measure the amount of time you spend doing e-mail, take an average, cut that number in half, and make that your target. Week by week, plot your progress toward that target. Keep it visual and in front of you—tack a graph on your wall, make a screen saver for your computer.

Keep score. You can measure and keep score on just about anything: anything to do with time, percentage of goals accomplished, success rate on selling a product or putting forth an idea, or the number of times your point is carried in a meeting. Get creative about what you measure, and notice how it forces you to pay attention to different things.

Get to the point. Structure your formal and informal communications to state your main point up front. This way of communicating (as in Dell's "Answer First") saves time in communication. State your point first, and then give your listener a few reasons to agree with you. This is similar to the way a lawyer argues a case: main point first (guilty or innocent) and then why the jury should agree. And as any good salesperson knows: never sell past the close. As soon as someone buys your main point, stop.

Set a stretch goal. Pick one area where reaching a stretch target would really take your work to a new level and set a leap-goal for yourself. Make sure it's a leap, not an increment—50 percent change, not 5 percent. Keep the goal in front of you, and let it inform your Top 3 or something you're measuring.

Reduce distractions. Whether working alone or with others, get clear about what you need to focus on and cut out distracting influences. This might mean clearing your desk, holding meetings where you won't be interrupted, and eliminating your own multitasking (e.g., buzzing Blackberry). Keep meetings short, to the point, and then go on to the next thing.

Enforce clarity and action. Drive conversation to the point of action: now what? Be clear in accepting or assigning actions (who, what, when). If you manage others, recap delegating conversations in terms of crisp actions and clear expectations.

CHAPTER FOUR

Step into the Organizer

SIT UP STRAIGHT

The Organizer

Let's slow it down a bit. In fact, let's just stop for a moment. Sit up straight, hold still, and you've stepped into the Organizer pattern. Already you may be recalling times when you've heard the irritating admonition to "sit up straight" or "shape up." Try not to be too annoyed; you may gain fresh appreciation of this pattern that loves to get it right. Place your feet flat on the floor and parallel to one another, with your knees together. Hold this book in both hands about chest level, as if it were a choir book. Hold your elbows out at chest level and you might notice a slight sensation in the middle of your chest; this is the physical center around which the Organizer holds its perfect form. Be as still as possible. Don't you just feel the urge to make a list?

We begin our tour of this pattern in a typical schoolroom, perhaps like one in which you sat up straight when you were eight years old. Here we might see straight rows of square desks, multiplication tables on the wall, and alphabetical order everywhere. Ahhh, the days of simple right and wrong when we were taught to think before doing, given gold stars for doing correctly, and praised for sitting still. The Organizer loves that order and attempts to create it whenever possible: numbered steps in a plan, large-to-small books on a shelf, and all hanger hooks facing the same way in the closet. Stepping into The Container Store (which even has containers for organizing other containers!) is a nearly orgasmic experience for Organizers.

At work, Organizers do the right thing and do things right. Here you'd meet leaders like Richard Clark, the head of

> *The journey of 1,000 miles begins with a single step.*
>
> —*Lao-tzu*

The Land of the Organizer—everything in its place

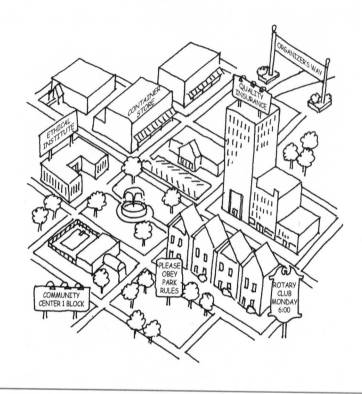

Merck, who is steadily steering a company grounded in ethics through the litigious wake of Vioxx—one lawsuit at a time—and winning most of them. You'd encounter the grown-up equivalents of Boy Scouts and Girl Scouts ("Be Prepared") in their adult versions of neat and tidy uniforms (i.e., business suits) doing what they do best: "Plan the work, then work the plan." And yes, I'd be among them, parsing big jobs into scalable steps, managing multiple workstreams with interdependent timelines, sorting out the best allocation of resources to the job, and sorting the paperclips while I'm at it. "The scissors go in the scissors drawer," I tell my Collaborator husband, who didn't even know there *was* a scissors drawer.

Organizers are people of character—they want to be correct—and tend to be good judges of character as well. The consummate askers of questions, Organizers also question themselves. In healthy doses, this leads to self-knowledge and humility but in large doses, it gives rise to self-doubt, perfectionism, even depression. Sometimes only their overactive sense of duty gets Organizers trudging through their days. If this sounds even remotely familiar, read on! There's hope!

Organizers have a sense of place: they like a place for everything and everything in its place. If the Organizer were a city it would be laid out on a perfect grid—like Chicago—which, owing to a disastrous fire in 1871, had the good fortune to be completely rebuilt with Organizers in charge. In Organizer territory, the pace is slower—certainly slower than in the Driver's lane. People walk calmly, step-by-step. They cross the street on the "walk" signal, stay within the lines of the crosswalk, and wait in queues for the bus. The clock tower in the central square keeps perfect time as it presides over carefully weeded gardens, properly mowed lawns, and trash placed in trash cans. If this seems like a scene from a slower yesteryear, well, there's some truth to that. It's easier to keep things Organized when they don't move around so fast.

Are you still sitting up straight?

The Voice of the Organizer

"Let's take this thing one step at a time."

What the Organizer Does Best

Suggest orderly ways to proceed, next steps

Too Much Organizer

Fixated and stubborn, caught up in details, perfectionistic

Not Enough Organizer

Undependable, unethical, inconsistent, disorganized

ORGANIZING YOU

Stacking alphabet-lettered blocks, lining up rainbow-colored rings in ascending order along a plastic rod, such are the vital preoccupations of many a young child. These simple activities help to Organize young nervous systems and develop coordinated movement. Since the nervous system reinforces the very pathways it uses, the more drawn we are to stacking those blocks or lining up those rings, the more sharply we're defining a sense of order that will be with us long after the blocks and rings are gone. When my wonderful father (if Organizer had an entry in the dictionary, his picture would be there) was deep in thought he would line up his thumb with the grid on the windowpane and the car across the street. "What are you doing, Dad?" we'd say in fun. And he'd laugh, caught again in his line-up act. But now I understand: he was just Organizing his thoughts. Some navy pilots, when they're trying to bring a faltering F-18 safely onto a carrier deck, steady themselves by studying the clock. Same idea: enter the Organizer pattern and it's easier to sort things out.

I invite you into an Organizing moment yourself—for some of you it may feel like an agonizingly long moment. But whether you make full use of it or not, you've got this Organizer energy, and there are times when it could be the prized player on your whole and balanced team. Set this book down in a place where you can still read it, and try this.

Sit with your back comfortably straight and feet flat on the floor, with your knees together. Fully extend your arms out to the side, shoulder height and palms up. Now fold in your forearms so that your fingertips rest on the tops of your shoulders. Hold this pose for a moment and notice the sense of composure. Picture your upper body as a Libra-sort of scale with the weight of your arms on each side. Keeping your lower body still, tip the scale of your shoulders slightly to one side, pause for two seconds, and then move to the other side; pause before returning upright.

As you tip from side to side, notice a quality of holding or "thereness" at the pivot point in your mid-chest area where your ribs come together. This is the Organizer center. In the Indian system of chakras, this corresponds to the "heart" center. While we don't need to stretch the metaphor too far, Organizers do embody a number of heartful qualities. In connection with others (usually one person at a time) the Organizer is a reliable friend, a good listener, and a responsible parent, worker, or boss. We might speak of someone as showing a lot of heart when he or she sticks with something for a long time—well past the endurance of most people—and that would pretty much define the Organizer. "You have more stick-to-it-iveness than anyone I know," my father once said to me. "You're the most stubborn person I ever met!" was the rather more blunt way Tanouye Rotaishi put it years later. Endurance, stubbornness, heart—we Organizers own it all.

SMALL STEPS AND GIANT LEAPS AT NASA

NASA's Johnson Space Center is a campus of more than a hundred buildings, each with a prominent number over its front door, arranged on a grid of paved streets and sidewalks separated by perfectly mowed grass. Neat and tidy, this is a place an Organizer could feel right at home. Here resides one of the icons of NASA's heritage, the nerve center of its human space flight program: the Mission Control Center. Roger that.

Organized Life at NASA

The Mission Control Center has neat rows of consoles, each labeled according to its distinct role in managing the mission. And each mission gets managed by the book, which is to say countless books and files of flight rules and numbered checklists for every possible procedure and contingency procedure. Long after there were automatic teller machines and a computer on every desk, NASA was still preparing for missions by re-wiring Mission Control consoles and changing out the paper labels under their plastic-capped buttons. It's not that people at NASA were dull or slow, but as a culture, NASA worked diligently to reduce the huge risks of spaceflight into pieces that were certain: checklists, wires, and plastic caps were certain. The Organizer at work.

NASA managed programs with similar micro-certitude. When the International Space Station Program was in its design phase in the 1980s and 90s, crisp milestones were laid out on a timeline: preliminary requirements review, preliminary design review, critical design review—like everything at NASA, they were known by their acronyms, PRR, PDR, CDR, and so on. Each review had a strict protocol for how it was to be conducted. Issues in the design would be numbered, sorted, reviewed, costed, and tracked by a five-digit action item tracking code. But all of this protocol and process did nothing to prevent the cost creep of the program, the cost cuts in the budget, or the inexorable slip in schedule. A criticism often levied on Organizer leaders, as it was on NASA, is that they manage the small stuff well, while the big picture reels out of control.

Enter the Disrupter: Dan Goldin

Bloated bureaucracy! Stuck in the past! These criticisms were lobbed at NASA, not by its enemies but by its new administrator, Dan Goldin, when he joined in 1992. There was no mistaking Dan's passion for all-things-space—he was like a little kid. But the agency was shellshocked that this Visionary "little kid" had just been given the keys to their candy store. Center directors hunkered down in what is often the Organizer's first reaction to change: "This too shall pass . . ." A campaign to discredit Goldin started up on e-mail. "He will destroy the agency!" one screamed. "He's unstable," another, who had known him in his former role, claimed, "he was nicknamed Captain Crazy at TRW."

Goldin came in with the manta, "faster, better, cheaper," and hammered that theme into every public speech and every private budget review.[33] "Which two of those three do you want?" was the stubborn reply at first. NASA and its contractors were used to a very logical, incremental, Organized way of working, "I can give you faster and better, but it won't be cheaper." But Goldin wanted paradoxical demands optimized,

Spotlight: Daniel Goldin

Former NASA administrator

Quote: *"You will send probes beyond our solar system and to the stars. You may look up and answer the question as old as humankind itself: Are we alone?"*

Expressed Profile: Visionary supported by Driver, a rocket scientist seeking the truth and the essence of our origins; unafraid to take a tough stance. He used the Visionary paradox of "faster, better, cheaper" to Drive NASA toward greater efficiency and effectiveness.

and a totally new paradigm for the space business. He truly was a Visionary leader, and to NASA's credit, the agency eventually got behind him. They may be stubborn, but Organizers are, above all, dutiful soldiers.

Goldin was able to launch aggressive management reforms that increased productivity by 40 percent, while cutting civil service headcount by a third. Through his pushing, the development time for earth-and space-science space-craft was cut by 40 percent, costs were reduced by two-thirds, and the number of missions launched increased fourfold. As for the pride-and-joy Mission Control Center, Goldin argued that NASA shouldn't be in the business of on-going operations—the private sector could do that. NASA should be focused on research and development. He wasn't interested in micro-certitude; Goldin wanted NASA "finding some life out there."

Dan Goldin ended up being NASA's longest-serving administrator. In naming him one the 100 most influential men and women in government, the *National Journal* wrote some years ago that "most space watchers say that Goldin is a brilliant visionary who brought NASA back from the brink of a black hole." NASA could never have launched anything without the steady energy of the Organizer. But sometimes the Organizer needs a kick out of the ruts of its own making. Roger that!

PLAN THE WORK, WORK THE PLAN

If you looked into the closets in Beth's home, you'd find the hanger hooks most assuredly facing the same way. "More than that," she told me laughingly in one of our early coaching sessions, "The clothes are arranged by category, suits on one rack, blouses on another. And when I pick out clothes, I try to draw from the right and replace on the left so that I'm rotating my wardrobe." Now there's a little Organizing tip for you. Beth had a system for everything, and a passion for her systems. Every day began with a checklist. "On my best days," she said with pride and humor, "every item gets crossed off."

A talented product manager in a high-tech company, Beth was being groomed for bigger things, a role in general management, where she'd be overseeing all of the company's operations in the UK. Described as sincere, straightforward, and responsible, she received solid praise from her boss and colleagues: "She never misses a detail; you know if you give something to Beth it will be handled 100 percent right." But—you knew there was a *"but"* coming—people harbored doubts about Beth's ability to come up a level and lead areas where she had no direct expertise. "She needs to look at the bigger picture," they told me. "She gets upset whenever things don't go according to plan; she has to flex a little more."

A Prescription for Flexibility

This wasn't news to Beth. "My family has been telling me this my whole life," she admitted. " 'Lighten up,' they'd tell me. 'Don't think you have to control everything.' " And by family, she meant birth family. Unmarried with no children, Beth was non-stop dedicated to her work. She worked 14 to16 hours a day and, far from making her more productive, this relentless schedule was making her more tense and less tolerant of deviations from the work she'd so carefully planned. More of the same, she started to see, would bring only bitter disappointment. As we talked, it became clear to both of us that our coaching was not going to be about getting a promotion, but about getting a life.

"Yoga, for starters," I suggested. "I used to enjoy taking yoga," Beth returned, "before I got too busy." If I had a minute for every time I've heard someone tell me of a healthy, renewing, enjoyable, they-used-to-do-it-and-know-it's-good-for-them practice that they no longer make time for, I'd have a day's worth, easy. I whipped out a small sheet of paper and mocked up a prescription: "Yoga—take class three times weekly and apply daily." Since I was only reminding her of something she already knew, she took my little prescription. Yoga was a perfect practice for Beth, taking what she was already good at as an Organizer—holding poses—and adding flexibility and being present in the moment, instead of planning for the future. It wasn't the only thing she needed to do, but it would underscore everything else.

I also had Beth take the FEBI so she could see the energy patterns behind the kind of feedback she was getting and the direction she wanted to move in. What was eye-opening to Beth was that the patterns showed four simple and clear ways to approach any situation. Not just the Organized one that she'd been using over and over, but three other options. She was already pretty strong in the Driver, now she had the option of the playful Collaborator, which would help her roll with the punches and get people moving more easily with her, plus bring more fun to her life outside work. And she could use the big-picture Visionary, a vital entry ticket to executive-level management.

The Payoff

Giving an Organizer an organized framework for managing her career was an easy sell. Beth went to work on it, trying out Collaborator and Visionary ways

---

Moving to Greatness: Balancing Organizer

Beth, product manager, country manager, technology products

Situation: Leader being groomed for general management needs to learn to flexibly manage beyond her expertise and get away from the details.

Expressed Profile: Strong in Organizer with Driver as her second pattern; weakest in Visionary and Collaborator.

Great Moves: Beth started her "flexibility training" with yoga classes three times a week. She also added social and creative activities to her time outside of work. She consciously worked to flex better with people and get them moving with her, and she cultivated Visionaries around her.

of working using the methods you'll find in the tables at the ends of chapters 5 and 6. I also sold her on Julia Cameron's wonderful idea of a weekly "artist's date,"[34] where you make an appointment with yourself or with a friend to do something fun and creative.

It's true that Beth felt like something of a slacker when her workday slipped from 14 hours. Such work habits are ground deeply into our being, and a certain anxiety is almost certain to erupt when we change things. But it's worth it. And that's not just me talking; that was Beth's experience as well. She started seeing people respond to her ideas more favorably when she flexed more with them. She felt new respect from her more Visionary colleagues after she'd gathered them together to brainstorm around new product strategy. "I need your big ideas," she had told them, and left open time in the agenda to really hear them.

Beth was given her promotion the following year. But what I found most satisfying about working with Beth was what she told me when she called me with the news. "Ginny," she said. "I'm happier."

MOVERS AND SHAPERS

"Shape" is Betsy's telling term for the Organizer pattern, as Organizers have a special skill for bringing form to new ideas and getting businesses (or communities, nonprofits, and everything else they run) in good shape. See how much you recognize yourself in these Organized leaders at work.

Bringing Order and Ethics to Citi

Chuck Prince was brought in to shape things up following the rambunctious and, in the end, scandal-tarnished reign of Sandy Weill. "Nobody thinks of Prince as a visionary or a great leader," said one of his detractors at Citi.[35] "He has the potential to be a great CEO," was the more measured assessment of Robert Rubin, a Citigroup director and former U.S. treasury secretary. As a *Fortune* magazine article on Prince summarized, "It seems almost unanimous—among employees, former employees, investors and analysts—that 2½ years into his job, Chuck Prince is still feeling his way." These hardly sound like enthusiastic endorsements. Yet Organizer leaders are often underestimated early on—and unsung heroes later on—as they work diligently to clean up messes and get things in shape.

Prince, for example, started by bringing ethics on par with profitability in response to a string of scandals, personally sermonizing to 45,000 employees around the world on the application of ethics to their work. (We might also guess there's a supporting Collaborator in Chuck Prince's leadership style from his stage presence and reputation as a being "the resident funny guy at Citi" before he became CEO.) He halted the growth-by-acquisition that was the hallmark of Weill's era in order to systematize and integrate the vast behemoth that Citigroup had become. Quoting John Reed, the CEO before Weill, Prince explained his approach to controlled growth: "John Reed used to say that the most important part of a race car is the brakes, and that you can't drive fast unless you have the ability to stop."

Spoken like a true Organizer! If you remember the fundamental muscle movement behind this pattern, it is to apply engine and brakes at the same time. How interesting to see this same pattern surface in a leader's mindset: an Organizer hardly moves anywhere without being sure they have brakes! Prince wants to make sure he has the brakes of an ethical culture and internal controls, or, as he tells investors, "We can't grow as fast as we want to grow."

Chuck Prince is doing what Organizer leaders do best: set the rules, establish quality processes, and do the right thing. It's too early to tell whether he'll be judged the right leader to bring Citigroup though troubled times or whether he'll be seen as having his foot too much on the brakes in a fast-money business. Either can be true for Organizer leaders. Given Prince's high profile, he'll certainly miss the trap that many Organizer leaders fall into, which is that people don't notice them at all.

Getting the Trains to Run on Time

In another part of the world, people are certainly noticing the effects that a quiet Organizer leader has had on the Indian train system. The trains actually run on time, which seemed impossible when Elattuvalapil Sreedharan took over as the managing director of the Delhi Metro Rail Corporation. Described by *The Economist* as "more like a monk than a manager," Sreedharan leads a very disciplined life of yoga, walks, jogging, and controlled eating.[36] His training as an engineer and his experience in railroads taught him to focus on two basics that may seem obvious, especially to Organizers, but not to many other developers of India's infrastructure: quality and ethics. Quality meant looking beyond favored local firms to the best suppliers globally. Ethics meant avoiding even the possibility of corruption by making vendor evaluation more transparent and objective. When the original 10 miles of metro rail service was installed in Kolkata, it took 22 years and 14 increases in budget. Under Sreedharan's leadership, the tripling of this network, which opened in 2006, was completed within budget and three years ahead of schedule.

Sreedharan is not one to blow his own horn over these accomplishments. Just the opposite; he deflects credit to others and exudes a quiet humility and get-it-doneness that *Good to Great* author Jim Collins says characterizes the

"Willful Humility"

This is the single most important quality in the most successful business leaders, according to management researcher and *Good to Great* author Jim Collins.

These leaders display a huge ambition for their company, a do-whatever-it-takes attitude (within the bounds of the company's values), combined with deflection of credit and personal humility.

Expressed Profile of Leaders with Willful Humility:

They're good enough in all the patterns—i.e., whole and balanced—and great in Driver energy, most generally supporting an Organizer Home pattern.

In this style, the ambition of the Driver is put in service of doing the right thing for the company, combined with the Organizer's persistence and humility.

most sustainably successful leaders.[37] At their best, what Organizer leaders lack in pizzazz and fanfare, they make up for in results and integrity.

GOOD AS YOUR WORD

When I think of integrity, my father pops to mind. "You gave me one too many," I can still hear him saying to the cashier in the grocery store as he handed back a penny. Okay, so maybe it was an object lesson for his young daughters (I never forgot it!), but that quality in my father carried over to everything he did. It made people trust him.

When people tease apart the elements of what makes one person trust another, three qualities stand out[38]: character, competence, and consistency. People of character are those who do the right thing and don't betray others. People of competence are capable of doing what we've put before them. People of consistency are easy to anticipate; they do things like start three sentences in a row the same way to make sure you get the three-part point. While any one of these qualities is possible in any pattern, the Organizer brings them together most consistently. Organizers do what they say they're going to do.

When my mother was due to give birth to my sister, my father practiced driving the route to the hospital. He had to get it right, plus find a suitable backup route that didn't cross the train tracks in case a train was coming at the same time as my sister. Always have a plan and a backup plan: that's how Organizers become people you can count on.

Like many Organizers who have a people-loving Collaborator pattern as their second pattern, my father emerged as a leader more by popular demand than by ambition. Chief troubleshooter that everyone would turn to at work, captain of his bowling team, convener of the golf foursome, my father has always been someone that people naturally want to Organize around. Plus, like many Organizers, he has a keen sense of service and is always doing things for others. When my brother gave him a snow-blower for Christmas—quite useful for winters in Michigan—he not only cleared away all the snow from his lot, but did the entire block, sculpting sidewalks and driveways into Organized perfection.

Organizers are as good as their word. And their word is good.

CAUTION: TOO MUCH CAN BE DANGEROUS TO YOUR HEALTH

All of this conscientious dependability goes too far when it starts to kill you, as it nearly did my father at age 48 when he suffered a heart attack. As with most heart attacks, this one had been a long time building. A bright, happy-go-lucky kid, my father claims he never felt like a responsible adult until he became a father. From the time I knew him, he never set the mantle down. He *had* to provide for his family! He *had* to succeed! Super-charged by the Driver, his sense of responsibility went into over-Drive and combined with the Organizer's fear of failure to create a pressure cooker. The flip side of doing the right thing is being afraid of getting it wrong, and Organizers can worry about this a great deal.

My father's sculpted snow-blowing; we're still laughing about this picture in my family. (Photo: John Whitelaw)

My father worried about remembering the right part numbers in his inventory work at Cadillac Motors (so he memorized the part numbers of every radiator grill component for every Cadillac built between 1941 and 1954). He worried that he couldn't keep up with the people who worked for him on these new-fangled things called computers (so he brought home books on Honeywell assembler language and studied nights and weekends). He worried about bills (so he took a second job). He worried about how to live up to the big promotion he was given when EDS took over the Cadillac Data Processing Center (so he worked harder still).

Do you recognize this cycle of worry and drive? You may be doing some version of the same thing. So many of the leaders I work with who struggle with work–life balance are caught in this loop. And many of them don't change their ways until after their first heart attack. I confronted one such leader, remembering my father's experience. This man's face blanched as he went on to tell me that only the previous week he'd had chest pains.

When the relentless pressure of the Driver combines with a get-it-right Organizer Home pattern, the work is never done. How could it be? The Driver is always raising the bar, pushing the Organizer to keep expanding responsibilities, not make a mistake, even as it moves faster to do new things, where more preparation is needed (but there's no time) or failure is more likely (but that's not an option). My heart gets tighter just thinking about it!

The Corporate Rib

Imagine putting your "best foot forward" or stiffening up a bit in defensiveness, and you've put on the Corporate Rib.

Sometimes you need it to help you through tough situations. But the more you become aware of when and why you're using it, the easier it will be to take it off, like a jacket, when you no longer need it.

When you're ready to let it go or shake it out, try the sidebar exercises that follow.

Releasing the Organizer Override

Let It Go

Lie down on your back with your knees bent, feet flat on the floor. Let out a few sighs ("Ah-h-h-h") of relief and let your body relax.

Raise your right hand about a foot above your chest, bending your wrist so that your fingers point down toward the midline of your chest.

As you exhale through your mouth ("Ah-h-h-h"), let your fingers touch down on the midline at your solar plexus and imagine the touch going all the way back to your spine. Let go of all the tension caught between the front and back of your chest.

Pick up your hand and drop it down at another midline location—"Ah-h-h-h"— working between your solar plexus and your sternum. With each landing, empty the tension in your upper body.

Getting Stuck in an Override

Short of a heart attack, tightness in the chest area is common among Organizers. In Betsy's movement work with clients, this knot of Organizer energy stuck in the middle of the chest is the most common pattern problem she sees; she calls it an "override," as it blocks our natural movement into and out of other patterns, especially the Collaborator. You might think this would only happen in native, Home-pattern Organizers, but that's not so. It's much more common in people who don't naturally prefer the Organizer pattern, but as a part of their "shape-upbringing" and socialization they've tensed their way into it. When we're stuck in the Organizer and holding it too tightly, our movements and behaviors appear stiff, forced, or too compulsive. What's worse is that if this is one of our weaker patterns, we're never fully discovering our strengths.

One way this Organizer override shows up is what Betsy calls the "Corporate Rib" (It's the rib Napolean touches inside his jacket in most of his pictures). Imagine being in a formal setting when someone points out that you've made a mistake. "What, me?!" you might protest, a little embarrassed or defensive, stiffening up a bit. It's exactly that stiffening up that locks the corporate rib. It tightens when we're holding ourselves in check, even unconsciously. You'd be amazed how common it is in corporate life! Especially in traditional Driver–Organizer companies where form matters a good deal. Dick, one of Betsy's clients who worked at such a company, described the Corporate Rib as part of the culture. "To be trusted in the company, you had to have on your Corporate Rib; it was as much a part of the uniform as the suit and tie." Dick remembered adjusting his posture whenever he entered the office building—"Upright; Rib in place"—and then taking off the "Rib" with his jacket once he entered his own office.

Freeing an Organizer Override

Overrides serve their purpose of getting us through a tough situation. But when we habitually fall into them and carry them well beyond their usefulness, they do more damage than good. This image of being able to take off an override like a jacket when we no longer need it is a good one to keep in mind. Two of Betsy's exercises that help people overcome

Organizer overrides are described in the sidebar. You might want to try them and see what they open up in you. A colleague of mine, Everett Ogawa, who is a master of deep tissue bodywork, says that when he works the Organizer center on people, they open to new bigness. "It's like our ego is locked up in there," he says. "It's everything we're trying to protect."

Indeed, the Organizer pattern, especially in large doses, is the most self-protecting, self-doubting, self-critical, self-explaining, self-righteous, and generally self-conscious of the patterns. Why? Because it moves through life like the engine and brakes example earlier, with both on! Try something—oops, better stop; is this right?—oh, need a slight correction; get going—oh, better slow down. It is always doing and judging its doing at the same time. This correct-as-you-go approach makes it possible to paint up to—but not beyond—the line, feel emotion up to—but not beyond—what one can handle (think British stiff upper lip), and think up to—but not outside—the box.

If this feels like something of a prison or a body cast, occasionally it is. It's the pattern we most like to rebel against, even when it's our Home pattern. Breaking the rules is a rite of passage for shedding what was once a workable structure, but now feels too small and tight, be those the rules of our parents, our childhood religion, or our first job when we had to punch a time-clock. Crises erupt in midlife and other times when the old rules don't work anymore, when even doing right by them leaves us feeling that something's wrong. The Organizer's strength is giving shape to things—which is great for fixing a business or getting trains to run on time—but that shape can become a barrier to further growth. Like a snail ever having to grow a shell, then shed it to keep growing, so do we need the Organizer's energy to give shape to our lives, even as we grow to discard it—and discard it to grow.

WHEN TOO MUCH GETTING IT RIGHT GETS IT ALL WRONG

Not only do we often struggle with the Organizer pattern in ourselves, but we can get mighty impatient with it in other people. I was at an intensive training session once where the expectation was that we would stay the whole time; this Zen training was designed to push us to (and beyond!) our limits. Bailing out in the middle was not considered an option. But one of the Organizer participants had pushed to his limit and that was all he was going to take. He told

Shake It Out

In the same position as the previous exercise, shake your arms out in a side-to-side bobble that starts at your spine, then moves through your shoulder blades and out through the ends of your finger tips, like a ghost trying to scare people. It's good to add sound effects; say "Blah-h-h-h" as you do this on the exhale. Repeat a few times.

my teacher, Toyoda Sensei, that he was going to leave, which was acknowledged with a nod and a grunt. Then he went on to explain himself. Organizers are forever explaining themselves since they want to be perfect so there's nothing to criticize and if you criticize them, they want to explain themselves further. He wasn't leaving because he was giving up, he explained.

"I have to get back. I just didn't want you to think . . ."

"Don't you dare tell me what to think!" Toyoda thundered. "I'll think what I want to think!"

That scene has always stuck with me, because of course, I've done this too. Countless times, I've tried to manage what others thought of me. What my teacher's ripping comment made me see was that my own need to get it right in the eyes of other people was, in a sense, a tremendous imposition on other people's eyes. Organizers of the world—I'm speaking to my tribe here—we have to let it go!

Questions upon Questions Lead to the Wrong Answer

Drivers, especially, can become impatient with Organizers. This is the case for so many leaders I've worked with who describe some sincere, hard-working Organizer in their group who drives them nuts. Clyde was one such boss, and Gayle was his over-self-explaining, self-certifying problem child. "Too much handholding," was the way he described working with her. "I can't stand answering all of her questions. She gets mired in the weeds, asks questions about questions!" Her barrage of questions signaled to Clyde that she was slow on the uptake and couldn't figure things out for herself. Yet to Gayle's Organized way of thinking, she was trying to get the directions straight, anticipate the obstacles, and understand all the rules so she could follow them. How could she understand if she didn't ask questions? All of which she would explain in detail to Clyde, which further irritated him.

Organizers love to ask questions, and sometimes they use questions as a way to slow down the arrival of new information long enough to chew on it and swallow it one idea at a time. Or they keep up a stream of questions to re-sort the information into the order in which they're prepared to hear it, which may be quite different from the way the other person wants to say it. Clyde continued his tale of exasperation. "I get one sentence out, as in 'Gayle, I want you to work with this team,' and Boom! that's it, she's on me with a question: 'Am I supposed to quit doing the other things I'm working on? Is

Signs of the Organizer Overdone

- Over-explaining
- Lost in the details
- Workaholism: "the list is endless"
- Asks too many questions
- Too self-justifying
- Overly concerned with what others think
- Excessive self-doubt
- Overly cautious, risk averse
- Too slow and deliberate

this more important?' " he says in a higher, squeaky, Gayle-like voice. "It never ends!"

Well, as you might imagine, it did end. The more Clyde lost patience with Gayle's questions and explanations, the more insecure Gayle became, and the more she looked for certitude through her questions and explanations. To Clyde, she became such an irredeemable pest that he fired her. Clyde's highly critical Driver certainly played into this drama; you can probably sense that he wasn't the most patient guy. The sad irony for Gayle was that her obsessive attention to getting it right—the Organizer completely unbalanced—led her to getting it so wrong that she derailed her career.

Thinking Too Small

Short of Gayle's extreme, far more frequent criticisms of highly Organized leaders—the "buts" that follow their string of laudable, dependable deliveries in a performance review—are "too low level," "caught up in details," or "not strategic enough." These Organizers often become the solid "B" players who are the backbone of organizations but are consistently overlooked for the Big Job. They might be the perfect and perpetual deputies or assistants, which might be perfectly and perpetually satisfying to them—or not. If they want to grow further, they will have to break through their own Organizer ceiling.

So how could Gayle have avoided over-Organizing her way to failure? How can workaholics break out of their relentless sense of responsibility—before their first heart attack? How can any of us break free from the Organized ties that bind us when it's time to grow beyond them? The key—as with all the patterns—lies in getting the best out of the Organizer, without it getting the best of us.

BECOMING UN-ORGANIZED

We overdo the Organizer in different ways, depending on which secondary patterns we use, or whether we use any at all. As pushed by the Driver, too much Organizer becomes the workaholic. Supported by the Collaborator, Organizers overdo it by getting spread too thin trying to please too many people. With the Visionary in the background, Organizers may just stay in the background, as these two more introverted patterns conspire to quietude.

In the extreme, when no other pattern is coming to the rescue, Organizers simply get stuck. They stop. Freeze. Can't make decisions, don't know which way to go, the things they try don't work—the brakes have overrun the engine. If this happens for you, the fastest way out is to release the Organizer override locked in your chest—go back to that override release exercise again and again—and get into the swing of the Collaborator.

If you think back to the muscle movements, the Collaborator is the other pattern that uses both engine and brakes, but it alternates the timing between them to create a swinging rhythm, rather than immobility. So you can unclog your Organizer by moving into the greatness of the Collaborator, where you swing, rock, sway, or even enjoy the bobbling feeling of a good belly laugh.

Play More

This same prescription applies if you're the Organizer–Driver workaholic. Give yourself time to play. And set up more playful people-interactive ways of working. The next chapter will give you many ideas about how to do this. It really *is* the case with Organizer–Drivers that less is more. Because only by working *less* and playing *more* will you set up the pulse of sustainability that truly moves you to greatness, and lets you move others there with you.

Get to the Point More

If you're more of the endlessly pleasing, overly detailed, overly explaining type of Organizer–Collaborator who puts too many words into a sentence, use more of the Driver's energy to cut to the point. Focus on the vital few, whether that's people, priorities, or points to make in a meeting. When you've made your point, stop! This is the sharp discipline of the Driver. Use the Visionary's bigness to keep opening up to new possibility. An occupational risk of Organizer–Collaborators is to cycle around the same few points over and over again, as in a Kafka-esque dream where we're always returning to the same corridor. The Visionary's expansiveness breaks you out of that loop.

Show Up More

If you're the insightful sort of Organizer–Visionary, you're already finding ways these two patterns beautifully support one another, as the Visionary dreams up ideas and the Organizer gets them done. But does anyone else know what you're doing? You might look for ways to use the Driver's bold-ness to push the most important of your ideas into a more public forum. Or to Collaborate on your well-Organized Vision with people who could help bring it to life. Using the Driver and Collaborator, you'll gain access to the extro-verted energy that takes good, well-organized ideas and makes them of greater impact, service, and value in the world.

ORGANIZER TO THE RESCUE

If all of these examples of Organizer-overdone lead you to regard this pattern as more of a liability than an asset, nothing could be further from the truth.

Like all the patterns, the Organizer is essential, as the leaders who have too little of it learn painfully.

A Manager Who Found Just Enough Order

Sarah was definitely under-Organized for her new management role in an advertising company, and she knew it. She used to interface with one or two clients at a time and "do the creative" on ads herself. But as the company grew, it had many more clients to service and needed to outsource jobs to vendors, rather than doing them in-house. Her new role required her to manage dozens of client and vendor relationships, juggle resources, manage interdependencies between projects, and coordinate with the other departments in the company.

"It's a nightmare," she said at our first meeting in her colorful, messy, overflowing, office. "I know what they want me to do, but it's just not working. I have one client who's always asking for things at the last minute and eats up more than half my time. I get so far behind in everything else that I lose track of projects or forget to contact a vendor, and then I'm stuck with even more work to do." "You need some systems and some rules," I told her. And then we looked around her tornado-struck office with its piles of ad copy, design books, client files, water bottles, and power bar wrappers and burst into laughter.

It probably wouldn't surprise you to learn that Collaborator and Visionary were Sarah's two strongest patterns. In the spirit of starting with her Collaborator strengths in graphic design, I suggested she come up with a big graphic timeline for her wall depicting all the workstreams she needed to manage—every client and every vendor. Laying it all out was initially overwhelming for Sarah, but it brought into clear focus one of the new rules she needed to follow: "I can't possibly spend more than half of my time on that one demanding client." She also starting enforcing the "Two Weeks Out" rule: barring emergencies with a capital "E," she would schedule all work at least two weeks out. This would give her time to coordinate with the other departments, find suitable vendors, and not be racing around like a chicken with her head cut off.

Sarah made some other great moves as well, such as joining her colleagues for their daily yoga class in the lunchroom. Just the discipline and composure

---

Moving to Greatness: Accessing the Organizer

Sarah, advertising creative director

Situation: Despite her highly disorganized style, Sarah had to grow from doing creative work to managing many client and vendor relationships.

Expressed Profile: Strong in Collaborator, with Visionary as second pattern

Great Moves: Sarah developed a bold graphic timeline for her wall on which all workstreams were visible and discussable with others. She set some rules for client management and partnered with others to free up time. She supported all of this with regular yoga class with her colleagues to help her composure.

Net Net: Her office is still a mess, but her leadership is not.

of daily yoga practice helped her settle down and focus better in the afternoons. She worked with her boss and a colleague on a team approach to handling that one troublesome client, and was able to free up a good deal of her time.

As is the case when we flip a vicious cycle into a virtuous one, success reinforced more success. Sarah found that having the three-month graphic calendar on her wall helped her see the ebb and flow of the business better. She could set better expectations with her vendors and they became more responsive to her. She could anticipate slower times in the business where she could slot time-flexible work. Her coordination with people from other departments became easier through a morning coffee circle where she gathered them into her office and together they reviewed what they called the Great Wall of Time. The last time I saw it, her office was still a mess by my standards. But her leadership was not.

Beg, Borrow, or Reveal Your Own Organizing Tips

Any number of books and articles have neatly packaged the Organizing tips of many a high-flying leader, answering the question, "How do they do it?" The answer for Sophie Vanderbroek, chief technology officer at Xerox, includes Organized delegating.[39] A two-page computer printout corresponding to the layout of the grocery story is posted on her refrigerator. Throughout the week, she and her children check off items they want, and she pays a high school student $10 an hour to do the shopping. The answer for Eric Horvitz, one of Microsoft's technology wizards, includes scheduling. It started when his wife, given access to his calendar, starting blocking out family commitments and included a two-hour slot for his reflection time. "I loved it!," he said, "I had permission to think!"[40] Part of the Organizing structure for Carlos Ghosn, the peripatetic CEO of both Renault and Nissan, includes traveling with a separate briefcase for each company.

We'll go into many more Organizing suggestions in the section and tables to follow. But maybe you just want to settle yourself into the Organizer pattern, put your feet flat on the floor, your hands neatly in your lap, and see if a good Organizing step for you doesn't naturally come to mind.

ORGANIZING FOR ACTION

You know you need more of the Organizer's energy when everything feels like a mess. Well short of the extremes, there are a number of early warning signs that we may need fuller use of the Organizer's gifts. If the Organizer is one of your least preferred patterns, you might recognize yourself in a number of these signs of being under-Organized.

- You lose interest in projects and don't follow through.
- You aren't able to consistently deliver what you say you will deliver.
- You have a hard time keeping track of things—e-mails, calls, actions, your glasses.
- You're frequently surprised by things you once knew, but forgot or neglected.
- You don't pay enough attention to the details.
- Your work sometimes lacks quality or good judgment.
- You pop off with imprudent comments.
- You're sometimes fast and loose with the facts.
- You jump around too much, and important things fail to get done.
- You have trouble articulating how you do what you do.
- It's hard for you to see the steps in things and to organize work processes for others.
- You often lose focus when reading or listening to somebody talk.
- You don't gather enough facts or data for important decisions.
- You don't slow down or take a breath.
- You have a hard time sorting out things and prioritizing.
- Your presentations are too scattered.
- You often keep people guessing and they just don't know what to expect from you next.
- Routine tasks, such as monthly reports or keeping up with accounts, bore you; you often put them off or forget to do them.

If a number of these limitations are getting in your way, here are some steps you could take to bring out more of the Organizer in you.

Building the Organizer Step by Step

In fact, steps are a good place to start. Putting things into steps helps Organize our thoughts. From to-do lists to process steps, breaking the big down into do-able chunks lets us take things or delegate them—one step at a time.

I find that walking around my office when I'm on the phone (thank goodness for wireless headsets) helps me concentrate and step through my thought process. Just stopping for a bit, holding still and allowing a moment of quiet to settle in can be a great step toward Organizing a fly-away mind with a bit of composure. One way to do this is described later in the chapter. Try it; even a few minutes of this Organized composure can disrupt the breakneck pace of your day with the pulse that sustains your best energy.

There are many ways to move into the Organizer pattern besides walking or sitting, though many of them are based on these basics. Slow and easy use of a treadmill, stair-stepper, elliptical trainer, or similar exercise machines offer variations on the theme of walking. Using a slow and steady pace (rather than the push-and-renew pulse that was recommended for Driver energy), invites the measured steadiness of the Organizer. Think of an academic march; anything you can do in that sort of rhythm brings out Organizer energy.

Just sitting—as in meditation—is my favorite practice.[41] But as a native Organizer, it's relatively easy for me to sit still. If you're a fast-action, jump-around kind of person, the idea of sitting still in meditation may sound like torture. For you it may be better to sit quietly and work a puzzle, sand a piece of wood, or stitch a needlepoint. Quiet, repetitive, stepwise activities bring out the Organizer.

Many people ask me about reading or watching television, whether that makes for a good Organizer break. It could, if you're reading something like the *101 Tips for Time Management* or watching the careful sawing, painting, and stepwise progress on a home improvement show. But generally the pattern we pick up when we get deeply absorbed in a book or show is the pattern of the book or show. I was never so struck by this as when my husband bought a DVD set of the first season of *24*. I didn't know what I was getting into when we watched the first few hard-Driving episodes. The hook of *24* is that everything happens in real time and through the season it tracks one very long, action-packed, heart-pounding, car-exploding, gun-popping, double-crossing, adrenaline-pulsating day. Whew! Let me tell you, watching *24* will *not* let you relax into the Organizer.

Organize from Your Strengths

In the spirit of starting from a strength, if Driver is your Home pattern use your Drive for performance. Install brief Organizer breaks as part of the rest cycle of your high-performing pulse of Drive and recovery. Often, just the chance to slow down will let you capture the details that otherwise get away from you. It can help enormously to take just a few minutes— 10 slow and easy breaths—to sit quietly, and then make a list of what needs to be done by the end of the day (week, month, etc.) or a list of anything that needs to be sorted out. Listening and patience may also be gifts you need from the Organizer. Activities that hone your hearing will help, such as listening to music (preferably nice, calm, Organizer music—think classical) or books on tape. In listening to conversation, you might

---

To access the Organizer, start with your strength.

If your Home Pattern is . . .

Driver—Set a goal around it. Make the Organizer break the renewing part of your performance pulse. Measure by how much your performance improves.

Collaborator—Play with it. Find fun or social ways to engage in Organizer activities. Play with self-talk to temper impulsiveness.

Visionary—Experiment with it. Make a study of different ways to use the Organizer and notice the relative benefits of each. Avoid perfectionism.

summarize the point periodically, even to yourself, to keep your own thinking sharp and attentive.

If you're starting from Collaborator energy, what you might need from the Organizer is a bit of prudence, even though the word itself makes you want to screw your face up into a prune. But seriously, look for ways to combine your sense of play and fun with more Organized actions. You might make a game of cleaning up your office (my colleague's basketball hoop of a wastebasket comes to mind); if you do this at the end of the day, you'll start in a more Organized place in the morning. You might develop a trick for catching yourself in impulsive acts and taking a second look at whether you really want to do them. "What would Queen Elizabeth do?" you might ask yourself. Or substitute your favorite ethical role model. What would Obewan Kenobe do? Even playing into the role of Organizer role models can help temper up-and-down impulsive you.

Nothing beats moving in Organizer ways for getting easy access to Organizer energy. But as a Collaborator, if you start something like yoga (or any of the activities in the Organizer table), do it with a friend. Make it a fun, social activity, and you'll be more likely to stick with it. Even if you don't stick with it, don't get discouraged. The Collaborator tends to operate in spurts. So if you stop for awhile, just start again. Buddy up with a friend—an "accountability partner"—and the two of you can keep encouraging each other.

If Visionary is your strong suit, approach the Organizer as something of a study. Use your willingness to experiment to try out different ways of moving into the Organizer to see which ones bring you the most benefit. You may be particularly successful using the arts and movement, since the Visionary is a more kinesthetic learner—you get a *feel* for things. You might try ceramics or sculpture done in a symmetric, Organized way. Or try movement calling for precise footwork.

Whatever you try, don't feel you have to take it to boundless extremes. Visionaries sometimes fall into a perfectionist trap when they try on the Organizer, probably due to the overriding tension we talked about earlier. If instead you approach the Organizer in a spirit of relaxed mindfulness rather than lock on, lock out, you can get to the essence of how little tension you need to do the job. You don't have to open a Container Store, you just need enough Organizer to get by.

Organize Your Senses

Whatever pattern is your strong suit, you can also develop easier access to the Organizer through your senses. Organizer art—whether you create it or hang it on your office wall—is orderly and well-composed. Fruit in a bowl, simple shapes in symmetrical arrangements, a four-square windowpane of the same tree photographed in four different seasons, such is the Organized order in visual arts. They're marked by simple symmetries, clear boundaries, and stillness at the surface.

Organizer music likewise has clear symmetries, as in a Bach fugue or a Mozart concerto. It extends to ballads and processional music, such as a wedding march, where it helps Organize walking down an aisle. You might try playing Organizer music as a break when you work, or listening to it might help you work (as schoolchildren who listen to Mozart better memorize their multiplication tables). A clock with a steady tick-tock-tick-tock is a great comfort to some people, as it helps them settle down and stay focused.

The sound of your inner voice can also be a source of Organized comfort, though you might have to root out an earlier voice from your "shape up!" childhood that drips with judgment and disapproval. If the only Organizer voice you have is limited to phrases like "you should be ashamed of yourself!" you're missing the best of the Organizer's inner wisdom. Can you listen for the voice that might say, in a turbulent moment, "steady as she goes" or "let's take this one step at a time"? Shop around for that voice. It might be your ethical role model. It might be Glinda, the Good Witch of the North (as she gently guided Dorothy home in *The Wizard of Oz*). It might start out as a borrowed voice, but if it's kind and wise, it becomes your own voice over time.

Organize Your Work

All of these methods can support and culminate in leadership behaviors that you do in a more Organized way. There are countless ways to be more Organized at work, even by counting what you do. You can use numbered lists in your speaking or presentations so people know where you're going and can gauge where you are. Making time to plan is another key to being more Organized, where you take a break from the action to look back on where you've been, look forward to where you're going, and lay out the most important next steps. You'll get more ideas from the tables at the end of this chapter, but don't be afraid to use your own creativity, too, one step at a time.

As with any of the patterns, if you want more Organizer energy, you have a choice about how much you develop that in yourself, versus surround yourself with others who have it in abundance. In this internal "make or buy" decision, "buy" is a fine option. But don't kid yourself into thinking you can buy the whole solution. Without enough Organizer in our style, we may not be Organized enough to get Organizers around us, or know how to work with them once we do. Similar to outsourcing information technology (IT), you still need enough in-house expertise to know what you need and when you need it.

Likewise, even if your strategy is to buy or borrow the good Organizing skills of others, make sure you develop enough Organizer "in-house" to do it well. Or at least well enough.

REFLECT ON THE ORGANIZER IN YOU

As our stroll through the world of the Organizer comes to an end, I invite you to take a few quiet moments to Organize your thoughts and capture a few words about how the Organizer pattern shows up in you.

1. Compared with the people you work with, would you say that you're more of an Organizer, less of an Organizer, or about in the middle? What are some implications for your work and leadership?
2. If there's one aspect of the Organizer that you get stuck in, what is it?
3. If there were one aspect of the Organizer you could personally use more of, what would it be?

ORGANIZER MINI-BREAKS AND BEST PRACTICES

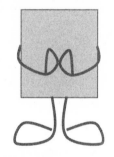

Your inner Organizer—holds it all together

The next few pages capture ways to step into the Organizer using breath, body, background, and everyday leadership behaviors. First, the **breath** exercises settle you in the moment and put a pause in the action. Second, the **body** activities not only place you in the Organizer pattern in the moment, but give you easier access over time. Third, the **background** suggestions will give you ways to surround yourself with Organizing cues. Fourth and finally, the **behavior** ideas will show you how to better Organize the way you work and lead.

The activities in this section are annotated for whether they're suitable for a mini-break (shown with the ❷ icon), or longer practice (shown by ◷).

A Time to Compose (❷)

1. Sitting comfortably straight, place your feet flat on the floor, and your hands flat on your thighs, palms down.*

Breath

Mini breathing breaks can return you to the calm composure of the Organizer.

---

*alternative hand position: place palms together, thumbs touching your solar plexus, fingers pointing to your chin, elbows held up level with the heels of your hands.

2. Half-close your eyes. Let your gaze drop, splashing off the desk or floor in front of you, not looking at anything in particular.
3. Let out a sigh of relief, letting the tension fall out of your neck and shoulders.
4. Close your mouth and, breathing softly and quietly in and out through your nose, take several breaths, feeling each one move into and out of your body. Allow each breath, especially the exhale, to grow softer and slower. Do for 5 to 10 breaths.

Walking Composed (❷)

Walk slowly with your hands at your solar plexus (the alternate hand position above). Remain aware of your breath, letting it be slow and even. As you gain steadiness, gradually increase your speed until you can walk at a normal speed without pushing into it.

Balanced Composure (❷)

1. Sit with your back comfortably straight and feet flat on the floor, knees together. Fully extend your arms out to the side, shoulder height and palms up. Move your arms just slightly forward so that you can see them comfortably in your peripheral vision.

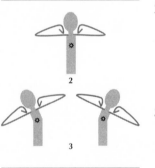

2. Fold in your forearms so that your fingertips rest on the tops of your shoulders. Hold this posture for a moment and notice the sense of composure and "thereness" in the solar plexus/diaphragm area; i.e., the Organizer center. Picture your upper body as a Libra-sort of scale with the weight of your arms on each side.
3. Keeping your lower body still, tip the scale of your shoulders slightly to one side and then the other. Let your upper body tip as one unit around the Organizer center. Feel the puppet-like quality of the motion.

Diaphragm Breathing (❷)

1. Stand with your feet shoulder-width apart, knees relaxed.
2. Interlace fingers, joining your hands in front of your belly. Inhaling through the nose, raise hands above head, turning them over so that palms

face the ceiling. At "top" of inhale, make a throat-clearing sound and feel the diaphragm set.

3. Exhaling through the nose, let palms come apart, as hands return to low, center starting position.
4. Continue with several more breaths in this way.

Diaphragm Circles (❷)

1. Sit or stand with your feet shoulder-width apart. Imagine a point of light in the center of your diaphragm. Breathe quietly in and out through your nose.
2. Keeping your lower body still and allowing your spine and upper body to move freely, move the "light" side to side five times and then back and forth five times.
3. Move it in horizontal circles five times and then vertical circles five times. Feel how the weight lifts and energy gathers in the upper body.
4. Finish with a few deep sighs of relief and feel the energy settle back down in your belly.

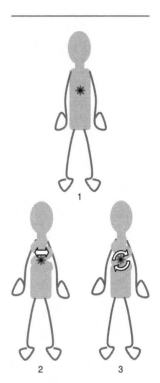

Add these elements to your office or home . . .

Add these elements to your workplace; your senses will pick up on their orderliness, inviting your mind to follow.

Organizer offices have a place for everything and everything in its place. Container stores, compartmentalized desks, and Ziploc bags were made for Organizers.

Organizer furnishings are neat and tidy, perfectly formed. Corners are square and every piece is perfectly placed. An audible ticking clock lends steadiness to the room.

Organizer art is still and perfectly composed: a bowl of fruit, a vase of flowers, with neat borders around everything. History buffs or geologists may display a timeline; scientists might put up the periodic table of elements.

Organizer music is easy to walk or march to (think of a wedding march and other processional music). Bach fugues and Mozart concertos, with their almost mathematical symmetry, are great organizers of thought.

Background

Surround yourself with order.

Organizer Activities (☯)

Walking—steady, measured pace

Cardio machines—slow and easy, such as a stair-stepper, elliptical machine, or other step-by-step activities

Yoga, Coordination Pattern training

Meditation, reflection, time to pause

Dancing to Organizer music or in an Organizer style—i.e., with precise form and footwork; e.g., ballet, waltz, contra dancing, some folk dances

Word puzzles, logic puzzles, Sudoku, solitaire card games

Ceramics—especially when done in with Organizer symmetry and precision and using a potter's wheel

Paint-by-number, classical oil painting, or painting within precise lines in a room

Dressage—i.e., formal horseback riding (other patterns, especially the rocking Collaborator, are also used in horseback riding, but perfect form and posture pertain to the Organizer)

Housecleaning

Organizing a space, cleaning out a desk drawer, putting files in alphabetical order, or sorting a jumble of items into containerized categories

---

Body

Placing yourself in the Organizer pattern gives you the deepest sense of its orderly composure.

Woodworking, or construction out of any number of materials when done step-by-step, with patience and quality

Needlepoint, cross-stitch, embroidery—patient stitchery for that stitch in time

Kayaking—slow and easy

Synchronized swimming, with attention to perfect form

Marching band and other drill squads

Creating visual art using Organizer energy—with well-defined objects, symmetry, and stillness. Organizer art conveys a sense of calm or character

Playing or singing Organizer music—that which has simple repeating patterns, mathematical symmetry; in slow, Organizer music, one assumes a posture and steps on the beat

Gardening—especially weeding a garden, planting flowers in rows, neat and tidy landscaping where there is a place for everything and everything is placed; think of a perfect English garden or a groomed golf course

Cooking in an Organizer way—following recipes, preparing ingredients ahead of time, creating perfectly shaped foods and well-balanced meals

Things you might say to yourself . . .

- "Let's sort this out—first things first."
- "You can do that (find that) later: the important thing now is to _____ ."
- "Take it one step at a time (one room at a time, one day at a time, one task at a time, etc.)"
- "Take it easy. Slow down."
- "Breathe."
- "You're doing fine. Hang in there. Stay with it."
- "Easy does it."
- "What would _____ do?" (filling in the name of an Organizer role model).
- "Hold still and take a minute to sort out what's happening."

Organizer Work Behaviors

Make a list. Find a way of making and using lists that lets you (1) sort your work, (2) keep it in front of you, (3) monitor your progress as you check items off, and (4) identify when you're getting overwhelmed and need to prioritize or get help. Try paper and electronic methods, sticky notes, color-coded lists, different places for posting lists, prioritized lists, pictures representing lists, audio lists—until you find a system that works for you. Start small and build.

Organize your day. Look for ways that you can take greater control over how you spend your time. Arrange your most challenging work for the times of day when you're at your best. Keep a reserve of necessary, but relatively mindless, tasks for late in the day or whenever you generally get tired. Look at blocking certain times of the day for specific purposes, such as e-mail, office hours, regular meetings, planning time, one-on-one meetings with key people, and time for yourself.

> **Behaviors**
>
> Organize your leadership and bring discipline into your day.

Break big jobs down into steps. Break large jobs into smaller steps, where each item gets put on your to-do list, or delegated to others. Think about what has to be done early, in the middle, or late to get the whole task done. Once you have the big job broken down into little steps, take it one step at a time.

Always know your next step. Whenever you're not sure of the next step on a large project, pause and take a look where you are and where you're going. Then parse the remaining work into smaller chunks and decide on the most productive next thing you could do to move it forward.

Make time for planning. Set aside specific time for planning to stay out of the rut of perpetual "react mode." At a minimum, tend to timeline planning; i.e., a task list set on a timeline becomes a plan. Depending on your job, you may also need to plan around other matters, such as the layout of a presentation, document, room, website, or big event. Plan a process improvement by mapping its current and desired state. Plan whom you need to engage around an important project or a better a distribution of work to others. Plan the budget or resources you need for upcoming work. Look at what you're working on right now and pick an area where a plan would be most useful, and build it.

Make a project plan. For more complex projects where the work of many people needs to be coordinated, make a project plan. A project plan can be as simple as multiple task lists (i.e., workstreams) on a timeline, noting the dependencies or deliveries between them. Try different methods—from a software project planning tool, to sticky notes on a large sheet of paper—to find one that works well for the projects you manage.

Under-promise and over-deliver. Deliver what others think you've committed to. If you have a track record of missing deadlines and underestimating the work involved, consciously adjust your estimates to what might feel like under-promising. If you have, in the past, delivered work of a lesser quality than was expected, consciously adjust your standards to what might feel like overkill. Once you're delighting others, rather than disappointing them, you can dial in your efforts perfectly.

CHAPTER FIVE

Swing into the Collaborator

LOOSEN UP

Are you ready to loosen up? Maybe move around after all that stillness in the last chapter? Grab a pen and piece of paper and start drawing lazy, sideways, figure-eights, letting one loop lead to the next. If you're mathematically inclined, you might recognize this as the symbol for infinity, which is appropriate for the pattern of the Collaborator, where one thing leads to another and then back again. As you keep drawing your figure-eights, making large, loopy turns, get your whole body into it, and you'll notice that you are rocking from side to side. Back and forth, to and fro, keep expanding the motion (let your head move, too) until you're swaying in your chair in a playful, easy rhythm that loosens the body, and maybe even puts a smile on your face. Even though you might hope that no one sees you right now, it's easy to feel why the Collaborator is a natural for engaging people, and playing in the give and take of relationships.

The Collaborator gets things moving. This energy gets people moving, gets parties moving, and sometimes even moves on before finishing sentences the way it started them. If you've ever gotten a car stuck you know that the best way to get it unstuck is to rock it. Similarly, the Collaborator rescues the Organizer from its ruts and keeps the Driver from landing too hard.

The Collaborator engages life and the people in it, not as a chore but as wonderful fun. This energy makes us able to roll with the punches, land with a bounce, and find our way around obstacles: this is a pattern of enormous resilience. Do you remember when President Reagan was wheeled into the operating room after being shot in the chest? (Hardly a time when most people find humor!) His comment to the attending physicians

The Collaborator

Even if you're on the right track, you'll get run over if you just sit there.

—*Will Rogers*

The Playground of the Collaborator—back and forth we go

was, "Please tell me you're all Republicans." Whatever one thought of his politics, one had to admire his engaging manner. Known as the Great Communicator, Reagan was easy with people and at ease with himself—the gift of the Collaborator. Or if you prefer a Democratic example, President Clinton had an abundance of the Collaborator's resilience, not to mention a dose of its impulsiveness. Of himself, Clinton said, "Do you know who I am? I'm the rubber clown doll you had as a kid, and every time you hit at it, it bounces back. That's me, the harder you hit me the faster I come back up."[42]

If the Collaborator were a location, it might feel something like a carnival or a cruise ship. That's not to say you won't find savvy leaders and successful businesses here. You'd surely see the offices of Southwest Airlines and might run into its Collaborative, Hawaiian-shirt-wearing chairman, Herb Kelleher. In the largely Driver–Organizer airline industry, Kelleher built Southwest into a distinct brand with fun colors, free beer, joke-telling flight attendants, and

"LUV"—of all things! You'd find teams coming here to bond beyond the dictates of task, gathering the fairy dust of the highest-performing teams, which is genuine caring about one another. Indeed, caring and connections between people abound in this land: customers are understood, employees are cared for, families gather, and communities are built. This is where influence matters more and hierarchical power matters less; people here know how to play, even in the multiply ma-trixed organizations of today.

> You might think, as I did, that one could be positive or op-timistic in any pattern. But the research shows that Collabora-tors really are more optimistic,[43] reminding me of a quote my husband often uses (did I mention he is the poster child for Collaborator?): "Optimists and pessimists agree on one thing: Optimists have better lives."

> Laughter breaks out. A cluster of people tumble out of the comedy club, stopping traffic as they spread into the street. "Don't worry, be happy," laughs a reveler to a driver she has stopped, handing him a free pass to the club's next performance. . . .

The Voice of the Collaborator

"You gotta roll with the punches."

What the Collaborator Does Best

Multitasks, gets people excited, engaged, and cooperating

Too Much Collaborator

Unreliable, over-committed

Not Enough Collaborator

Brittle, humorless, loner

JOINING WITH THE COLLABORATOR IN YOU

Funniest boat name I've ever seen: "Eat, Drink, and Remarry." If I could get you to laugh out loud you'd instantly find the center of the Collaborator pat-tern in you. It's right there, down in your belly. I don't know if Collaborators are happier than most because they're always triggering this center with belly laughter, or whether they're laughing because they're happy, but the two are most assuredly connected.

> If I didn't get you to laugh out loud, here's a simple exercise you can do to feel this center and experience the Collaborator's rubbery resilience. You can do this sitting where you are right now (unless you're in the middle seat on an airplane).

Cross one leg over the other so that the ankle of one leg is on the thigh of the other. Wrap your hands around your ankle, holding it from the top and the bottom. Lift the foot slightly and gently shake it up and down, side to side, al-lowing your whole body (including your head) to move like Jell-O. Notice that as you bobble your foot, the mus-cles in your belly, just below your belly button, move in and out; this is the Collaborator center. Do both sides.

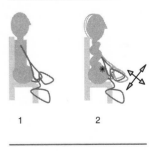

1   2

Notice a general loosening in the joints; see if you can get an easy, bobbling feeling through your whole body.

By another name, I'd learned about this belly center some 30 years ago when I first started aikido. On the first day of aikido training, we were taught its basic principle to "Keep One Point," which is a point just below the navel—the Collaborator center—from which all aikido motion is to emanate. Collaborator movements abound in this art, which is based on the give and take of joining with the energy of an attack to lead into a throw or pin. Moving from this center creates the grounded fluidity that you see not only in aikido practitioners, but also in great golfers, sensuous belly dancers, and basketball players who land with a bounce. It is fitting that aikido's exuberant founder, Morihei Ueshiba advised his students that the art "should always be practiced in the spirit of joy."

But Ueshiba was, in fact, building on an even longer tradition, deep in the Japanese culture, and for that matter in cultures throughout the world (e.g., yogic, Taoist, Sufi, Hopi, and many others), which understands the belly as our center of vitality. The Japanese word, *hara* refers both to the physical belly and to its energetic role as a furnace and conduit of vital energy—*ki* in Japanese (*chi* in Chinese). Developing this center and its energy develops the entire human being, physically, emotionally, mentally, and spiritually. A number of Japanese phrases express this connection: a fully matured person is one who has "finished his belly" (*hara no okii hito*). To think with your belly (*hara de kanganasai*) is to tap into your inner wisdom, what we might call gut-level knowing. Using a "belly voice" (*hara-goe*) is to speak with integrity, confidence, and presence.[44]

This belly center is your connection to that vitality, grounding, confidence, presence, and deep wisdom within you. Collaborator energy lets you light up a room and spread a sense of can-do optimism. Like Driver energy, it is extroverted in its direction and intention. But unlike the Driver, it is oriented *with* people, not pushing against them. As such it rounds out executive presence with a user friendliness that makes you the kind of leader others readily want to follow, not out of fear or duty but out of a sense of fun, excitement, and joy.

MAKING "LUV" AN AIRLINE

Back when airlines served free food and charged for alcohol, Southwest served only peanuts and gave away beer. When most planes were painted austere shades of blue and gray, Southwest's were bright orange. Walking through the airport, pilots of other airlines were distinguished by their crisp, military-like uniforms, while Southwest's pilots swaggered around in bomber jackets. In every respect, Southwest has been a different kind of airline: a Collaborator jewel in a rough industry.

It's also been the only U.S. airline consistently making money. For years it has been the most profitable airline in the U.S.—and in some years, more profitable than all of the other carriers combined. According to *Money* magazine, Southwest was the best-performing U.S. stock from 1972 through 2002, going up more than 25 percent per year. Not to bore you Collaborators with a bunch of financials, the punch line is: far from being frivolous, fun can be mighty profitable. People—from paying customers to loyal employees—are drawn to fun.

Herb Kelleher: Two Men in One

People are drawn to Herb Kelleher, the wild and wacky founder of the company he created largely in his own image. As *Fortune* magazine described Kelleher, "He has some of the best people skills on earth. He is also a walking paradox. As brilliant as he is batty, Kelleher is half P.T. Barnum, half Will Rogers, half Clarence Darrow and half Jack Welch. (Yes, that adds up to two men—but if you drank as much Wild Turkey and smoked as many cigarettes as Kelleher does, you'd be seeing double, too.)"[45] Sounds like a whole leader—or two—in the zany way of the Collaborator.

Kelleher came up with the concept for Southwest while scribbling on—what else?—a cocktail napkin. Its business formula was a model of Driver simplicity, combined with the Collaborator's gift for finding a practical way to do everything. Forget the added costs of maintaining a diverse fleet of planes; Southwest would fly only 737s. Erase the process costs of seat assignments; Southwest would seat people in groups of 30. With hawk-eyed attention to keeping costs low, Southwest was able to undercut competitors' prices and still keep the best margins in the industry. Then, removing the green eyeshades and donning the Hawaiian shirt, Herb Kelleher would become the very personification of the brand, swaying the hula in a Southwest commercial.

Southwest's Collaborative Culture

But Southwest's fun-loving brand runs much deeper than its ads, and much wider than Herb Kelleher. "In the unlikely event of a water landing, you have the unlikely chance of becoming a champion swimmer. But first, reach for that vest

---

Spotlight: Herb Kelleher

founder, Southwest Airlines

Quote: *"Listen, we have an incredible esprit de corps here . . . The intangibles have always been more important than the tangibles. Plus we run this company to prepare ourselves for the bad times, which always come in the business."*

Expressed Profile: Collaborator-exemplar with great support from the other patterns in the ability to focus, drive costs down (Driver), fly with a good safety record (Organizer), and build a different kind of business (Visionary). Note the overall emphasis on joy, practicality, people, and building in resilience.

under your seat . . ." joshes a Southwest flight attendant in the preflight warnings that nobody listens to, except on Southwest. Southwest did something for flying that no other airline did: it made people laugh. Laughter, it turns out, is good medicine for flyers. They keep coming back for more.

The laughter starts at home, in the Southwest headquarters in Dallas, which has the feel of a Romper Room set up for boisterous kids. An article in *Fortune* magazine described the scene: "The walls are festooned with more than ten thousand picture frames—no exaggeration—containing photos of employees' pets, of Herb dressed like Elvis or in drag . . . Then there are the teddy bears, and jars of pickled hot peppers, and pink flamingos.[46]" The overflowing abundance of the Collaborator!

"It's comfortable," says COO Colleen Barrett, principal keeper of the cultural flame. "We celebrate everything. It's like a fraternity, a sorority, a reunion. We are having a *party*!" Yes, doing serious, safety-conscious, profitable business, but still a party. "We really do everything with passion," Bartlett continues. "We scream at each other and we hug each other." While many companies discourage or prohibit couples from working together, Southwest celebrates it with family-friendly policies that help families stay together.

Its heart-shaped logo and ticker symbol—LUV—say it all for Southwest, both inside and out. That inside matches outside is also what makes it so hard to copy, even when a low-cost, spin-off competitor adopts a piece of its winning formula, for the Collaborator's fun, warmth, and vitality are impossible to fake.

LOVABLE LEADERS

People may feel pushed to greatness by Driver leaders, and stabilized along a path of solid execution by Organizer leaders, but they are positively swept up by Collaborator leaders. We know from studies of what makes change efforts work or communication successful—or even what brings good ratings on television—that emotion trumps logic every time. Emotion makes us remember things: the stronger the emotion, the longer the memory. No one works with emotion and the heart of a group better than a Collaborator. And the affection runs both ways.

Winning Affection against the Odds

John Lasseter is a good example. Fired by Disney in 1983, Lasseter joined the computer division of Lucasfilm, which later became Pixar. He was the genius behind the new digitized technology (and lovable characters) that made *Toy Story* the top-grossing, Oscar-winning film of 1995. A couple of years later,

Disney and Pixar entered into a partnership, out of which came a string of box office hits from Lasseter and his protégés. But the partnership didn't fare as well and was scheduled for abandonment when Disney's then-new CEO, Bob Iger, made a surprising move. Rather than split from Pixar, he bought it. And rather than put Pixar's creative department under Disney, he did just the reverse: he put Pixar and Lasseter in charge of Disney's ailing animation department.

This is what's called "reverse integration" in the merger and acquisition business, and let me tell you, it is the hardest cultural change to sell in an organization. The pride of people in the Big Company, in this case Disney, is hurt. People often feel awkward, angry, and anxious about their jobs. The boss from the Little Company generally gets a cool reception and lukewarm support, and in Lasseter's case, this was a boss who'd been fired by the Big Company years earlier. Generally, this spells double trouble.

But this is what happened: 500 Disney animators were gathered in a warehouse building the day after Disney announced its acquisition. They weren't sure what to expect. The chairman of Walt Disney Studios addressed the crowd and then introduced the man who would become their new boss: John Lasseter. The crowd burst into cheers, was on their feet, and on and on the applause went. Lasseter, in his jeans and Hawaiian shirt (is this the standard outfit of Collaborator leaders?), blushed and beamed.[47] Nothing cool about this reception. As lovable as his characters, Lasseter was certainly feeling the love that Collaborators can inspire.

Spotlight: John Lasseter

Chief Creative Officer, Pixar, Disney

Quote: *"I believe in the nobility of entertaining people . . . if ever a child anywhere in the world leans over to their daddy during one of my movies [as his own son did watching dull parts of someone else's movie] and asks 'How many letters are in my name?' I'll quit."*

Expressed Profile: Lovable Collaborator whom people (even when they might have reason to resist) love to follow.

Spreading That Loving Feeling

I worked with a similar, lovable leader who was the Collaborative CEO of a terrific nonprofit organization called Big Thought. Big Thought's mission is to bring engaged learning through the arts into urban communities, and Gigi Antoni is all about that mission. "Whip 'em into a frenzy!" one of her colleagues rooted, as Gigi left the office to go speak at a fundraiser. "Talk 'em into a stupor!" hollered another colleague, who added after the door shut behind Gigi and the lights seemed to dim a bit, "She has an amazing charisma." Asking people for money ranks right up there with root canals in my book. But Gigi was telling me one day why she enjoys even the fundraising part of her job. "At first it wasn't easy for me, either," she admitted. "But then I noticed that people sort of lit up when they gave to our programs. They knew they were helping kids, and it made them feel good. I re-framed my fundraising role as giving people that good feeling." This is the contagious good feeling of the Collaborator.

IMPULSE CONTROL

That's not to say life is all sweetness and light for Collaborators or for the people who work for them. The fundamental movement of the Collaborator pattern is back-and-forth, engine-and-brakes. This to-and-fro movement shows up emotionally as up-and-down mood swings, and Collaborators are often known to be royally dramatic. It shows up mentally as going back and forth on decisions. Only half-jokingly, I tell my Collaborator husband, Mark (who actually does *not* wear Hawaiian shirts), after he's voiced a strong, loud, unequivocal answer to something, "Okay, got it. I'll ask you again in a few days to see if it changes." Collaborators approach a decision more through asymptotic oscillation than a direct stab. And they have no qualms about impulsively changing their minds, something hard for us "if-I-said-it-on-Tuesday-it's-still-true-on-Thursday" Organizers to get our stable little heads around.

This can create some confusion in organizational life, as it did for Gigi and Big Thought, especially as the company grew larger. When the organization was small, it could operate something like a family band, picking up and adding a gig in Houston at the last minute. But when it became a huge network of partners and volunteers attracting national grants and being asked to scale their success nationally, Big Thought could no longer operate on the impulses of its leader, no matter how beloved or charismatic she was.

"They're telling me I have to manage my impulsivity and that's what I'm going to do," Gigi owned in her good-natured way. It became clear that some of the problem was that people—probably responsible, steady Organizers—started acting on ideas that were still oscillating through various Gigi conversations. We developed a code phrase among the management team under Gigi—"Is this thing cooked?"—to test when an idea from Gigi was fodder for conversation versus a serious new direction.

Gigi had plenty of Vision and Drive to go with her charismatic Collaborator, and it was reflected in her expanding vision for Big Thought and her ambitious goals. She realized

---

Moving to Greatness: Rounding out the Collaborator

Gigi Antoni, CEO, Big Thought

Situation: Nonprofit organization has grown to national prominence and the entire organization and its leader have to scale up to new capacity.

Expressed Profile: Strong in Collaborator with Driver and Visionary as healthy supporting patterns. Weak in the Organizer.

Great Moves: Gigi used her Driver strength to focus on the priorities of her new, larger role. She put in a few Organizing systems with her assistant. And the best move she made was bringing in a strong Organizer COO.

that the sheer number of things she was juggling was contributing to the churn in the organization, and that she needed a strong COO to Organize Big Thought's operations. Her weak pattern was the Organizer, so what better solution than to bring in a native?

Enter Melody. Melody knew all about working with Collaborators, having once been part of the family at Southwest Airlines. But she also had an instinct for process and order that was exactly what Big Thought needed. Gigi and Melody, working as CEO and COO became a great combo: Gigi Collaborating and Visioning up and out, with Melody Organizing down and in. You could almost hear the music: Gigi would be approached with an idea, she'd socialize it, improve it, whip it into a magnificent vision; Melody would sort out its process implications, and set plans for its execution.

Individually, Gigi and Melody became whole and balanced *enough* in all of the patterns. Together they became a powerhouse. Though Gigi would never say she mastered the Organizer, this smart Collaborator collaborated her way to getting it.

TWO SIDES TO EVERY STORY

"There are two sides to every story," I once heard a Driver leader say, "And one of them is wrong." For Drivers locked into their single-point focus, it often is "my way or the highway." For Collaborators, there really *are* two sides to every story—sometimes more, and sometimes they want to tell you all of them. "I can have an argument with myself," Mark laughs after he's laid out the point, the counterpoint, and the reason why the counterpoint matters more than the point, all before I've said a word. Collaborators are usually in motion—no wonder it's easier for them to see more sides to any issue. As a result, it's easier for them to get people moving with them, to influence others, and to build consensus.

The Art of Building Consensus

John Thain brought the skills of the Collaborator when he took over the troubled New York Stock Exchange in 2004. He faced a delicate balancing act between investors who wanted faster, electronic processing of transactions and floor brokers who had long been involved in every order and who resisted change. But presiding over delicate balancing acts and reconciling differing points of view played right into Thain's strengths. "I have often been struck by how he can build consensus in a very short period of time," said a colleague who knew Thain from earlier days at Goldman Sachs.[48] Thain was known for bringing people to the table and going back and forth with much debate, synthesizing and integrating their points of view until he could craft a way forward that everyone could buy into. Thain's Collaborative strength (probably supported by the Organizer's measured approach and good ear for listening) helped him lift the New York Stock Exchange out of its past and give it a future.

"Understand before you seek to be understood," is the way Stephen Covey puts it in *The 7 Habits of Highly Effective People*. We know it works. From my practice of aikido, I even have a physical understanding of *why* it works. When we move off our position to literally see what someone else is looking at—a very Collaborative thing to do, what's called a "join" in aikido—we not only obtain additional information, but we physically position ourselves to move people in ways that are most natural and easy for them. People who practice this technique physically—again and again—get pretty good at it, not only physically, but mentally and behaviorally as well.

Influence

The Collaborator's Two-Sided Tip Sheet on How to Get Others Moving with You:

1. Know where you want to go.

2. Know where the other is coming from and where he or she wants to go.

   Be willing to come off your position to really understand the other's point of view.

3. Connect where the other person wants to go to where you want to go; Show where your interests intersect.

   Start by moving others in the direction that is easiest for them.

The Art of Influence

Robert is a good example. A skilled aikidoist, he also had a background in sales and a friendly way with people. Even though the Collaborator was his not favorite pattern, it was one he could use easily, especially after years of aikido practice. He told me once of his "system" for influencing people. "If someone doesn't agree with me, I start by understanding what they do agree with," he said. "I completely move into their position until I can repeat it back to them. I also try to understand where they're going and how I might help them get there. And then I horse trade—this for that—so we both get something we want." This was a good case of Tanouye Rotaishi's advice from years earlier: "Become the other person and go from there."

This ability to go back and forth, to weigh my position and then your position, to trade this for that, is the easy way of the Collaborator, and how they make leading other people to their way of thinking look easy. Conversely, people who try to influence others out of a "my way or the highway" mindset do more to create resistance than to generate cooperation. Collaborator energy greases the gears between people and jostles a little this way, a little that way, until those gears match, making coordinated movement possible.

CURB TO CURB

Too much of a good thing becomes a bad thing. When seeing both sides is taken to the extreme it can mean endless delaying of a decision, or breaking trust with one side by changing your mind, going back and forth, curb to curb. "He weathervanes," my boss used to complain about our division head. "He waits to see which way the wind blows. You want to get to him last, because he'll keep changing his mind up until the last minute." That's the sort of reputation that follows the Collaborator overdone.

At the extreme, Collaborators can seem wishy-washy or as though they're trying to "have their cake and eat it too." Juggling between commitments, bobbling between relationships, at work or in their personal lives, they may become so overcommitted and unreliable as to do justice to none of them. A good juggler can inadvertently create an overstuffed life that always needs juggling.

A Juggling Leader Who Dropped the Ball

Overstuffed certainly described Regina's life. She ran a small consulting firm that specialized in applying improvisational comedy techniques to leadership communication and team building. A fun and funny gal, she was completely at home on an improv stage, and, in fact, every aspect of her life had a sort of improvised quality. A rag was stuffed in the gas cap hole of her car because she'd forgotten to put the cap back on after fueling, and hadn't gotten around to ordering a new one. She'd go into a meeting "winging it"—completely unprepared—which worked now and then for client meetings (she was, after all, selling them on improvisational techniques). But it didn't work when she had to meet with a loan officer from the bank or with the rather surly auditor at the Internal Revenue Service about back taxes. All of her finances seemed backed up; today's income was already spoken for by finance charges on top of interest on top of debt from last year.

She went through the jumble of her day with a breathless quality of trying to get "caught up," and yet her everyday choices (as in taking on a client she didn't like, couldn't work with, and had no time for because her mortgage was past due) perpetuated the juggling act of borrowing from the present to pay the past, and overstuffing the present to compensate. Even her clients started to sense the disorganized desperation growing beneath her sunny veneer.

I'd like to tell you that Regina learned about the patterns, moved into the quick-calculating Driver's seat, sorted out her finances, Organized her client commitments into a workable schedule, and lived happily ever after. But so far as I know, Regina is still struggling to juggle this overburdened life (Regina,

---

Signs of the Collaborator at the Extremes

- Unreliable, missed commitments
- Life feels overstuffed and out of control
- Muddled finances
- Overly impulsive
- Inappropriate behavior or humor
- Talks way too much
- Sees conspiracies everywhere
- Not taken seriously
- Wrapped up in political intrigue
- Melodramatic; won't get off the stage
- Cycles around same point or emotion, especially anger, again and again

---

are you reading this!?). Another truth I've learned is that no one changes one tiny little bit until they're ready.

But, my, can we suffer as we dig the rut of our favorite patterns into an inescapable chasm! And when the Collaborator is the pattern we overdo, its rubbery resilience, always helping us land with a bounce and keeping us laughing, helps keep this insidious game afoot.

Political Animals and the Politically Incorrect

There are other ways that Collaborators can overdo themselves into difficulty. Collaborators may take humor to the point of being inappropriate or not taken seriously by others. Part of what Regina struggled with in her business was the impression that her work was "clownish" and not suited for serious businesspeople, even though her techniques were terrific for building teams and executive presence. Many humorous leaders I've worked with receive feedback that their humor sometimes makes them seem cavalier or sarcastic. The very thing that makes humor funny—its ironic twists or irreverent way of looking at a subject—can also cause offense.

Collaborators are known to love a good story and "spin a good yarn." But when that story turns dark, it can become trust-breaking gossip, multilayered political intrigue, conspiracy theories, or terrible dreams of being in an endless loop à la Kafka's castle. Collaborators can also loop around in the castle of their grudges. They may seem to be over their anger, but not for long, and then they're back to being angry again.

Have you heard the one about the Collaborator who never got to the point? That happens, too. And they may fail to deliver as one thing leads to another, as in:—"Don't worry, doll, I'll get to that report right after I make this call . . . ." But before the Collaborator makes the call, he checks his e-mail, and while online . . . .

BALANCING THE COLLABORATOR WITH THE OTHER PLAYERS ON YOUR TEAM

If you know the end to that story all too well—and you've had enough of it—you'll appreciate that three other patterns are ready to rescue you. And they're already on your team. Here's how you might put them to into play.

Cut out the Extra and Focus

The Driver comes to your rescue if you need to simplify your complicated, Collaborator life. Clear the desk. Set some priorities. Focus on the vital few. The Driver is also your friend if you need to get on point in your communication and set a clear direction. "Answer first." Make your point. Don't sell past the close. You might read through the suggestions in the Driver chapter for ways to bring that edge into your communication. Wandering, roundabout instructions—on the one hand you could do it this way, on the other hand that way—do not for clear delegation make.

Do What You Say You're Going to Do

Once you've gotten your work (or life) down to simpler proportions, the Organizer is your player for setting up a few systems to keep things running. Don't hold out for one great, big organizing system where everything connects to everything else—you'll never get there. Just a few modules of Organization should do the trick—a way to keep your calendar, track your accounts, or maybe find your dry cleaning. Put a mini-system in place to Organize one thing and play with it. Let it prove its benefit to you, or throw it away and try another. Don't get discouraged if your first attempt at Organizing doesn't work. Think of it as a game that you get better at by playing.

A little Organizer energy can also help you get realistic about your commitments and keep your life to its simpler proportions. A simple rule, like: "Say yes or no, but don't say yes and do no," plus a bit of disciplined tracking can help you clean up the disappointed wake of missed deliveries. In a 30-second pulse check on Friday morning you could mentally review your week and ask, "How many times did I *not* do something I had committed to doing?" Maybe this week it was three times. But through this kind of awareness, chances are good it will be fewer next week.

Get over It

If you struggle with cycling around the same point again and again, from a grudge to an obsession, Visionary energy can help you open up and break out of it. "Let it go," your Visionary consciousness can remind you. Accessing the Visionary by getting out in nature and opening up your senses will help you clear the Collaborator loop.

And finally, if your good humor is leading to misinterpretations, lightweight dismissals, or red-faced embarrassment, I might suggest the Tanouye method of starting by knowing your audience, not simply valuing them for their applause or laughter, but knowing them with a perfect join that makes everything you say perfectly appropriate. "Become the other person and go from there."

WHEN YOU NEED TO LIGHTEN UP

On the other hand, maybe more Collaborator energy is exactly what you need to lighten up. From picking up your own spirits to lighting up an audience and "whipping them into a frenzy" of support around your message, nothing plays like the Collaborator. And if you've been trying to lead without it, the only directional energy you provide to other people is the Driver's push. If you can round that out with a good dose of the Collaborator, you both push and pull people to greatness.

A Leader Who Needed to Listen

Johann learned how important Collaborator energy could be, and, if he could jump into this sentence, I'd bet he'd tell you that even he was surprised by the difference. The direct and to-the-point head of operations for a medical device firm in Europe, Johann had a crisp, direct style that people understood and respected. But they often didn't feel heard by him. "You don't listen well," they told him in feedback. "You cut off conversation and aren't open to new ideas." This feedback was familiar to Johann—he'd heard it before, including from his wife—and in another year, it might not have mattered enough to be worth changing.

But this year was different. The company had entered a period of turmoil in which its entire business model was threatened, and it needed to drastically cut the time and cost involved in its processes, or it would not long survive. This called for radical new ideas for how the various groups in operations could work together. All of which was in the back of Johann's mind as he was reading about himself as part of the problem: "You don't listen well . . . aren't open to new ideas."

"I have to change," he said with characteristic intensity, connecting the dots. "If I don't open up and listen to their ideas, they will not listen to each other, and we will not find the ways we need to work to survive."

Well alright then. Johann had a disciplined way of working, so we identified a few Big Rules he could follow to flip his communication style from pushing to pulling. One was: More questions, fewer answers. When he'd hear an idea, rather than pop off with his opinion on the matter, he would make it a practice to always start with a sincere question, as in: "Tell me why you see it that way." He was determined to start that very day.

"They don't quite know what to make of me now," Johann told me a few weeks later when we were talking about his progress. "They like the new, open meetings and having more say themselves. But you know how people are; if they see you trying to change, they think 'This isn't going to last. He'll be back to telling us what to do in no time.' And as soon as you do anything close to your old ways, they say 'Aha! We knew it!' "

Johann had a good point. The context surrounding you as a leader, just like your family context, has a way of holding you in place. Like a pair of old shoes, the people around you hold some memory of what it's been like to fit with you for a long time. When you change, they may or may not be ready to follow. That's why good executive coaching has to work with the people surrounding a leader, not just with the one person. And that's why, when you undertake change, you do well to make it a social event.

Enlisting Support for Change

A best practice for this, and something Johann did in true Collaborator fashion, is to enlist others in your change. He told the head of human resources about his new rules and asked her to observe him and give him feedback when she saw him following or breaking them. He also made a bet with another colleague that he could keep up this "open and asking" style for three months or he'd owe his friend a steak dinner. He brought in humor. At one meeting, he set up a small child's chalkboard like a picture frame in front of him, facing his colleagues gathered around the table.

"What's that for?" one asked.

"*That*," he responded with mock seriousness, "is my blank slate."

Over time, the more he asked questions, the more he saw it sharpening the thinking of his people, resulting in better dialogue and more well-considered answers. The more he allowed for idea generation and debate in meetings, the more engaged his colleagues became. Meetings became energized, and people pursued agreed-upon directions with the vigor of real buy-in.

Johann was quite pleased some months later when we spoke again. "I could never have pushed through the kind of change we're undertaking now,"

Moving to Greatness: Asking for the Collaborator

Johann, head of operations, medical devices

Situation: Company is in turmoil and must find radical new ways of working; Johann has a reputation for not listening and shutting down new ideas.

Expressed Profile: Johann was at home in the Driver, with strong support from the Organizer. He needed to foster more Collaborator (and Visionary) in himself and in his organization.

Great Moves: Johann shifted his leadership style from telling to asking, and set up meetings that became increasingly engaged around how to cut cost and time out of processes. He also asked colleagues for feedback on his success with the new style.

he admitted. But with the brightness of Collaborator energy, he certainly helped pull people toward it.

Sometimes Collaborator Distinguishes the Best from the Rest

Even in healthy organizations, Collaborator energy can be the difference between good and great leaders. Mark, who, in addition to being a non-Hawaiian-shirt wearing Collaborator, is also a terrific leadership consultant, did some work with a cruise line to discover what traits differentiated the best from the rest of the captains. The company had a red-yellow-green scorecard for how well the captains performed possibly the most diverse leadership job on earth, with responsibilities ranging from safely maneuvering gargantuan cruise ships to creating a happy climate onboard, from driving revenues to saving costs, and from caring for employees who became like family to enforcing policies that employees didn't like. A handful of captains consistently scored "green" on every measure—they had it all. Mark's job was to find out what they had that others could either develop or that the company could select for over time.

While the best captains had plenty of the Driver and Organizer, the rest of the captains did too. What made the best stand out was their engaging Collaborator energy and characteristic optimism. These were captains who loved their people, their ships, and their jobs. One took Mark out on deck to ooh and ahh at the sunrise, "Don't you just love it!" he gushed. They had the Collaborator's way of engaging people and being approachable. They knew what was happening on their ships well beyond the content of formal communication because they were always out and about, asking after the sick mother of a cabin steward or hamming it up with the guests. In mastering the "soft stuff," these captains made the best hard numbers in the fleet. The rest—able as they were—needed more of the Collaborator if they were ever going to come up to the bar set by the best.

Play is the exultation of the possible.   —Martin Buber

WHEN MORE OF THE COLLABORATOR IS MERRIER

What might be some of the signs that you could use more of this engaging Collaborator? Ask yourself how many of the statements below are true for you and whether they're seriously limiting your effectiveness or joy. Right there—having little joy—was all the diagnosis I needed at a point in my life when I knew I had to get more of this pattern. Here are some other warning signs you might look for:

eam player.

at work or socially.

l fun—pure and simple fun!

oo hard.

d humor in difficult situations.

ver whom you have no direct au-

people are coming from.

way around obstacles.

rything feels like work.

ing with you.

rator

f the Collaborator, well, start right there.
nents, especially as you engage that Col-
ediately draw out this pattern. No wonder
m in swinging chairs to keep them happy.
s bring out the Collaborator's "don't worry,

one with a swing, such as golf, baseball, or
se activities, make sure you move from your
sitting next to a scratch golfer—not a super-
ountry club pro—and we were talking about
e said tapping the middle of his chest, "It's so
me from here?" "What?!" I countered, not en-
share with him the aikidoist's view of center. To
by my rather urgent explanation and thought
ould run golf clinics. Move from the belly and
etter.
another way to enter the Collaborator. You may
d, but if you do and you've used it, you know how
ravels through your whole body and makes it hard

To engage the Collaborator, start with your strength.

If your Home pattern is . . .

Driver—Use your focus and goal-setting ability, and measure your progress at the end, but allow for a messy, indirect middle.

Organizer—Plan and schedule time for Collaborator fun; do it with a friend whom you don't want to let down.

Visionary—Ground yourself in the Collaborator center so you don't drift off; make a study of different ways to reach people.

not to smile. If you do them slowly and easily, any number of activities with repeating movements invite you into the Collaborator. Dribbling a basketball, bouncing a soccer ball up in the air using various body parts, bicycling, swimming, ice skating, or rollerblading—all of these activities have a gentle oscillatory feel if you do them with ease. As you speed up (you might try this experiment sometime), you'll notice a threshold where you start going into the Driver; back off and you rock your way into the Collaborator.

Laughter Is Good Medicine

Virtually anything that makes you laugh welcomes the Collaborator. From going with your team to a comedy club to having a night out bowling, groups bond over laughter. I was once facilitating a meeting for 70 senior leaders in a rather proper British company. The quirky conference organizer—a great, high-energy, effusive Collaborator—mocked up a county fair as the setting for an evening team-building event. Teams roved from stall to stall (drinks in hand, as you might imagine), trying their luck at tossing rings over bottles and whatnot. But the big hit of the evening, what everyone talked about later, was the completely silly, laugh-out-loud, hopscotch game.

Find Your Rhythm with Others

Depending on what you most need from the Collaborator, and which Home pattern strengths you're starting with, you can pick the most appropriate Collaborator behaviors or activities and tailor the way you do them. For example, what Drivers most often need from the Collaborator is a better way to engage people. If this is your situation, you'll want to make sure that the way you practice the Collaborator involves other people. For you, jumping on the trampoline alone may be a warm-up, but it's not enough. You might try basketball or another team sport, aikido (which is the most Collaborative of the martial arts), or dancing, especially swing, jitterbug, or square dancing.

Yes, dancing. "Most men hate to dance," Mark tells me, and he probably *is* speaking for most men. Like it or not, partner dancing—especially with instruction—is one of the fastest ways I know for tight people to get a sense of rhythm and for loners to get a feel for moving with (or leading) others. So often, Driver–Organizer leaders want to get a tangible formula for addressing the intangible, people side of their work. "If I commit to having lunch with a colleague three times a week . . ." such a formula begins. But they find, as you'd find, it's not much of a lunch or a better relationship if these conversations are tackled with too pointed an agenda and are lacking the easy rhythm of the Collaborator. "You got to feel it—like music," I tell these guys and gals. "You can't formula your way there." And when it comes to music, the sounds of jazz, reggae, disco, Swing-era big bands, and island music are just the thing to bring out the Collaborator in you.

Drive toward Indirectness

If you're a Driver seeking more Collaborator energy, use your focus and goal-setting ability to set some goals. Who are the most important people you need to engage? By what date do you want to have them moving with you on a specific project? Once you're clear on your targets, set them aside. You'll come back in the end and measure how you did, but first you want to pack some play into the messy middle. Become quite intentional about using an indirect (e.g., inquiry) approach, rather than a direct (e.g., advocacy) approach.

This intentional indirectness was what Johann modeled with his "more questions, fewer answers" approach. Rather than racing right into a new relationship, think about who could introduce you. Rather than starting from the mindset of "how can I get you to do what I want?" flip that to: "How can I get to know who you are, how you think, and how we might work together?" In the give-and-take of relationships, it's no accident that the "give" part comes first!

Similarly, if you're trying to improve the teamwork or climate in your group, use your Driver strength to set up measures of where it is today and targets of where you want it to be tomorrow. Then set all that aside and create some back-and-forth play in the middle. The tables at the end of this chapter will give you more ideas for Collaborator activities you could try (I promise: they don't all involve dancing).

Discipline Yourself to Play

If Organizer is your strong suit, you might especially need the Collaborator for its fun aspect and for unknotting that tension in the middle of your chest. Lighten up. Use your planful ways to schedule some fun for yourself (Collaborators are scratching their heads at this, but it works for some people). You want to keep that playdate as diligently as you would your work appointments, so you may want to make plans with another person whom you wouldn't want to let down.

Among the greatest masters of play are children. If you already have children in your life, this avenue into the Collaborator is especially available and important. But even if you don't have youngsters of your own, you might think about children of friends or children in the community. My friend Janet used to visit a local children's hospital once a week to play with kids, and found it to be the most fun and fulfilling part of her week. So you might make space for some playtime with children, not to teach them or lecture to them, but just to *play* with them. They'll be eager to show you how and even suggest what you should play!

Exploring Influence

If you're starting from the Visionary, the Collaborator's connectedness to people—and grounding in the belly—might be exactly what you need to bring your ideas to life. Use your Visionary strengths to paint an inspiring picture of the future, but then experiment with how to sell it to people. Think practically. Sense the essence of others' interests and see if those interests connect with any of your ideas. Play with positioning your story in ways others are ready to hear.

Having Fun with Your Senses

If the Collaborator's optimism and resilience are what you're after, your Collaborator practice doesn't have to involve other people, but it does have to be fun. It has to be genuine, look-forward-to-it play. Mark calls this a "nonnegotiable passion," something you enjoy so much that no one can talk you out of it. And how often do you need to engage this passion? Mark's answer is simply: *enough*.

As with the other patterns, you can also enjoy doses of the Collaborator through what you see, hear, touch, smell, or taste. We didn't talk too much about the smells or tastes of the other patterns, but with this pattern, you can almost smell the festival, taste the barbeque, and breathe in Rome's Piazza Navone, with its jugglers, rickety stalls, and outdoor cafes, where one scent leads to another. You can hear the sounds of the *beautiful Italian language* with its *up* and *down* modulation (and *up* and *down* hand gestures), drawing you into the swing of the Collaborator. Learning Italian and traveling to Italy or going to the Caribbean islands, where tiny umbrellas stick out of coconut shell drinks, or to "no hurries, no worries" Hawaii, where *everyone* wears a Hawaiian shirt—there are worse ways to immerse yourself in the Collaborator spirit.

But back in your office, what can you do to remind yourself of this pattern that plays with life? Well, you could doodle. You could make loopy, cartoonish characters (the sillier the better), even preparing yourself for what your Collaborator might say at the next meeting. Or maybe you prefer art from others. Collaborator art is colorful and playful, whimsical and bright, often child-like or simply drawn by children, maybe your children. You could put photos and pictures on the walls, hang balloons, or sprinkle sentimental knickknacks around the shelves—and if this is starting to sound like the offices at Southwest Airlines, so be it.

Many organizations are creating playful congregation space where people can come together for a break or for casual idea-swapping. You can create Collaborative space by turning natural intersections into workplace piazzas. "It's much more conducive to conversation," says Jennifer Becker of Proctor and Gamble, one of the companies that has done this.

Collaborator music could also swing its way through your office. Don't laugh: I've been playing Collaborator music as I write this chapter. Organizers and Drivers especially might access a more Collaborative frame of mind for those afternoon meetings after listening to this kind of music over lunch. Collaborator music makes you swing or sway on the beat, as in most jazz, reggae, salsa, the swinging (non-stomping) parts of Latin music, Hawaiian folk music (think ukulele), island music in general, and, of course, big band swing music. You can generally pick out Collaborator music by the urge to move to it—this is foot-tapping, finger-snapping, head-nodding music that may even make you want to dance. Well, *some* of you.

The sort of self-talk that emerges in the voice of the Collaborator is resilient, encouraging, funny, and sometimes humorously self-deprecating. "Just roll with it, baby," is one of Mark's lines that now the Mark-in-me voice says when something utterly ridiculous or irritating is happening, as in the tipsy colleague telling secrets at a team dinner, or the bank closing just before I arrived. "Don't take it personally," you might say to yourself. Or "that was then, this is now."

Humor may come to your inner rescue. Mark was about midway through a six-hour driving trip one time when he pulled into Wal-Mart to pick up some additional toiletries. He bought some toothpaste and shaving cream, opened the trunk to stick them in his suitcase, and found no suitcase. He had left it behind. As he told me later, "I took one long, look around the Wal-Mart parking lot and knew with certainty that I was the dumbest person there." He adds this piece of wisdom for those crazy-angry moments when we're ready to scream: "I know when I tell the story later, it's going to be funny. So it's funny now!"

Making Work Social

More than in any other pattern, Collaborator self-talk can become talk-talk; Collaborators generally love to talk. It's not just that they love to be the center of attention, though some of them do, but they also clarify their thinking by talking. If you need more of the Collaborator's perspective and your self-talk can't get there, chat with a Collaborative friend. He'll be glad to talk.

Your inner Collaborator
rolls with the punches

The more you can swing your way into Collaborator energy, the more natural you'll feel engaging in Collaborative leadership behaviors. You might apply Collaborator energy at work by practicing seeing other points of view "until you can repeat it back." You could make a practice around *giving* to relationships before *taking* from them. Or you might just find a few ways to make work more fun. If you're not so good at this, enlist help from the most effusive, enthusiastic person who works with you. No one can have your fun for you. But as the most social of the patterns, Collaborator energy surely doesn't have to be learned alone.

WEIGHING THE COLLABORATOR IN YOU

As we finish our swing through the carnival of the Collaborator, you might take a few minutes to have a conversation with a friend or jot down your own inner dialogue on how you engage this pattern.

- If you were to weigh your Collaborator energy relative to that in the people you work with, would you say that you have more, less, or about the same as they do? What are some implications for your work and leadership?
- If there's one aspect of the Collaborator that you might take too far, what is it?
- If there were one aspect of the Collaborator you could benefit from, what would it be?

COLLABORATOR MINI-BREAKS AND BEST PRACTICES

Here's what you've been waiting for: ways to rock and roll your way into the Collaborator's easy rhythm. Over the next few pages, you'll find ways to engage the Collaborator using breath, body, background, and everyday leadership behaviors. The **breath** exercises will give you a resilient sigh of relief. The **body** activities let you fully immerse yourself in Collaborator energy, which makes it easier to engage the next time you need it. The **background** suggestions give you ways to surround yourself with a more Collaborative environment. All of which will help you put the Collaborative **behavior** ideas into practice in your everyday work.

As in previous tables, icons indicate whether an activity is a mini-break or warm-up (❷) versus something you'd do for 20 to 30 minutes as part of a practice (❷).

Loosening Relief (❷)

1. Take in a breath through your nose and exhale—Ah!—a sigh of relief through your mouth.
2. Repeat a few times, feeling tension drop out of your neck and shoulders with each breath.
3. Sitting in a chair with your feet touching the floor, shift your weight from side to side, from your left "sits bone" to the right and back again. Feel a loosening through your torso and neck as more and more of your body gets into the motion. Think of your spine as a worm where every little segment is flexible.
4. Let your head bob from side to side, as each ear takes turns moving closer to your shoulders.
5. Gradually make the motions smaller and smaller until you feel like you're only imagining them. Notice the sense of warmth and ease in your body.
   Note: You can do steps 3–5 standing, by shifting your weight from foot to foot, gradually reducing the motion to the point you only imagine it. Once you get the hang of moving side to side, you can repeat the same steps moving forward and back.

Sitting Bounce (❷)

1. Sit on the floor or on a chair, crossing one leg over the other. Wrap your hands around your ankle, holding it from the top and the bottom.
2. Lift the foot slightly and gently shake the foot up and down, side to side, allowing your whole body (including your head) to move like Jell-o. Notice, as you move your foot, that the muscles in your belly move in and out; this is the Collaborator center.
3. Repeat on other side.

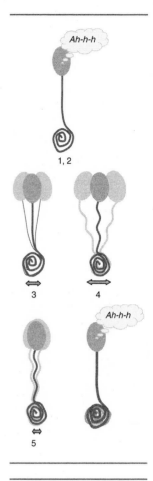

Breath and Body

The bounce and ease of the Collaborator are available at a moment's notice.

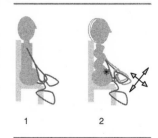

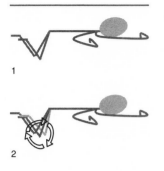

Side Pedaling (❷)

1. Lie on your side with both legs bent, thighs at right angles to your torso. Rest your head on the bottom arm and place the palm of your other hand on the floor in front of you.
2. Slide the top knee back and forth across the bottom knee (not lifting up). Let your whole body come into the rocking motion, including your head.
3. Make small pedaling circles with your top leg. Try both directions (backward and forward pedaling), and large and small motions.
4. End by gradually shrinking the size of the motion until you just imagine it.

Lying-Down Blahs (❷)

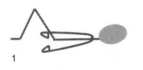

1. Lie on your back with your knees bent and the soles of your feet on the floor, hip-width apart. Relax your arms at your sides.
2. Breathe in through your nose and out through your mouth. Let out a couple "sighs of relief," saying "Bla-h-h-h-h" as you exhale. Feel where tension releases in your body.
3. As you exhale, say "Blah-h-h-h-h" and shake your arms, shoulders, chest, and head (keeping your chin down), as if the motion were coming out from the spine through your fingertips. Picture a silly ghost scaring people; in fact, feeling silly or playful helps you get into it.
4. Relax. Notice where warmth (energy) is present in the body.

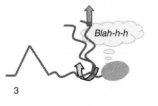

Standing Blahs (❷)

1. You can do the above exercise standing with your feet hip-width apart, knees relaxed. Let out a few sighs of relief.
2. Shake your arms in front of you with the movement extending out from your spine through your fingertips. Go ahead and laugh if you feel like it—or picture a ghost scaring people.

Bounce Backs (❷)

1. Stand with your feet hip-width apart and gently bounce up and down, keeping your feet on the floor and letting every joint loosen. Let your head and neck move as well.
2. Keeping your bounce going, start shifting your weight from foot to foot.
3. Keeping your shifting bounce going, start lifting each foot slightly in an easygoing hop, like a boxer bobbing and weaving. Try different directions (side-to-side, forward and back) and different rhythms as you bob with a spring in your step.

Add these elements to your office or home . . .

Add these elements to the places you work, inviting your senses to play.

Collaborator offices are full, with everything leading to something else, conveying a sense of bounty and colorful brightness . . .

Collaborator furnishings are bright and cheerful with overstuffed cushions, rounded edges, and chairs that rock . . . walls are softened with carpet and sensuous curves suggest a sitting area. Toys are scattered around and conversation pieces capture attention.

Collaborator art is rich, sensuous, and often playful, from Monet's water lilies to Dilbert's comics. Imagine photographs of family members, team trophies, and a miniature basketball hoop positioned over the wastebasket.

Collaborator music from big band to makes you want to swing to the rhythm with a partner or an audience.

Things you might say to yourself . . .

- "Roll with it, baby."
- "Lighten up."
- "Don't sweat the small stuff."
- "Don't worry, be happy."
- "Don't take it so hard."
- "That was then, this is now."
- "Roll with the punches."

- "When you tell this story later, it's going to be funny. So it's funny now!"
- "How can I play with this?"
- "Give before you take."
- "Let's celebrate!"
- "What's the most practical way to make this work for people?"

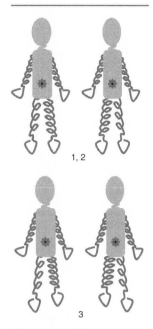

1, 2

3

Background

One thing leads to another . . .

The office of a Collaborator . . .

Hardly a place for everything, and everything all over the place. (Photo: Mark Kiefaber)

Collaborator Activities (☯)

Aikido or tumbling or swinging aspects of other martial arts

Skating, ice dancing

Golf—making sure the swing comes from the belly center

Rollerblading—slow and easy, side to side

Dancing of many forms, including the Charleston, swing, the twist, hip-hop, belly dancing, square dancing, hula

Team sports—with focus on the team aspect, especially sports where jumping is involved and you have to learn to land with a bounce or control a bouncing ball

Bowling—especially the swinging delivery and social aspects

Swimming—slow and easy, with rhythm, or bobbing up and down on waves

Bicycling—slow and easy, with friends

Skiing—slow and easy

Jumping on a trampoline

Coordination Pattern training

Rocking in a chair

Playing with children—best if you let the child choose the game or decide what you're going to do; resist urges to teach, lecture, or criticize; just play along!

Playing with animals

Weaving

Parties—especially with costumes!

Learning Italian—if you don't already know it; speaking it with your hands if you do!

Creating visual art in the spirit of the Collaborator—using fun, bright colors, cartoons and caricature, rounded edges, things tumbling into other things; Collaborator art often conveys a sense of joy or overflowing abundance

Playing or singing Collaborator music—makes you want to swing or sway on the beat, includes jazz, reggae, salsa, the swinging (non-stomping) aspects of Latin music, Hawaiian folk music, island music in general, and big band swing music

Landscaping with Collaborator energy—creating overflowing abundance; think of Monet's garden, where everything grows into everything else, or of gardens replete with playful colors, captivating fragrances, textures, and the occasional gnome

Cooking in a Collaborator way—creating a feast for the senses, with aromatic spices, fun touches, and flavors toppling together

---

Body

Ways to immerse yourself in the energy of the Collaborator in larger doses.

Collaborator Work Behaviors

Put some fun into your day. Think about what makes work fun for you, and put some of those elements into your day or week. It could be a humorous conversation, a practical joke, lunch with a spirit-lifting friend, a team-building game with colleagues, balloons and parties in the office, or a pizza lunch celebrating a special accomplishment or event.

Build your network. Think about the number of people you work with routinely or talk to on a frequent basis and imagine doubling that number. What might you be able to learn, influence people on, or make happen with a larger network? Think about the people you could add to your network right now who could help you recruit, tell you about your competition, give you insight into future trends or technology, take some work off your plate, help you take on a larger project, open an opportunity, support you in selling an idea, or give you feedback on how you're working. Identify where you most need to build your network and commit a conversation-a-week to it.

> **Behaviors**
>
> Ways to lead through people, make it fun, and build resilience.

Help build and bond a team you're working on. Pick a team you're working with or starting soon where trust and mutual support will be highly important. Identify ways for the team to get to know each other better. You might try cooking a meal together, going bowling, participating in an improvisational comedy workshop, or doing a community service project. Get a book on team-building activities, such as *Teamwork and Teamplay*,[49] and pick a few that would work well for your team.

Celebrate. Find excuses to celebrate: birthdays, arrivals of new employees, work anniversaries, hitting milestones, beating a competitor, or getting through a tough time. And find ways to celebrate that stir up energy and lift spirits, such as quirky awards, photo clips set to music, inviting families, or just having fun gathering around food and drink.

See both sides. In making decisions or settling conflicts, consciously talk about and see the issue from multiple points of view. Put yourself into the position of others, and consider the impact of your decisions or solutions on them.

Weigh your alternatives. Consider multiple options in making decisions, not just the first idea that pops to mind or the way things have been done in the past. Have a Plan A and a Plan B. Recognize that sometimes decisions must be made quickly, but other times a decision serves only to prematurely close off options; ask if a particular issue really needs to be decided now.

Find your way around obstacles. Maybe you're running into a wall of resistance, or don't like some of what is going on. See if you can figure out how to turn it. In the spirit of aikido ask, "How can I use this?" Be willing to come off your position (even though you have an end in mind), and sense where others are coming from and how they can move with you. Practice turning the energy in a direction that you want to go, and that others are able to follow.

CHAPTER SIX

Drift into the Visionary

WHAT'S POSSIBLE?

The Visionary

Drift for a moment into the Visionary pattern, the final frontier. What's possible? Here you might simply "Invent . . .," to borrow the Hewlett Packard tagline, letting go of old boundaries and inviting your mind to expand like air filling space. Hang back. Your eyes soften to take in everything around you and thoughts arise from the edges, the lateral, random connections that others might miss. Here you might encounter a leader like Steve Jobs, the CEO of Apple Computer, who has reinvented two industries (and counting) in one lifetime, hanging out in the space of "thinking differently" before charging into Driver territory to make his great ideas happen. Or you may connect with Tom Anderson and Chris DeWolfe, the entrepreneurial founders of MySpace.com. For a time the fastest growing website on the Internet, MySpace was created as a place to simply hang out and, as DeWolfe says, "Let people be what they want to be."

You might notice a sense of harmony with nature in this pattern, where outside comes inside and offices are light and airy. Movement is chaotic but not frenzied. Here people chill, hang out, leap, and drift, exposing the essence of ideas, the meaning of work, and the unseen needs of the market. Visionary leaders scan for possibilities and land on what to pay attention to with something between uncanny intuition and exasperating randomness that, in either case, can be confounding to others. "The trouble with the Visionary," admits one of my Visionary colleagues "is that it's only Visionary on a good day. The rest of the time it's more like daydreaming." Indeed, Visionary adults were often the bored, disorganized, underachieving daydreamers in the classrooms of their childhood. Visionary flunkie Albert Einstein could be their patron saint.

113

Visionary leaders focus on the future and on what's possible in the present. All ideas with no one implementing them does not a leader make. But leaders who can connect the dots to a brighter future can inspire others to extraordinary greatness. Conversely, leaders lacking "this vision thing," as former President Bush (the first one) once called it, struggle to inspire others from a deep well of truth.

Ah, this land of the open mind and the mind that opens others to new possibility. The blue sky knows no boundary as a kite drifts overhead, its tail telling of the subtle currents providing directionless direction.

GETTING THE HANG OF THE VISIONARY

Some of you find your Home in this pattern; others of you might enjoy a chance to hang out here for awhile. At its best, the Visionary invites you into a flow state, or *samadhi* condition, where your doing is so effortless it becomes being. Rather than standing apart from time that you have to manage, this pattern invites you into the slipstream of the eternal Now. Unlike the other patterns, the Visionary does not have a fixed center in the body, but instead is manifested as a freely moving fulcrum and ever-expanding energy. Drifting movements or opening any sense can be your port of entry, but many people find it easiest to enter the Visionary using, not surprisingly, *vision*.

Hold your hands out at the side of your head as if you're in a stick-'em-up position. Relax your neck. Without turning your head, use your peripheral vision to see both hands at the same time. Notice that you also see everything between your hands, but in a softly focused, all-at-once way, what we call 180-degree vision.

Wiggle your fingers and move your hands slightly behind your head until you can sense, but not quite see, the motion of your fingers. Let your vision keep expanding without boundary, taking in the entire space around you, even seeing yourself sitting there seeing right now. That's the bigness of the Visionary, taking in everything all at once, where ideas float in.

The art of being wise is the art of knowing what to overlook

—William James

You might remember a time—we've all seen children do it—when you were gaping in wonder at the world, completely absorbed in the moment. If you relax, open yourself to

The Visionary Landscape—opening to new possibility

the moment without agenda or judgment, invite 180-degree vision, and breathe without effort, something can reveal itself to you that you never expected . . .

For some people, this pattern may seem foreign to the driving, execution-oriented work of leadership. And yet, people who can't get here pay a steep price, as do those who stay too long!

TOO MUCH, TOO LITTLE VISIONARY AT BIGTIME INVESTMENTS

"Bigtime" is a made-up name, but the story that unfolded at this investment house is true, and is telling of the ups and downs of Visionary leadership.

The Voice of the Visionary

"Let's see how things develop."

What the Visionary Does Best

Promotes harmony, tries new things

Too Much Vision

Irresponsible, too impulsive

Not Enough Vision

Lack of openness and flexibility

It starts back in the 1980s with Tim, a highly imaginative, technologically brilliant Visionary leader. He'd led the team that built one of the first successful data warehouses. His reward was a dream assignment leading a new team to develop an investment portfolio management tool. In today's world, that might not seem so novel or exciting, but this was well before the Internet, and it took a leader like Tim to envision the power and potential of this product. Such a tool would put Bigtime in a class all its own among the top investment firms. With a bright new division and a big new budget, Tim set to work.

Aesthetics came first. Tim moved his senior management team into corner offices with spectacular views of Boston. He declared that people could wear whatever they wanted, no more dress code requiring jackets, ties, heels, or stockings; the team was ecstatic. Next, he hired additional software engineers and designers to conceive of this futuristic product. The bounds were broadly sketched: it should perform sophisticated analyses of a portfolio offline, and let people manage their holdings and make trades online. The product was technically complex and—in this era of primordial personal computing and 1200 baud phone lines—well ahead of its time. Everyone was enthusiastic and swept up in new possibilities, except for a seasoned secretary who knew Tim all too well. She shook her head and said, "Tim up here unsupervised? That could cause trouble."

It did. Plans for the system grew more grandiose, as Tim thought of more and more ways to improve it and encouraged his team to be equally creative. The specification was always a work-in-progress. The team missed all of its early delivery dates, and pressure from outside mounted. Tim's senior people began spending nights and weekends at the office, throwing more hours at the work. Morale remained high—everyone believed in the vision, and Tim did his part to keep spirits high. He served beer on Friday afternoons, arranged for team dinners (also with beer), installed a large-screen TV so people wouldn't have to miss their favorite sporting events while working late (as everyone started doing with the project so far behind schedule).

Tim's boss, the company's CEO, remained hopeful, and initial feedback from users of a trial version suggested that the product would be a big hit. But two years after the original delivery date had come and gone with nothing beyond the trial version delivered, the company forced Tim out. And in came Bruce, who quickly established that things were going to change around here. In his unvarnished Organizer–Driver style, he instituted daily status meetings for all senior managers to begin at 8:00 A.M. sharp, weekly code reviews, and a new mantra: "Focus and finish. Focus and finish."

But Bruce ran into trouble, too. When he tried to speed development by cutting features, the trial users complained. Bruce had hired a number of project managers to keep things on track. When they tightened control, the best and most creative people quit. They felt that Bruce and his managers stifled them, didn't appreciate them, and valued schedules and process too much: "Without people like me in the organization, you won't have anything to focus on and finish!" an exiting engineer told an uncomprehending Bruce.

Other people also left, bored by having no new features to develop and complaining that Bruce lacked vision himself and didn't "get" it in others. "Bruce just isn't very bright," said another engineer on his way out.

Two more years went by, and then—with tens of millions of dollars spent, a team that had swollen to over a hundred people, and the product still not shipped—Bruce, too, was fired.

If Tim and Bruce could have been melded into one whole and balanced leader, Bigtime could have had an unbelievable success story with this product. Instead, struggling with these two partial leaders whipsawing the organization in radically different directions, the business suffered an enormous loss. The people suffered as well, including Tim and Bruce. Tim went on to an even more powerful position—inspiring Visionaries have a way of doing that. But he was fired from that job, too, in an even more spectacular debacle. Bruce, whose career never recovered its momentum, became a midlevel manager in a middle-tier company. Too much or too little of the Visionary is dangerous—both extremes cry out for balance.

WHEN VISIONARIES ARE WHOLE AND BALANCED

David Dotlich is just as brilliant a Visionary as Tim but he gets things done. One of the founders of a small consulting company, CDR (its real name, since this is a happy story), Dotlich grew his business considerably over a short period of time. "Every morning David wakes up determined to make the company better," praised one of his CDR partners. David then engineered its purchase by a much larger company, Mercer Delta (which became Oliver Wyman), and proceeded to become the leader of not only the CDR portion in the larger firm, but of Mercer Delta's entire North American operation.

Balancing Big Ideas

David is a person of big ideas. "Why not?," he asks, with that sense of possibility that makes the Visionary fearless when facing risks that freeze others. "I create a picture of how things can be and get everyone on board," he says. The way he does it is not always orderly. As the managing director who runs the business day-to-day puts it, "David has 101 ideas, but doesn't try to do all of them. He distills them down to five or six big picture things he wants to have happen and shares them with three or four people, who then work in parallel, either knowingly or unknowingly, as David moves on, and assumes things are in motion. David doesn't do a lot of tracking until he needs to know where things are at." This may seem chaotic, and sometimes it is. But two things make it feasible. "It works," as the managing director put it, "when whatever David has suggested is absolutely right for the firm, right for the business, and people know that." And it works because David has a keen eye for talent, as many Visionaries do, and surrounds himself with great people who balance his tendencies. Julianna, for example, one of his executive assistants, was impressed by the "utter finesse and flexibility" with which David goes after opportunities.

"I'm not so flexible," she said. "I don't go with the flow." But she sure helped David stay organized. "When I first got here, there was no system for following up on what was a real opportunity or a casual conversation. Now I send him a spreadsheet of all the opportunities he's identified. We look for which need further action, making sure we're following up on the right things. It keeps both of us focused."

David blends the Visionary's scan with the Driver's intense focus and love of winning. In David's words, "I keep my eye on the bigger picture of where we want to go—I build a picture. Then I run a mental calculus: of all the things I'm facing, which will contribute most toward the goal. I let go of those that don't have high payoff." In a sort of Visionary–Driver two step, he's able to scan, target, and let go of the rest.

When David does run into trouble, there's usually a pattern to that as well. "My strength is creating an exciting picture and assuming everyone is onboard. But it can also be my weakness, because I may think people are with me when they're not." In a painful example of this early in CDR's development, David was sued by another company that he had earlier helped launch. The "exciting picture" ended up being viewed quite differently by the different players, leading to misunderstandings and a lawsuit. "If I had to do it again," David reflected, "I'd go step by step, put everything in writing, laying it out step by step." In other words, more of the Organizer.

David's Balancing Practice

Yet on the whole, what makes David so effective is that he does blend the grace and ease of the Visionary with plenty of focus (Driver) and people skills (Collaborator) and he surrounds himself with good Organizers. Organizers like Julianna, who observes, "He's a cool cucumber when it comes to meeting his hot goals!" Where does he get this balance? David's lifetime of learning has led him to a number of practices—activities he puts into his day and week—and the connection to physical balance is as clear as daylight.

"I meditate," David saysof his formula for greatness. "At night before sleep, I reflect on the day and think about the next day—generally process what's happening in a detached way. I work out doing Pilates, which does a lot of work with the body's balance. I have a trainer who has convinced me that balance will be the secret to my health. So I practice walking with balance, lifting one foot then the other—doing all kinds of Pilates exercises to work the core muscles and spine. I'm also running about four times a week."

The balance evident on the outside in David's leadership style starts on the inside with the way he balances the patterns and even pays attention to physical balance itself. David's trainer's comments are true for all of us: balance is the secret not only to our health, but to functioning at the top of our game and endlessly rejuvenating ourselves from the spring of our natural potential.

WHEN VISIONARY IS NOT ENOUGH

Holly was a chemist by training and a successful manager at a water treatment plant. But she was also not one to stay put; a gifted playwright and teacher, she now combines all of those skills making university science understandable to nonmajors. Beyond her own classroom, she's a leading innovator in science education across the country. In Holly's science programs, molecules have names, hydrogen and oxygen like each other, and free radicals roam the classroom. Holly's students adore her and the classes are always lively—but getting ready for them used to be quite a drama:

"I have trouble getting out the door in the morning," Holly told me. "I yell at myself the whole time trying to stay on track—when I finally actually reach the door, I see the hole in my sock, remember that I'm missing an earring, and have to scream at myself to keep going. I try to prepare my lectures in advance but always end up thinking of the best ideas in the car on the way to work. There's a moment of terror—the image of facing all those expectant faces with nothing to say!—and then the ideas start popping up." It was as though she needed the adrenaline to pull everything together. By the time she got to work, she was routinely in a state of mild panic. Holly's Visionary ways—never planning ahead—showed up in her personal life as well, such as when she threw a birthday party for herself that was so last-minute it was nearly a surprise. Her Organizer husband was aghast: "It drives me crazy! You're not

**You know your
Visionary is
overexposed when
you're . . .**

- Unfocused
- Disorganized
- Dropping important details
- Lacking follow through
- Jumping around too much
- Starting many things and finishing few
- Drifting off
- Leaping to new ideas no one else can follow
- Daydreaming a great deal
- Always looking for where you put something

planning this party—you think you can just handle things when they come up and deal with problems as they arise. You need to plan for them."

"Well, that's how *you* do it," Holly responded, trying not to sound defensive.

"That's how all adults do it! Everyone plans!" her exasperated husband assured her.

Organizers, yes, but not Visionary types. Not Holly. Somehow, trying to plan and organize was always a losing battle. Even in kindergarten she got an F for not being able to put on her wraps properly (she could never find them) and a D for "works in a neat and orderly manner." Probably more than children in any other pattern, Visionary kids collect messages of failure amidst all the "shaping up" rules of early school experiences.

Even getting ready for school was a daily battle with her parents; now she has more sympathy for their frustrated screaming as she devises schemes to help her own children make the school bus. When her equally Visionary daughter was young, Holly drew and taped a picture near the front door titled "Everything I Need to Have When I Leave for School." It showed a little girl with everything she needed to be properly dressed and all the things she's supposed to be carrying: a backpack, lunchbox, homework. Holly's daughter would get dressed, look at the picture, get something, come back and look at the picture again, then go get something else.

But when it came to her own life, it took more than a drawing by the door to whip Holly into shape, and instead she developed the voice of her own inner drill sergeant. "You're playing guitar! You're supposed to be arranging a meeting! Put that guitar down!" Or screamed at herself: "No, you can't work on that now! You have to review these reports now!" This monitor voice was an anxious, irate companion, a "constant inner jabbering."

This wasn't pleasant, and it took quite a toll on her health—she developed respiratory trouble, sleep problems, and jumpy legs. She was wakeful much of the night and tired when she woke up. While she was gifted with abundant energy, it shot through her more like chaotic lightning than well-channeled electricity.

"I need an Organizer primer," Holly said, after learning of the patterns. And she went about finding creative ways (naturally) to be more organized. She put a few organizing points into her day, such as daily walks and a time to write. And she used her playwriting strengths to play around with finding an Organizer voice, even stepping into an Organizer role that was more friendly, less punishing.

A year later, she was much more optimistic and effective as she recounted her journey: "The patterns have helped me more than anything I've ever come across. First I learned what I'm good at—what pattern is Home for me. Before that I was wandering around in my parent's patterns feeling like a failure. Second, I realized that staying in my Home pattern was not good enough; there were many things I would never be able to do well. Third, I wanted to make forays into other patterns, and the patterns gave me the map and tools to get there."

If, like Holly, you're strong in the Visionary and ready to make forays into other patterns, here are some ideas for how to do that.

BRINGING VISION INTO BALANCE

Start with your strengths, which are likely to include a wonderful imagination and natural inquisitiveness. No matter what pattern you want to cultivate, the process itself will engage you more if you make it something of a study. But beware! Don't go to extremes. A number of Visionary leaders have difficulty managing their attention, especially if the Driver is one of their least preferred patterns. They often alternate between hyperfocus and complete lack of focus. Visionaries can also get caught up in not starting something they can't finish and thinking they can't take anything far enough to finish it (since everything has to be done 110 percent). Don't feel you have to become an expert Driver, Organizer, or Collaborator. But if you can get very curious about how to *be* each of these characters, how to ease into each pattern and feel it in your body, together with an appreciation of what each is good for, you'll find your own natural balance. So relax your standards, allow some risk, and explore. . . .

Regardless of the pattern you want to access, the first step is to Get Here Now, and a quick Driver mini-break is a good way to do it. You might try the exercise in chapter 3 that taught you how to Push into the Driver's seat in less than a minute. When you're in need of a quick energy boost or a fully present, focused mind, you can summon Driver energy that will focus your intention.

To figure out which pattern you need more of for balancing vision, start where your need is the greatest, which is generally related to your weakest pattern and strongest source of resistance. The places you don't want to go hold the most potential for balance and breakthrough.

Organize Your Vision

If your need is around parsing and planning work and getting things accomplished, Organizer is the pattern you want to cultivate. You might warm up

Let's take this one step at a time. . .

Your need: Focus, edge

Your resistance: Pushy people, competition

Your great move: Enter the Driver

Your need: Organization, discipline

Your resistance: Rules, routine

Your great move: Warm up with Driver, then creatively explore the Organizer

Your need: Socializing your ideas, influencing others

Your resistance: Frivolity, social scenes

Your great move: Warm up in the Collaborator on your own, then Collaborate with others

with a Driver mini-break to build some focused determination and with that, enter the Organizer. Since Visionaries tend to be kinesthetic learners—people who learn in their bodies—physical activities for entering the Organizer are probably best for you. Visionaries also learn through imitation; you might doodle your own Organizer action figure and imagine how you could become *that*.

Use your creativity to make the tools of the Organizer your own. For example, no Organizer tool is more common than a list. But who said lists had to be confined to words? They could include a picture by the door ("Everything I need for . . ."), a set of reminder tones played on your computer, or colorful graphics on a timeline around the walls of your office. You might pick a particularly hectic or challenging part of your day—your morning routine or getting ready for a meeting—and experiment with how you could use a list, drawing, map, poem, song, or even a video clip to step through it. Forget trying to develop one grandiose system for your whole day—that's not your style. Use your strength—your wonderful imagination—to evolve mini organizing cues that work for you one situation at a time.

Feel free to get creative about how you organize your thoughts. For example, keep a notepad or recorder handy to collect thoughts when they happen so you can organize them later. You can also get creative about how you organize your space. You may never have or want the neat and tidy office of a native Organizer, but you do want to be able to locate that file or find your keys. You might create a special place for items you need to find quickly, for example a "key drop" or a basket for urgent items. Visionary Betsy has learned to ask herself, "Where should this item live?" Later, when she can't find it, she asks the question again—holding really still—and the answer usually comes to her.

Creating an order you can see is another Visionary aid. If your current "file system" consists of stacks all over the place, forget trying to go all the way to sequestered, alphabetized file cabinets. But you might try clear plastic file boxes so that you can still see what's inside. Betsy swears by color-coding as well: red for action files, blue for idea files, and so on.

Ed, a Visionary colleague at Bell Laboratories, had a notoriously messy office. (We used to take potential new hires by Ed's office just so they could be impressed with what creative, free spirits we had working at the labs.) His organization scheme started with a bulletin board on the wall behind his desk with large numbers "1" and "2" pinned on it. Underneath the "1" were push-pinned papers and reminders of all his top-priority, must-do items. Underneath the "2" were important, longer-term assignments he had going, and he'd make a point to work on them at least once a week. A large "3" was taped to his wastebasket.

Almost any activity, done consistently, will add the Organizer's discipline to the way you lead and work. You might experiment with different activities in the spirit of inquisitiveness—what helps most? If I write out each step of this project plan as I take a walk, does it come out better? If I hold still when I put something down, is it easier to remember where I put it? If I move slowly around my office as I read something, do I remember it better? Again, don't get hung up in perfectionism! You don't have to be a model of discipline; you just want enough for balance.

Drive Your Vision

If your need is for greater focus, ambition, hitting your goals, or keeping a sense of urgency, the Driver is the character you'd do well to find within yourself. You know the formula: push on something. The clock is an easy target. Set a deadline for yourself to finish something you've been putting off—even make a bet with a friend if you're really serious—and finish absolutely on time. You might picture a Driver friend and, for a few moments, move into their way of being and doing. Or draw your own Driver action figure and find its qualties in yourself.

At work, one of your most important tools as a leader is how you focus attention—both your own and others'. Use your Visionary strength to sense the big picture and pick out *what* is worth paying attention to. Once you have the *what*, don't lose it; name it specifically, precisely. Driver practices such as always knowing your top three priorities, setting measurable goals, and measuring progress against them are good ways to capture your insight and focus attention on it.

Focus here!

Socialize Your Vision

Finally, if what you really need is to inspire others and get people moving with you, turn to the Collaborator. You might draw a clownish Collaborator character for yourself and feel your way into making that fun engagement your own way of being. You might give your character a voice and hear what it has to say.

When I used to teach aikido classes, we'd do bouncy, loosening individual exercises to warm up. Otherwise, people would be too stiff when they started working with partners and their movements would be stiff and awkward. Similarly, you might want to warm up to the Collaborator's easy frame of mind on your own before engaging others, so that you don't come across as too stiff and awkward.

Once you've warmed up, the best practices of the Collaborator involve others. Outside of work, if you have children available (or pets), play with them—and the sillier you get, the better. With adults you might explore social activities that help you develop a sense of rhythm, timing, and sensitivity to other people. Think of it as something of a study: in what situations are you able to really *listen* to people and sense them? These are the conditions you want to keep creating and learning from.

At work, you can look for similar conditions. You might try having lunch with colleagues, becoming a mentor, doing someone a favor or having her do you a favor, and see which methods work best for building business relationships. You can experiment with different ways of building a team: does the team gel better by having a crisp agenda or by enjoying a potluck dinner at your house? This spirit of easy inquiry will eventually enable you to move more easily with others and them with you.

In the field of leadership development, people vacillate on whether it's better to play to your strengths (the new mantra) or to find and fix faults (the old model). I prefer a mixed model. Certainly, we want to win on our strengths—we can do so with less energy and more natural ease. But strengths alone give rise to partial leaders. Only when we bring in enough of the other patterns—the Driver's focus, the Organizer's discipline, and the Collaborator's playful engagement—to stay out of trouble can our Visionary self be expressed at its best.

WHEN VISION BECOMES BLINDING

What happens if you're not able to balance your Visionary strengths? Or if you're in a leadership situation that calls for more Driver, Organizer, or Collaborator than you can develop? That was Brian's situation, and it forced him into a tough choice.

When Brian joined a high-flying Global 1000 computer company, his glib intelligence was immediately recognized and he was soon promoted into management. After a scant two years, he landed a position as the executive aide to the company's CEO. Brian and the CEO, both strong Visionaries and great strategic thinkers, got along famously and would often debate the future of the computer industry, where technology was going, and why. After that plum assignment, and with friends in high places, Brian breezed through a few more promotions. Everyone knew he was brilliant, if somewhat arrogant, and if they had any doubts about his ability to deliver results or manage day-to-day, he was promoted before those doubts could be proven one way or another. One year he was opening offices around Europe. The next year he was starting up a new line of business.

From Visionary Heaven to Visionary Hell

But then several things happened. The CEO left. The new CEO downsized the company, and the new line of business Brian headed was shut down. For a while, it wasn't clear if Brian would even have a job, until finally he landed in a position that was as Organizer-demanding as jobs come: project manager for a set of cost-cutting initiatives. The job required Organizing meetings and lists upon lists for action tracking. It played to every one of Brian's weaknesses. He kept trying to make it a strategic, big-picture job. But Brian's Organizer boss became increasingly frustrated that he wasn't getting the basic, day-to-day job done. She reacted by tightening the reins even further, wanting more reports, more lists, more details, and, to Brian's dismay, treating him like a "low-level gofer." For the first time in his career, he was frightened.

Develop, Acquire, or Exit

Develop, acquire, or exit: those are the three options Brian or any of us has when we realize that we're in a situation that is not working. The "develop" option is the one we've been talking about, where you develop easier access to counterbalancing patterns. This is a great option if you're a leader like Holly who is largely successful and doing work she loves. But it's not a good option if you hate your job, let alone the person you'd have to become to do it well. The more strongly we prefer a single pattern—as Brian did the Visionary—the harder the "develop" option becomes. For Brian, it was not worth the effort.

The second option is to "acquire" people who shore up your weaknesses and give balance to your strengths. This is a great option for someone in a position to take on a partner, hire people, or assemble a team. Earlier you saw how David hired good Organizers to balance his weakest pattern. I watched

Dan Goldin artfully use the partner approach when he was the administrator of NASA. Goldin was a great Visionary with the wonderment of a child when it came to exploring space. While this was fine for setting a vision, it wasn't much good for getting things done in a huge government bureaucracy. For that he brought in General John Dailey, the personification of Organizer stability and follow-through, as his number two. If you are able to find Drivers, Organizers, and Collaborators to offset your Visionary excesses and you can work with mutual trust and respect, you can turn a potential mismatch into a huge collective win.

Brian was in a position to hire several people, but he brought in others like himself. He didn't "resonate" with Organizers (including his boss) or respect detail-oriented people. Until he developed some awareness of how he was hiring in his own image, he kept digging his hole deeper. Eventually, he did bring in a couple of Organizers who could ably manage a project plan. But it wasn't enough to mask the fact that Brian was adding little value himself. By that time his unproven track record and recent failures had washed away his credibility in the company. "Exit" remained the only option.

For Brian, it turned out to be a good option. He learned a lesson from his painful experience and sought a very different kind of role, one that was more consultative and played to his strengths as a great ideas guy and downplayed his weakness for follow-through.

But even the "exit" option is not always an answer. As Tim found in exiting Bigtime, the same problems often follow leaders to their next jobs. This is especially true when strong pattern preferences combine with weak awareness of them, a trap you now know how to avoid!

VISIONARY ON THE RISE

If Brian's story makes you think the Visionary is somehow not as important in business or leadership as are the other patterns, nothing could be further from the truth. In fact, the Visionary is on the rise, both in our popular culture and in leadership specifically. A potential death knell to the careers of many ambitious leaders is being told in talent reviews that they're great at this, that, and the other thing, *but* "not strategic enough."

A Leader Needing to See the Big Picture in a New Way

That was the case with Susan, a terrifically talented, down-to-earth leader who excelled at getting results. A senior executive at a telecommunications company with more than 7,000 people reporting to her, Susan turned around the quality of the company's networks and the satisfaction ratings of its customers.

Excellent at day-to-day operations, Susan was challenged by the CEO to be more Visionary: "He's telling me I need to be more strategic, 'change the playing field,' and talk about some sexy new technology at the next analyst's meeting," she said. All this was hard for Susan, because she was not one to speak about things she wasn't sure of. "I'm from the Midwest," she said, accounting for her basic-as-bread values. "When I listen to my colleagues talk about the "big picture" or visionary technology, I hear a lot of fluff. And yet, I get it. I know what they're asking me to do. I'm just not sure how to do it in a way that's true to me."

At first, Susan thought that she already *did* see the big picture—she was just more "realistic" than some of her "fluffy" colleagues. Most leaders say (and sincerely believe) that they can see the big picture, but each pattern has a very different view of it.

Using the metaphor of forest and trees, Drivers scan the big picture by looking through a roving straw until they see the tree that they want to cut down. Organizers see a million trees that they want to sort into some kind of order. Collaborators collect the big picture by swinging, Tarzan-like, from tree to tree as one thing leads to another and back again.

Only Visionaries, hanging in the expansiveness of Now, take in the entire forest all at once, seeing no tree in particular, yet each in all. Drifting in a timeless, open space, without agenda or judgment, new possibilities spontaneously emerge until the Visionary leaps—doesn't push, step or swing—but *leaps* to an entirely new place. The leap doesn't always lead to a new category-crushing strategy; sometimes it leads nowhere, which is all right, too. To become too agenda-driven is to automatically exit this Visionary pattern. The utter pointlessness of "chill time," the surrender to the universe, is exactly what's needed to enable breakthrough, and is also what makes this pattern irritatingly difficult to pin down or depend on.

Giving up Control

No one gets more irritated by this unpredictability than the Organizer–Drivers and Driver–Organizers who have largely shaped the businesses of today. This Western business model (which has been exported to many global organizations) emphasizes competitive spirit and taking charge. But this model has come under a great deal of pressure in recent years because there's simply too much going on to try to control it. As a recent *Fortune* magazine article

Seeing the Big Picture

Most leaders think they see "the forest for the trees," but each has quite a different view . . .

Driver: Rapid, single-point scan to find a tree to cut down.

Organizer: Tree, tree, tree—isn't there some way to sort this?

Collaborator: Swinging from tree-to-tree—Wheeee!—one tree leads to another and back again.

Visionary: All trees at once, nothing in particular, each in all.

observed,[50] "If you want to take back control, begin by acknowledging that you really can't. The earth will not slow its spin."

The key becomes figuring out *what* to pay attention to, which requires the Visionary's immersion in the flow and leap to the essence. At its best, the Visionary invites us into a state of *wu-wei*, a Taoist ideal that roughly translates as "effortless effort." As the *Fortune* article continues, "*wu-wei* describes a state in which the world seems to be working for us." This is very different from seeing the world only as a place we have to control or it will destroy us. Not that the Driver's view is wrong. It can be quite correct in certain contexts. But by itself, it's too limiting.

The Visionary's view opens up much more possibility, including possibilities that solve the problems facing us. As jobs migrate quickly around the globe to wherever they can be done most cost effectively, the most enduring source of value comes through innovation. Innovation only happens through that wonderful quality of seeing what everyone else sees, but seeing it differently—this is the gift of the Visionary.

The Visionary's ability to leap to the essence is also our indispensable ally in dealing with the pace of life today. Knowing what to pay attention to and what to let go of is an essential skill in everything from breaking paradigms to building strategy to balancing work and life. "It would be one thing if I just had 10 percent too much work," said Dennis, expressing sentiments felt by many leaders I've worked with. "Maybe then I could just work a little faster or longer. But I couldn't get this job done if there were two of me." Dennis, like others, tried the work-harder, work-faster strategy for awhile. But it was leading to utter exhaustion. Somewhere not far from breakdown, his Visionary self emerged and he started letting go of details, trusting his seasoned intuition, and leaping to a few essentials. Please don't wait until your first heart attack to find the freedom of this pattern!

EXPANDING INTO THE VISIONARY

The Visionary's gifts can be unexpected. In Susan's case, better work–life balance was the surprise bonus; she went after more of the Visionary because she wouldn't settle for being seen as "not strategic enough." She started adding Visionary mini-breaks to her day, times when she would expand her vision to

180 degrees and relax into deep, centered breathing. "Though I learned not to do it during executive meetings," she told me laughingly in one of our coaching sessions. "Last time I did it I got so relaxed and drifty that I was saddled with an action item before I could snap to and say 'no!' " Outside of work,

> *Every atom of my being as good as belongs to you.*
> —Walt Whitman

she also integrated more Tai-Chi-like motions into her yoga practice and learned to do the moves with an effortless *wu-wei* quality.

At work, Susan fostered more Visionary activity in her organization. She started scheduling quarterly strategy sessions with her senior managers for which they prepared by interviewing key customers and studying competitors to get the big picture. She also brought the most respected junior engineers in the organization together for brainstorming sessions.

As Susan added Visionary insight to her already great skills at getting things done, her star kept rising in the company. Moreover, she felt the payoff in personal balance and wholeness, as she understated in her usual way, "I feel better and I've grown some."

You have a pretty good idea of where the Visionary pattern fits among your preferences based on your FEBI results. You might also want to develop more access to the Visionary if you recognize yourself some of these symptoms:

- You feel stuck.
- You hate randomness and chaos.
- You're mired in details.
- You're trying to deal with a quickening pace by doing the same things faster and faster.
- You feel life is boring, has no meaning, or is too predictable.
- You find yourself trying to control everything.
- You're having big trouble coping with loss or adjusting to change.
- You distrust intuition or think it cannot give you any insight.
- You have difficulty imagining solutions to problems.
- You want more imaginative spark and big-picture thinking.
- You want some breathing room in your life, and the sense of new possibility.
- You're afraid to go out on a limb even though you know you are right.
- You never "chill" and you are burning out.

Invite Some Chaos

What can you do? For starters, any of the Visionary activities will more effective if you completely immerse yourself in them. No multitasking. It's also great if you can do the activities spontaneously, when the spirit moves you, not at the same, regimented time every day. This is completely opposite to what I'd tell someone who wants to develop more of the Organizer. If it's more Visionary you want, invite a little chaos wherever possible.

David's way of inviting chaos into his leadership approach was to give the same assignment to several people, resulting in parallel streams of work. Sometimes the people would find out about one another and join forces, some-times they didn't. Either way, something creative emerged: the synergy of spontaneous teamwork or the variety of multiple approaches. Organizers tend to complain when they discover someone else is doing the same thing they are—they think it's disorganized and wasteful. Drivers tend to compete. But Visionaries know that Nature plants more than one seed.

Similarly your activities outside of work—even if they're not specifically Visionary activities—can be done in a Visionary way by allowing them to be more chaotic and expansive. For example, if you wanted to paint in a Vision-ary way, you might use a medium with its own element of chaos, such as wa-tercolor. Or you could paint in a wide open space, inviting abstract visions to express themselves. Modern art that conveys essence, infinity, or chaos invites the Visionary spirit. Even if your only painting project consists of walls in your home, you could use textures or glazes to create some randomness. If garden-ing is your pleasure, you might introduce some chaos by allowing a patch of sage to grow into the impatiens or let your beans to grow up your corn. Or you could create garden spaces that are so in harmony with their environment that they don't need extra watering or weeding.

Immersion through Your Senses

Every one of your senses can be used to enter the Visionary. You can start by simply softening and expanding your Vision to 180 degrees. You can take that a step further by getting out in open spaces. It's best if you can reach a bit of alti-tude: walk on a ridge, mountain, mezzanine, or a lookout on the upper floor of your office building. Ron Heifetz counsels leaders to "get up on the balcony"— and it can literally *be* a balcony—to get a fresh view of what is going on.[51]

The sound of your inner dialogue can take on the role of the Visionary. Vi-sionaries are inquisitive and they welcome, even need, a level of risk in their undertakings. "What wants to happen here?" you might hear yourself saying as you open to a Visionary frame of mind. Other wisdom from your Visionary voice might include:

- "Let it go."
- "You are where you are meant to be, doing what you are meant to be doing."

- "It's perfect, you just have to figure out why"
- "Come up a level. What's out there?"
- "What's really going on here?"
- "What's possible?"
- "What *else* wants to happen here?"
- "Hang loose."
- "Celebrate the paradox . . . the question is the answer!"
- "How are these the same?" (for example, a rose and a typewriter)
- "What if . . . ?"

The next time your catch yourself bemoaning an unwelcome change or fretting over a future possibility, see if you can flip that voice into one that accepts "It is what it is," or "Okay, my worst fear happens," and then ask, "How could I use this?"

Music also comes in all patterns, but Visionary music floats in the air with an expansive bigness that is never oppressive, always opening. Hildegaard von Bingen's lilting medieval chants have this quality—it's no accident that her music has been remixed and reintroduced to our increasingly Visionary culture. Where Driver music moves you to stomp on the beat, Visionary music invites you extend, flow, fall upward, as with modern dance, and you may not even discern a beat. I sometimes play New Age or Chinese music to add Visionary extension to my Tai Chi practice. You might play some Visionary music when you need to get bigger, let go, think outside the box.

You can also add Visionary elements to your office. Invite some randomness by bringing the outside in: a branching vine, a bubbling waterfall, an open-air breeze that stirs the mind. Bring in more natural light, or try lightbulbs that mimic it. Torchiere lamps that aim light toward the ceiling, or pools of light that define spaces without hard boundaries all create a feeling of openness.

If every part of your office is neat and tidy (Organizers, you know who you are!), you might allow some chaos in your desk drawers, in a creative corner, or with a random quote that emerges on your screensaver. You might try hanging something Visionary on the wall, such as an abstract painting, an evocative photograph of outer space, a poem, or a quote: "The problems we face cannot be solved at the same level we were at when we created them," beneath a black and white photograph of Albert Einstein.

The Visionary may never feel as natural as your Home pattern—and that's all right. But developing enough ease in this pattern to be able to let go and leap to unexpected insights is exactly what's needed for your drive, discipline, and people skills to come to full fruition.

THE WHOLE AND BALANCED VIEW AT BIGTIME

Even after developing greater ease in the Visionary, or in any of the patterns, we're unlikely to be mistaken for natives. As a result, whole and balanced leadership often comes in the form of a great partnership, which was the saving grace for Bigtime. Fred, who replaced Bruce on the troubled software project, balanced his Visionary nature with a strong Collaborator–Organizer lieutenant who had worked with him for years. Kathryn was really good with people, gentle, soft-spoken, well-organized, and able to get things done. Fred and Kathryn, in discussion with the demoralized team, established new rules without having to spell everything out: come in when you want, leave when you want *but* be here for core hours; be creative *but* build things the users want and will pay for; deliver on time; have fun, get along, work as a team *but* work.

The team, which had shrunk to 30 people by the end of Bruce's disastrous tenure, had been hidden away in a small annex nicknamed The Clubhouse. It might have been more appropriately called The Doghouse when Fred and Kathryn first took over. But all of that changed when the team won the company's respect by redesigning the entire website, miraculously on schedule!

They went on to other successes, including delivering a version of the original investment product, which was now able to connect to the Internet. They became known as the "creative engine that could"—could get things done, that is. The Clubhouse cadre knew its stock had gone up when it was moved into the best part of Bigtime's new building, a large corner with glass walls and views of Boston Harbor. Fred and Kathryn had all the internal walls torn down and replaced by screens and modular furniture. The screens could be rolled up or kept down; the furniture and computers could be joined and reconfigured into any kind of workspace. The whole area had a sense of freedom, lightness, and efficiency that reflected the way the team worked, both inspiring and effective.

The Visionary's insight is essential to leaders and their organizations, but without the balance of the other patterns, great ideas get lost in the chaos and nothing gets done. As the team at Bigtime found, when the Visionary is brought into wholeness and balance, the possibilities are endless. And the view is awesome.

REFLECT ON YOUR VISIONARY ESSENCE

As we finish our tour through the last of these essential energies, you might reflect for a few minutes on how the Visionary manifests in you.

- How much do you operate in this pattern relative to others around you: more, less, or about the same? What are some implications for how you work and lead?
- If there's one aspect of the Visionary that you might take to extremes, what is it?
- If there were one aspect of the Visionary that you would like easier access to, what would it be?

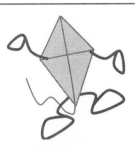

Your inner Visionary

In the flow; seeing and being the essence of things.

VISIONARY MINI-BREAKS AND BEST PRACTICES

The next few pages summarize numerous ways to enter the Visionary using breath, body, background, and everyday leadership behaviors. The **breath** exercises will help you immediately access a Visionary frame of body and mind. The **body** activities will help you access the Visionary with greater comfort and less effort: the more you do them, the easier that access will become. They'll help you build awareness of what your version of the Visionary pattern feels like—when it's present for you and when it's not. The **background** suggestions will help you keep Vision "top of mind" by engaging your senses using Visionary elements. And finally, the **behavior** ideas will give you concrete ways of adding Visionary behaviors to how you work and lead.

The breathing and body exercises can be stand alone or be used in combination to create two-minute, Visionary mini-breaks during your day, or in 20- to 30-minute journeys into the Visionary as an ongoing practice. As in previous chapters, icons indicate whether an activity is more of a mini-break or warm-up (❷) or something suitable for longer practice (❧).

Visionary Seeing (❷,❧)

Breath and Body

Entering the Visionary through all of the senses combined with effortless breathing.

1. Lean back and hold your hands out at the side of your head and, while looking straight ahead, see them only in your peripheral vision. Relax your neck. Wiggle your fingers and move your hands back until you only sense their motion, letting your vision expand to 180 degrees. Use these eyes in the following exercises.

Entering the Visionary through Sound (❷)

1. Sit quietly for a few minutes and invite your breath to slow down, breathing in and out through your nose.

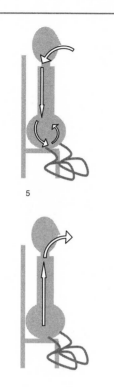

5

2. Let your eyes soften to 180-degree vision, taking in the entire dome around you and seeing nothing in particular.

3. In the same all-at-once way, absorb all of the sound energies in the room, without judging what they are or whether you like them. Simply enter the stream of energy they represent in the moment. Let yourself hear how the sound moves, or gently, almost internally, move with it. You may notice a change in sound quality as you're able to enter the sound stream more completely. This takes some practice, but the resultant peace and sense of flow are well worth it!

Visionary Breathing Break (❷)

1. Soften your eyes to 180-degree vision. Invite every sense to open in the same way. Your ears hear all sounds and the space between all sounds. Your skin feels every air current. Every sense is brought immediately to the now.

2. Relax your jaw, letting your mouth drop open. If your jaw feels tight, say "Em-ma-a-a-a" a few times. Allow breath to move in on its own accord, filling your body from the bottom up.

3. When the breath is through filling you, allow it to turn around and flow out through your still slightly opened mouth, endlessly expanding to the furthest reaches of the universe.

4. Now in it comes again from those farthest reaches, effortlessly breathing you, and now out it goes again, without effort or obstruction. With the exhale, invite any tension in your body—in your neck, shoulders, and chest especially—to flow out as well. Let go of whatever you're carrying.

5. After a few open-mouth breaths this way, close your mouth and breathe a few more breaths in and out through your nose, with each one becoming quieter and more invisible. As you breathe in, let the breath be drawn deeply into your core (i.e., lower abdomen, deep muscles along the spine). As you breathe out, connect with that core and imagine sending it infinitely, invisibly out to the world.

Float into the Visionary (❷)

1. Stand with your feet hip-width apart and your knees slightly bent. Invite your vision to open to 180 degrees and breathe calmly through your nose.

2. As you inhale, gently press your feet into the ground and use this downward energy to let your arms effortlessly "lift without lifting" straight up in front of you, not ramrod stiff but in a flowing way, until they reach shoulder level.
3. Extend your arms out to infinity, letting everything float for a moment; breathe in and out through your nose as you hang, suspended for a moment in the Now.
4. Bring your hands back toward your chest, breathing in, palms facing the earth. Let your elbows bend and hands draw back until they're close to your shoulders.
5. Let your hands drop back down to the starting position as you breathe out. Repeat several times.

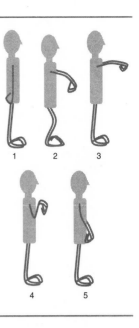

Shift into the Visionary (❷)

1. Begin as in 1 and 2 above. As your hands lift effortlessly to shoulder level, let them drift wide to the side. Let your arms hang effortlessly for a couple of breaths, feeling an expansion through your body.
2. Shift your weight onto one foot and let that downward force express itself through further extension on that side. Shift onto the other foot and allow extension through your other arm.
3. Explore shifting your weight randomly—not just back and forth—varying the pace. Let everything move, especially your head. Let each downward push of the foot rebound through your arms, back, neck, and head. Let these different parts of your body take the lead in the movement and feel how it shifts. Leave no part of you behind as you invite this randomness to flow through you. Perhaps do a mental scan of your body to see if anything is being held still, then let it move.

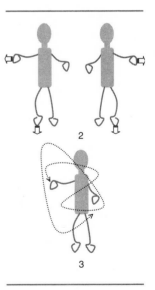

Visionary Moving (❷)

1. Begin as in the shifting exercises above, but now add further, random movement. Bring your index finger near your thumb, as if you were making a small kite. By shifting weight in your feet and letting that expand through the kite, let your kite fly a random path, as it would on a windy day.

1, 2 on chair
Front view

1, 2 on cushion
Side view

Breath and Body

Entering the Visionary in meditation, inviting a *samadhi* or flow condition.

2. Gradually invite the random meandering of your kite to infiltrate more of your body, until your whole body is moving to this imaginary wind. Remember, no repeating motions; surprise even yourself.

Visionary Meditation (☯)

1. Sit on a cushion or chair, with your spine naturally extended, not ramrod straight. Your hip joints should be slightly higher than your knees. Eyes are relaxed in 180-degree vision.
2. Arc your arms into letter "Cs," with your shoulders relaxed and your palms coming together a few inches below your navel. One hand rests on the other, fingers over fingers, open, both palms facing up, with the middle finger of one hand touching the center of the palm underneath it. Your thumbs touch at their ends. Move your elbows forward or back to bring them to the same plane as your shoulders and hands, so your arms together make a perfect circle.
3. The blades of your hands solidly contact your center, a couple of inches below your navel. Here they can feel the breath move to and from your center.
4. Breathe in through your nose. Feel your tailbone relax down into the chair or cushion; let your jaw relax and your mouth open, and exhale slowly. Take a few breaths this way, dropping any tension you feel in your body.
5. Settle down into breathing in and out through your nose, letting the breath move freely, deeply, into your center. Just follow the breath with a count, beginning with "1" and working up to "10." If you lose count, just go back to 1. Invite your awareness to rest on the breath itself, completely experiencing the breath. If any thoughts arise, don't worry about chasing them away, simply blend them with your breath and notice any changes they make in your body.

Visionary Activities (☯)

Tai Chi, Chi Kung

Aikido—practicing multiple-person attack, called Randori ("seizing chaos")

Sailing

Surfing, bodysurfing—becoming one with the wave

Snorkeling

Figure skating—effortless leaps and turns

Scuba diving (also brings out the Organizer, with its safety focus)

Coordination Pattern training

Photography, filmmaking—done spontaneously and in the moment, as of a butterfly in flight, a fleeting smile; not planned or contrived, yet with perfect timing

Meditation—cultivating the *samadhi* condition, where mind and body disappear and you hang in the eternal now

Hang gliding, paragliding, skydiving—activities in the air

Creating visual art in a Visionary style—with elements of randomness and spontaneous timing; drawing on an infinite scale, with strokes that give a feeling of nature's flow; Visionary art conveys essence or chaos

Playing, writing, or singing Visionary music—Gregorian chants, Chinese music, or New Age music—anything expansive, with a random, flowing rhythm; think of a Gregorian chant soaring upward to fill the spaces in a cathedral

Dancing to Visionary music or in a Visionary style—with movements that are random, extended, graceful, including spontaneous leaps and "falling upward," or just moving with the flow

Writing in a way that isn't planned—pouring your thoughts out in a stream-of-consciousness journal entry or free verse, for example

Reading that puts you in a Visionary state of mind, for example, stream-of-consciousness poets, futurists, or big-picture strategists

Regularly experiencing the Visionary through the arts—by attending a live concert or dance performance, visiting a modern art gallery, attending a poetry reading, or watching a Visionary film that conveys a state of being (e.g., *American Beauty*, *Lost in Translation*)

Gardening in a naturalized, organic style—harmonious with the earth

Cooking in a Visionary style—without a recipe, using whatever is in the cupboard or refrigerator

Body

Enter the Visionary through activities that drift, float, or are somehow suspended, activities that encourage creativity, chaos, or harmony with nature.

Background	*Add these elements to your office or home . . .*
Creating a Visionary space	Include stacks of reading material, Internet access, and places to congregate or dream alone. Bring nature indoors, with vines that hang and wander, all in harmonious blend.

Visionary furnishings are movable, reconfigurable. Walls are few and ceilings are high. The pieces invite freedom of movement. The essence of boundaries suggests regions: a four–panel screen or a see-through fish tank.

Visionary lighting is open, expansive, natural, and includes skylights, high windows, and lamps that shine upward rather than down.

Visionary art is evocative, symbolic, and open to interpretation: a photograph of outer space, leaves blowing in the wind, a Jean-Paul Sarte quote against an ethereal background, "Being is what it is."

Visionary music floats in the air like Gregorian chants, with New Age bigness; it is more background than foreground, arrhythmic, ethereal, and changing in style. Examples: Enya, fusion.

Background and Behavior	*Things you might say to yourself . . .*
Self-talk in the voice of the Visionary . . .	• "What's possible?"

• "You are where you are meant to be, doing what you are meant to be doing."

• "It's perfect, you just have to figure out why."

• "Come on in—there's plenty of room." (To invite new ideas into your mind.)

• "What's the real essence of the problem (situation)?"

• "What wants to happen here?"

• "What else wants to happen here?"

• "Let's see what develops."

• "Let go. Hang loose."

• "What if . . .?"

• "How can I use this?"

• "Celebrate the paradox . . . the question is the answer!"

• "How are these things (situations, people, etc.) similar?" (When they appear dissimilar.)

Visionary Work Behaviors

Add spontaneity to your day. Get out of your office and just sense what is going on in the workplace. Engage in random, spontaneous conversations to take the pulse of what's happening. Or pick an issue that you want to get different points of view on and run it through several spontaneous conversations.

Make time for reflection. Get a journal or start a log in which you write for five to 15 minutes several times a week. Keep it free-form, but reserve it for important issues at work; explore them in your journal to get at the essence of what is really going on. Also use your journal to record learnings. Keep a notepad or recorder handy to collect random thoughts.

Brainstorm. You can do this alone or with a group of people. Write down a problem you're struggling with and then give yourself a couple of minutes to think of as many ways as possible to restate it. What's the *real* issue here? Once you pick what you think best states the real issue, brainstorm again to find as many ways of solving it as you can. Try improvising with whatever is available. Net down your ideas by picking one or two that you want to take a step further.

Surf the net. Open up your field of view for any problem you're working on. Plug it into a search engine on the Internet and see what's out there. Find out who has dealt with this issue and identify a thread of information that looks promising.

Get the big picture. Take a reflection break and virtually or literally, if possible, come up a level: stand on a balcony, overlook, or a place with a big view. Let your eyes expand to see the whole picture and reflect on an issue you're working on. What's the bigger picture? What's essential in the end? What are the trends and patterns? What's possible? Let expansive questions like these help you explore your issue with lateral thinking.

Stir things up. Not for the sake of being mischievous or malicious, but stirring things up adds energy to situations so new order can emerge. Invite a contrarian point of view into your meetings. Start parallel tracks of activity to see who can run with a project or what emerges first; run an experiment that might fail; test two or three ideas to see which is best; do something that surprises your competition; bring in a focus group of 12-year-olds to test out your strategic plan.

Location, location, location. Consider creative venues for holding meetings or doing your work that could inspire new thinking, e.g., a park, a museum, an aquarium, an art gallery. Or travel virtually, with Web cameras.

Flip your reactions to chaos. Anytime you catch yourself or others bemoaning an event, flip it. Assume it's meant to be and ask," How can we use this?" Improvise and identify the opportunities present; follow up on those that seem most promising.

CHAPTER SEVEN

Pick a Barrier, Break Through

YOUR INNER TEAM

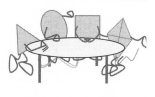

Let's call a meeting and pull together all four pattern players on your inner team. It's a good way to find your "voice"
in each of the patterns, and you can even imagine the different ways they'd walk into the room and gather around a
table: Driver first, followed by the Organizer, both right on
time. A few mind cycles later, the Visionary drifts in, an-
nouncing to the group that Collaborator is on the way.

DRIVER: We're always waiting on that one! Who called this meeting, anyway?

"I did," you might answer in whatever voice is your team leader—most
likely that of your Home pattern. This meeting unfolds in different ways depending on which energy is running the show. But here is one way it might
play out.

DRIVER: Let's get to the point: what are we going to do with what we've
learned? How can we use it to win!

VISIONARY: Not so fast. You always want to jump into action. Let's take
a moment to reflect and explore. Now that we're all together, some things
will be possible for us that have never been possible before.

COLLABORATOR: Yes, let's talk. We need to get to know each other. I'll
tell you one thing that strikes me: we don't all get the same voice at this table.
Some of us are "on" practically all of the time, and others of us struggle to
play at all. I'm not sure we even respect each other.

DRIVER: It might help if you'd show up on time.

ORGANIZER: We never really saw each other clearly before. If we think about the process steps in this book, first we got to know that there were four of us. Second, we learned that some of us function more than others. Third, we toured each of our territories and saw what each of us is good at, and where we get into trouble.

VISIONARY: So much more freedom is possible now . . .

COLLABORATOR: . . . if we work as a team.

DRIVER: Only if we *do* something! Let's figure out what we need to do more of and get on it.

VISIONARY: Well, what really *are* our goals? We might rethink what winning means. We might explore . . .

DRIVER: That's fine, explore away. But then let's focus on a vital few priorities—a key goal.

ORGANIZER: Right. And once we know what we're shooting for, I can figure out the steps to get there.

COLLABORATOR: Oh, you both make it sound like such work. We can play with this, you know, make it fun!

Can you imagine such a meeting for yourself? Maybe you've never thought about it before, but inner dialogue is always in the voice of one of these patterns; the patterns we don't use much, don't get to "speak" much. Who would be the quiet player on your team? How well would the characters get along? We'll be consulting the whole team in laying out a plan for moving to greatness, as each of these players owns a key step in the process:

1. **Explore** what's possible. With the openness of the Visionary, you'll reflect on your work situation, the opportunities presenting themselves, and recurring barriers that get in your way.
2. **Focus** on a key goal. The Driver will help you target the most productive change you could make right now. What change would have the most impact?
3. **Plan** a practice for reaching your goal. With the discipline of the Organizer, you'll step through a process for identifying which pattern is most needed for your goal as well as best practices for developing it.
4. **Engage** others in your plan and make it fun. In the playful spirit of the Collaborator, you can think through ways to get support for your plan and keep it enjoyable.

Now we are starting the third leg of our journey in moving toward greatness, which is gaining freedom to use any pattern when it's called for. Some people spend months or years simply recognizing the patterns and seeing their individual limitations. You might be landing on this chapter well before you need it. Even if you don't want to change a thing about how you function in the patterns right now, this process will help you recognize how these four energies can work together in practice toward your greater good. You may find that this chapter is one you come back to again and again.

EXPLORE WHAT'S POSSIBLE

VISIONARY: It's always wise to start with a Vision of what you're trying to bring about. Sit back, relax, and imagine what's possible. What opportunity approaches? What is the essential problem you must solve?

Your inner Visionary is especially useful for this first, exploratory step in developing a practice. You might coach yourself through these questions, similar to the way I coached Eric.

Eric was pushed to the point of change by a challenge from his boss, who told him he had to change or retire. Twenty years a cruise ship captain, Eric reflected the values and skills of the field when he'd entered it, before computers were commonplace and ships were the size and complexity of a city (with an ice rink, no less). His safety record was second to none, but he was an old-fashioned captain who ruled by dictates and kept a distance from his crew and—whenever possible—from the guests. The ships he captained would consistently fall near the bottom in rankings of crew satisfaction, guest satisfaction, and revenue. Change or leave was the rather stark choice Eric was given. A proud, Organizer–Driver, he most assuredly did not want to end his career on this low note.

To explore possibilities, Eric needed to dig into the same basic questions you can ask yourself about any challenge or opportunity facing you right now:

- What is the opportunity or challenge?
- What's possible for you if you meet it? What will that do for you? (And what will *that* do for you?)
- What are your personal barriers to meeting it?

EXPLORING THE CHALLENGE

Eric's challenge was simple on the surface: change or leave. But change how? "I'd have to communicate more, get out with guests more, find more informal ways of interacting with the crew," he started down his list. As you might imagine, these were not activities Eric enjoyed at all, and he'd made scant time for them in the past. The more we talked, the more his resistance surfaced. He voiced concerns about losing his dignity if he lightened up and losing respect if he got too friendly with the crew. "I'm just the way I am. This is my personality and I'm too old to change," concluded this man who was younger than I.

"Well that's pretty simple. It sounds like you're going to retire," I said. I'm often struck by how quickly people move from denial that they need to change to hopelessness that they can without pausing in between to question the fixedness of the personality they think they're saddled with. Sometimes I flip it around for them: look around, everything is changing. If something is staying the same, what's holding it in place? But in Eric's case, I didn't have to say anything. He was already on the other side of the debate.

"No, I can't retire," he countered out of his Organizer's strong sense of integrity and duty. "I can't leave things this way. I have young children. I can't let them see their father give up."

Exploring the Benefits of Change

Eric felt trapped between a rock and a hard place, which is a perfectly fine springboard for change. So we moved to the second question, which is a drill-down effort to connect the opportunity or challenge to what is personally essential.

"If you do make this change, what's possible for you?" I asked Eric.

"I suppose my ship would get higher ratings," he started with the external evidence. "And maybe the crew would work better as a team."

"And what would that do for you?" I asked. This is a great question for getting from out-there to in-here and to the essence of what someone really values. We can ask this of ourselves. By connecting a change we're contemplating to something deeply important to us, we remind ourselves why it's worth doing, why it's essential that we do it. Then, instead of thinking about all our resistance and all the reasons we haven't been able to make this change in the past, we can focus instead on how this change leads to something really valuable to us. Moreover, this crucial question can be asked several times. When you try it yourself, you'll see that each time it's asked, the answer goes deeper until there's no deeper to go.

"I suppose I'd feel better about myself as a captain," was Eric's first crack at what change would do for him. The more we probed, the more he saw that he wasn't satisfied with his performance, hadn't been for a long time, and he was getting grumpier and more distant from his crew as something of a defense. Even during his weeks off, he was becoming more grumpy and distant from his family. What was in it for him to turn his performance and attitude around? His sense of accomplishment was at stake, as was being a good role model for his children, proving to himself he could do this, and, ultimately, his own happiness.

Exploring the Barriers to Change

With a good deal riding on making this change, we could move into the third question: what gets in the way? "Time." Was Eric's first response, hitting the most common excuse ever given for solidifying ourselves into our habits. I get the logic of it: we think we can't do anything new because every piece of our life holds every other piece in place like a jigsaw puzzle and it was packed before. But, if we could start to see every piece of our puzzle with flexible edges or even as interwoven waves, not "pieces" at all (here's where you need some Visionary energy!), we'd see our enormous power to reconfigure it to match changes in our situation. In Eric's case, he faced a totally different captain role than the one he'd faced 20 years earlier. Far from not having time to change, it was truer to say the situation had changed faster than he had and he needed to catch up.

"Setting time aside for the moment," I suggested, "what are your personal barriers to making this change? Tell me one or two specific ways in which you might be getting in your own way when it comes to communicating more, or being more informal with the crew?" Likewise, when you get to the third question in this exploration, I'd encourage you to look inward, not at the clock. In looking inward you'll see some of your habits, which represent the hard edges in your puzzle-pieced life. Once you can see how you're playing into hardening those edges, you take back the power to soften them.

"Well, I suppose I'm shy," Eric answered. "English is not my first language, and while I can speak it and understand it, I don't make jokes in it. I suppose I speak English quite formally. Sometimes I don't know what to say to people. Of course I know how to give orders and how to run the ship. I'm not talking about that. But I don't ask the crew about their families and such; I wouldn't know what to say anyway."

As we talked about his lack of informal communication skills and interpersonal ease, it was clear that these were

Exploring the Time Barrier

It's easy to think of time as a barrier. But it's far more useful to flip that thinking around and explore the recurring themes in the things you never make time for, and ask yourself why that might be.

recurring barriers for Eric. I'm sure there were others, but we just needed one or two good barriers to get started. Otherwise—as your Driver voice might say—we'd end up boiling the ocean. I offer you the same advice when you explore for yourself.

Phase 1: Explore

To support your own exploration, and all of the phases of designing a practice, you'll find these questions in a downloadable worksheet on our website: www.movetogreatness.com.

To start, consider what **opportunities and challenges** are in front of you right now. You might reflect on your pattern preferences and a potential weak link in your leadership. You might consider feedback you've received from others, or what's changing in your situation and whether you're on top of it. In the end, pick one opportunity or challenge to attend to right now.

Next consider the essential **benefits** of attending to this change. Keep asking, "And what will that do for me?" until the answer goes no further. When you get to that point, you've traced the chain to one of your core values.

Finally, consider one or two personal **barriers** that get in the way of making this change. Try to word them in such a way as to highlight your role in them, which is your power to address them. So it's not "time" that is the barrier, but rather, "I consistently don't make time for 'small talk' because I'm not comfortable holding it."

In the spirit of your broadest Visionary mindset, explore . . .

- What is an opportunity or challenge facing you right now?
- What's possible for you if you meet this challenge or opportunity? What will that do for you? (And what will *that* do for you?)
- What are your personal barriers to meeting this challenge or opportunity?

Flush with the insights of exploration, we can invite the Visionary to sit down, and call up the Driver. It's time to focus.

FOCUS ON A KEY GOAL

DRIVER: It's simple. Pick your target and set a goal. Identify a few measures of success and a way to keep score. If you don't measure it, you can't manage it.

The art of this step is to pick the right goal and the right measures, where a little change means a lot. In my conversations with Eric I likened this to the rudder of a ship, where small changes can have a big impact on the ship's direction because the change is being applied where it has leverage. You might think about your change and the type of goal that would represent the rudder of your ship.

A GOAL TO LOWER BARRIERS

The barriers you exposed in the exploration phase are a good place to look. What do they have in common? If you keep running into these barriers, what goal would lower them? "I'd have to be easier with people," Eric concluded when he thought about what it would take to reduce his barriers. We played around with wording a goal that would point Eric toward developing ease with informal communication, but as we talked it became clear that his self-consciousness would never go away if he kept focusing on himself (a trap Organizers frequently fall into). So we flipped it around: Eric's goal was, in six months, to become so skilled a communicator that he could set others at ease. Worded this way, the Collaborative energy of this goal was clear; his work was not going to be about finding clever ways to string words together (which would be his typical Organizer approach), but rather genuine ways to connect with people, out of which the right words would flow.

Just thinking about his communication goal this way was a breakthrough for Eric, but it made him uncomfortable. More than once he had to review his reasons for change to remember that it wasn't just to be a nice guy, that it really did connect to something deeply important to him. That's okay. You might find that you need to do the same thing, which is why you were asked to make those connections in the exploration phase. If you truly believe this change is nonnegotiable for you, nothing will stop you from making it.

Measuring Success

"Soft" as this goal may seem on the people side, Eric went back to the hard business reasons for it in order to identify three measures of success. It was known in the company that the best captains rated highly on measures of approachability, which included this quality of putting others at ease. Eric had just received 360-degree feedback showing his approachability score to be around three on a five-point scale. "Six months from now, I want it to be a four," he committed, which would put him in the top half of the captains. He also wanted to see positive movement in the metrics around crew satisfaction and guest satisfaction. We wrote down his starting numbers and he chose his target numbers. Since cruise ships measure everything, Eric had a built-in way to keep score. He would see these numbers updated every few weeks.

Eric was comfortable with this crisp, measurable focus. In fact, it anchored him as he ventured into the much less comfortable world of engaging people. You may find this to be true for yourself, as well. Or maybe you're just the opposite: you may love engaging people but hate being measured. Stretching ourselves to use all of the patterns gives us all an equal opportunity to be uncomfortable with something! I would encourage you at this stage to be accountably crisp with your measures of success. As anyone who has done biofeedback knows, watching numbers works. If you're monitoring your heartbeat, you can reduce it. Likewise, if you're counting how many times you lose your temper in a week, you can reduce it. With such clear intention, the next time you're on the verge of losing your temper, instead of being totally sucked into the emotion of it all, some little part of you will remember that—darn it—if you lose your temper you'll have to increment your counter, and that little slice of perspective (which is not, itself, upset), can remind you to exhale. But don't take my word for it. Run your own experiment with your goal. Just be sure you measure the results.

Phase 2: Focus

With the sharp focus of the Driver, write down a goal you can leverage, a goal that takes aim at the barriers you've run into in the past. Make sure you put a time window on it. Three to six months is best. Give yourself more than six months, and you'll put off starting; give yourself less than three and the changed habits will not be deep and results may not yet be apparent. If you tend toward perfectionism, reel yourself back to a realistic target and timeframe. You might try restating the goal in different ways; for example, how would your Collaborator voice say this? How would your Driver put it? Trying the goal in different patterns was how Eric came to flip his goal to one that focused on his effect on other people rather than on himself.

Once you have your goal, see if you can identify three measures of success. How would you know you got there? What would be clear evidence that you could see, hear, touch, count, poll, or otherwise experience? It's one thing to say, "I'll be more approachable"; it's a much stronger measure of success to say, "I'll average a four in approachability when I poll people on that part of my 360-degree feedback six months from now." Sometimes a measure of success is something that happens or doesn't happen: a stronger relationship, a new assignment, being invited to executive-level meetings, or even not being fired. But the best measures of success are on scales that you can measure incrementally, so you can see progress as you go. A way to think about success measures is this: what would you really like to see three months from now? Six months from now?

- What is your goal and its timeframe?
- What are three measures of success for your goal?

With this focus and precision, our Driver has done its work. Time for the Organizer to develop a plan.

PLAN A PRACTICE FOR REACHING YOUR GOAL

ORGANIZER: Oh, I love a good plan. Here are the steps for how to build one for reaching your nonnegotiable, clearly defined, easily measurable goal. First, identify which pattern best supports your goal. Second, refer to the chapter on that pattern for numerous ways to strengthen it. Third, construct your own best practice using your strengths. The best practices combine specific work behaviors with ways of steeping yourself in the pattern from other activities or background cues.

It's a pretty straightforward process. Moreover, the first step is done for you if your goal came out of reflecting on a weak pattern. In Eric's case, Collaborator energy was clearly needed for his goal, and it was also his weakest pattern in the FEBI. If you're not clear which pattern would best support your goal, take your best guess and then go back to the chapter on that pattern and reread the symptoms of needing to strengthen it. At least one of the items in the bulleted list near the end of the chapter should relate to your goal and the barriers you want to overcome.

Simply knowing which pattern best serves your goal is a big help. It stops you from trying to act on the surface without changing the way you feel underneath. If Eric tried to put people at ease in his normal Organizer–Driver style, they'd quickly pick up on his agenda-driven, fault-finding, perfunctory approach. Knowing he had to get into the Collaborator frame of body and mind to truly put people at ease showed him how he had to work with himself to become more at ease with others.

Pick a Work Behavior to Practice

Eric looked through the set of Collaborator work behaviors for ones that would work for him and serve his goal. Informally networking or coaching people seemed to be in the right direction, but Eric knew he couldn't just wade into a group and start chitchatting. What he could do, however, was use a strength to approach a weakness. By parsing the task he could focus on putting people at ease one person at a time. He'd start with one of his favorite people and open up that relationship with a bit more care and support, and then move to another direct report and focus on that relationship. In each case he'd ask himself: What did he have to offer this person? What did they need most? Simply asking these questions would help him step into the other person's perspective.

Build Deep Support from the Right Pattern

Given that the Collaborator pattern was so weak for him, it was important for Eric to support this new work behavior with other chances to get in the swing of this playful pattern. We shopped through a number of possibilities, landing on a couple of activities he was willing to do during his next time off. Normally, I don't recommend putting practice off until vacation, but in the case of a captain who works ten weeks on and then gets ten weeks off, vacation is long enough and frequent enough to build new habits. "Besides, it's probably better that no one I work with sees me," Eric said of his first commitment to take an improvisational comedy class. When he agreed to this idea, I knew there was hope for Eric; this class would be a challenge, and yet some playful quality in Eric seemed ready to come out. Playing with improv, he'd be forced to listen to and build on what others were saying, and he'd have to do it spontaneously, exactly the skills he'd need for informal communication back on the ship. Plus, he didn't think he was able to be funny or lighthearted in English and this would push him to discover otherwise.

The other activity was one his wife had been asking him to do for some time and could even be useful in his role as a captain—ballroom dancing. He and his wife were going to sign up for classes at a learn-to-dance studio near their Florida home. "Especially do swing dances," I told him. Dancing well, he'd learn to set his partner at ease. Finding an easy rhythm in movement would help Eric convey that ease in other respects.

Finally, I suggested he put something in his shipboard office to remind him of his intent. While poking around a trinket store for gifts for his sons, he came upon a bobble-headed, bobble-handed, happy-faced island figure, tacky enough to make him smile. Perfect.

To build a similar plan for yourself, start with the work behaviors table associated with the pattern that would be most helpful. You might find the perfect prescription right there in the table, or you might have to extrapolate

TABLE 7-1 Strengths You Can Use to Approach a Weakness

Strong pattern	*Possible strengths*	*Ways to use them for approaching practice*
Driver	Winning, keeping score	Set numerical targets; measure progress; set some easy goals
	Likes speed	Do fast things or in short bursts; get some quick wins
	Competitive edge	Make a bet with someone on your progress; race with someone toward your respective goals
Organizer	Disciplined, orderly	Do the same thing regularly; plan your practice then practice your plan
	Takes big tasks one step at a time	Break activities down into one thing at a time
	Likes lists	Keep a log of practice, check off activities successfully done
Collaborator	Sense of humor, fun, play	Use your humor to stretch your comfort zone; play with your practice as you would a game
	Sociable	Practice with a friend, combine practice with social activities
	Sense of rhythm	Find a natural rhythm to your practice, go back and forth between a couple of activities
Visionary	Imagination, openness, spontaneity	Let your creative mind explore new directions in your practice; change it up now and then
	Inquisitiveness, likes to learn	Treat your practice as a study; become curious about what works best; enjoy new insights
	Likes risk	Practice as an adventurer, pushing the envelope of your comfort zone; enjoy change

or brainstorm a bit to get one that's right for you. Once you have an idea of what you could do at work to move toward your goal, if it seems especially difficult or uncomfortable, ask how you could do it in a way that builds on something you're already good at, as Eric did by approaching each person at a time. Table 7-1 summarizes a number of the strengths of each of the patterns and may give you an idea of how to use what's relatively comfortable to help you move out of your comfort zone.

The more uncomfortable you are with the pattern you're practicing, the more important it is to warm up with a mini-break to get into the pattern and also to practice it outside of work. You might want to spend a couple of weeks just getting comfortable with the mini-break exercises of the pattern you want to develop. Outside of work, you might pick one item from the desired pattern's activity table that you could commit to. If you're crunched for time, maybe commit to only one or two mini-breaks a day. Or take something you're already doing, such as cooking, gardening, or spending leisure time with your family, and do it fully in the energy of the desired pattern.

At the Top of Your Mind

Finally, beyond anything you are doing, look for some way to *be* with the pattern you want to develop. Find a way to keep it at the top of your mind. A desk knickknack, a screensaver, art for your walls, the right kind of music, anything that particularly reminds you of the pattern could be a good cue. When I run programs teaching the FEBI, I often ask participants to bring something to the following day's class that symbolizes a pattern they want more of, and I am amazed at the creativity unleashed in that simple assignment. One woman who wanted to develop more of the Visionary brought a Ziploc bag full of air to class. "When I unzip it and open it up," she said demonstrating, "Air flows into air." What a wonderful image for ourselves!

Build Your Own Best Practice

So let's recap this planning phase and give you a chance to run through it yourself.

> **Step 1:** Identify the pattern that best supports your goal.
> **Step 2:** Look through the work behaviors table for the appropriate pattern. Lift, extrapolate, or brainstorm from the tables and pick one or two work activities that would move you toward your goal.
> **Step 3:** Suggest one strength (probably from your Home pattern) you could build on to approach this activity successfully.

Step 4: Support your work practice with mini-breaks or outside-of-work activities. Check the appropriate pattern tables for ideas and write one (or two) things you'd like to try below.

Step 5: Identify a supporting cue in your environment that would remind you of this pattern and your intention.

With your plan sketched out, the Organizer has done its duty. Now, let's look at how to make it practical, fun, and involve other people. Collaborator, take it away!

ENGAGE YOURSELF AND OTHERS IN YOUR PLAN

COLLABORATOR: Let's get real, sweetheart: if there's not a thing you enjoy about this plan, you won't stick with it. You need to figure out how to get other people involved and have some fun with this. Getting others involved isn't just for the fun of it, though if you ask me, it does make it a lot more enjoyable. Telling others about your plan makes it more real and more likely to be successful. Plus, as you change, every relationship around you changes, and if others are cheering you on or giving you feedback on how it's going, you're just going to get to your goal more easily.

Marshall Goldsmith, a great executive coach and leadership researcher, compiled some data around what made leaders successful in following a plan for personal change. He found that the single most important factor in successful change was the willingness of the leader to involve colleagues in the change, and seek their feedback along the way.[52] So, even if much of your practice is done solo, involving others in some way—even telling a friend about your goal, your plan, and where you want to be in six months—has a very practical payoff. We give things energy when we talk about them. When we tell another person about our commitment, our commitment doubles.

Invite Feedback

I experienced this again just recently. I was in a leadership program, seated with the group I was coaching that week at a round table, in the center of which sat a dish of hard candies. This is standard fare in conference centers and I tend to eat way too many of these sugar-spiking, mouth-numbing, junk candies. That week, I was determined not to do it and,

The Best Practices

1. A specific work behavior that moves you toward your goal.

2. A supporting mini-break or activity that develops the same pattern.

3. A supporting cue in your environment that reminds you of your intention.

The Key to a Successful Practice

. . . is telling someone about it and inviting his or her feedback on your progress.

on the first morning, I said to the gentleman next to me, "I do not want to eat those candies. Please, if you see me reach for them, tell me to stop!" Of course he agreed, and, you know, he didn't have to do it once. Every time I remotely thought about taking a candy, I flashed to the embarrassment I would feel at having him correct me. It's such a small example, but I've seen it play out again and again in my own life and in the lives I've had the privilege to step into as a coach: tell somebody what you want to do and have them hold you accountable and you're already miles toward your goal. Who can you tell about your goal? Who might be able to give you feedback on whether they see you making progress?

The more the merrier. Even shy Eric shared his goal with each direct report—one at a time, which was his way—as he opened up the relationship with them. Without putting them on the spot individually, he told them that he wanted to be more visible and easy with the guests and crew and to tell him if they saw it happening or not. Unbeknownst to Eric, he was further serving his goal of putting people at ease by simply inviting this feedback. When people know that we're open to hearing from them, they relax with us a little more. When we do hear from them, we have to remember that we *did* ask for it, and accept their comments—good or bad—graciously.

If you think about it, the unwillingness to share our goals with another or to ask for feedback comes from our fear that we won't succeed. It means we haven't reached that inner tipping point of commitment to our change. If the fear gets the better of us, it becomes a self-fulfilling prophecy. If you ever feel caught in this fear between the rock of change and the hard place of not changing, well, welcome to the human condition. Please know that if you own that fear—own it as in saying to yourself, "I'm afraid I'm going to fail and embarrass myself, but I must do this anyway"—it won't get all of you anymore. Every time you stare down one of those fears, you'll get bolder. Don't take my word for it. Try it yourself—but first tell somebody about it!

Invite Fun and Friends or Make Your Own

Another way to engage people in your plan is to do things with them. If you're a Collaborator by nature or want to develop more Collaborator energy by practice, you'll especially want to engage in activities with other people. Eric chose dance classes with his wife, somebody he trusted, and with whom he could stumble around a bit without feeling foolish. The improv class itself had other people in it and the fact that they were strangers gave Eric more permission (than if they'd been friends) to act and play in new ways. They had no expectations of him; they didn't know he didn't think he was funny in English. They found his understated delivery and unexpected wry-ness an absolute hoot.

I think it's fair to say that Eric had more fun with his practice than even he was expecting to. Since he was trying to develop more Collaborator en-ergy, fun itself was a good sign of progress. But there was more. When Eric came back to the ship for his next rotation, he started off by meeting one-on-one with each of his direct reports, sharing with them the higher satisfaction ratings (and revenue targets) he was shooting for and how he personally would work to bring that about. He asked for their feedback and what they could do to further these goals. And on that first Sunday night of the cruise when captains have to do their captain thing and greet all the guests and in-troduce the ship's management team, it was not the perfunctory performance of the past. For a brief few moments he was back in the improv class, and the guests applauded with their laughter.

Phase 4: Engage Others

"Thank you very much!" says your Collaborator self to this invitation to come forward and inject some fun, play, and people into your plan.

- Who can give you feedback on your plan and what do you want to ask them to watch for?
- Who could you involve in an activity in your plan?
- What would make your plan even more fun?

And with that, it's a wrap. You now have a plan that will move you to-ward greatness; that is the greatness of breaking through a barrier, over-coming fear, and finding freedom of movement and genuine expression of the patterns within you. You can revisit this process again and again; use it often and well!

AVOID THE LIKELY PITFALLS

We can't leave this part of our journey—flush with high hopes for our plans and our goals—without acknowledging that we've been here before, and it's not always pretty. How many New Year's resolutions have we made that were forgotten by January 15th? How many times have we heard the same basic message in 360 feedback, even after our earlier attempts to change? There are several reasons for this: old habits die hard, plans can derail, and some goals are simply not worth it to us. Having the patterns at our disposal doesn't necessarily change the last reason; some goals will still not be worth reaching. But the patterns certainly give us fresh ammunition for eliminating the first two barriers. No matter how deep our habits or how our plan might derail, one of the patterns will dig us out. Let's take a look at likely pitfalls of practice and how to avoid them.

Habits, like arteries, can harden with use. Tanouye Rotaishi used to say, "The body of a baby is soft and pliable. The body of a corpse is stiff and rigid. We're somewhere in between." As we age, we lose the plasticity and possibilities of our less mature selves. Babies regenerate nerves more readily than do adults. Young children learn languages with much greater ease and fluency than do older people. But we don't all age at the same rate. Some people, as they get older, become hardened caricatures of their younger selves. While others—those who Jung would call fully mature adults—explore their shadow side (which we might think of as weaker patterns) and the possibilities that come with each stage of maturity. So we're somewhere between corpses and babies. We're somewhere between being hardened caricatures and free expressions of our full selves. But as long as we are alive, we can change. As long as there is movement in us, we can move toward greatness.

The key, and this is where the patterns are especially useful, is to work with the body. Deep habits are stored physically. They physically represent channels of least resistance carved by years of use. It is as if we are constantly shoveling paths through the snow for ourselves. The deeper the snow, the more we feel confined to the paths we've already made. The unused paths aren't *un*available to us, they're just harder to use at first. We have to trample down some snow, and at first, it can be uncomfortable and slow going.

If you try to change your behaviors on the surface with your mind alone, without your body agreeing to its role in the change, you smack against one snowdrift after another and change feels impossible. When you work with your body, it's like you're out there shoveling new paths, paths that will allow you access to new places.

So if you find yourself slipping back into old habits, the key is to work more deeply with your body. Your breakthrough will come if you can physically engage the supporting pattern more thoroughly, more deeply. Personally, I've also found meditation to be enormously beneficial as a companion to developing ease in any pattern (perhaps being an Organizer makes me like to sit still). It gives me a chance to see what's going on inside, where I'm holding tension, and where I need to relax to find new openings, first in my body and then in my life. Many people find yoga or Tai Chi to be hugely beneficial in the same way. Sometimes a helping hand is what you need, in which case deep bodywork or deep tissue massage can help point out and release the tension that holds old ways intact.[53] So if you're feeling trapped by the gravitational pull of old habits, my suggestion is to find some way to become more aware in your body.[54]

The Pitfall of No Time

Another pitfall to practice happens when we try to make time for our plan and can't. Or this week we can, but next week we're busy or on the road and will miss that yoga class we signed up for. And then discouragement sets in. We break stride and we can't seem to get going again. In this case, we do well to call on our inner Organizer to break down the problem. First, what do we have time for? Surely a mini-break. If we don't have time for a mini-break, we're dealing with resistance, not a lack of time. Let's nail down what we can do. Second, how can we make at least part of our practice portable? If we know we're going to be on the road next week and will miss yoga class, maybe we can take notes in class this week and commit to 20 minutes of yoga in our hotel room.

The specifics aren't as important as the thought process here, which is to break the problem down into smaller chunks and come up with small solutions to each one. With the problem of time, you can also look at things you have to do anyway—walk to the restroom, cook a meal, brush your teeth, answer e-mail—and see if they can be done in the energy of whatever pattern supports your goal. If you want a plan that takes virtually no extra time, break your typical day into smaller pieces and see how some of them could be reworked to serve your goal.

The Pitfall of Perfectionism

Another trap some leaders fall into is going to extremes. They become so all-or-nothing that "nothing" becomes the only possibility when "all" doesn't fit. The Driver and the Visionary are your allies here. With Driver clarity, cut out the extra. Don't get caught up in the weeds. Apply the 80/20 rule to glean 80 percent of the benefit of your practice by focusing on the most important 20 percent of things you could do. Don't try to do too much. But what you do,

---

No Time Required . . .

Betsy has her clients put the patterns into their daily lives by doing them for just a minute at breakfast, lunch, and dinner. No special exercise is required . . . just eat or drink in the desired pattern.

She also has them connect a mini-practice to discrete points in their day. For example, whenever they sit down at their desk, they might take a minute to think or put something away. Or whenever they walk to their car, they might consider possibilities.

do completely. And with Visionary ease, let go of the rest. Come back to the essence of your goal and why it's important to you.

The Pitfall of Boredom

If you're a Collaborator, boredom often derails your plans. Collaborators don't like to do the same thing over and over, and while they may marvel at the steadiness of the Organizer, they frankly find it boring. To avoid this pitfall, find a rhythm in your practice. The same thing day after day isn't your way. You might try alternating between a couple of activities, and occasionally blow off practice and just do something fun. You can try blending your practice—say, walking on a treadmill—with something you enjoy—jazz music, for example—to make it enjoyable enough to do three days out of seven. Collaborators tend to be more start and stop with their practice than are Organizers or Drivers. If that's the case for you, just find your own rhythm for restarting.

In both broad and subtle ways, each of these energies can balance the others not only in practice, but in life. If we're Driving too hard, we can recover in the Organizer's calm, the Collaborator's fun, or the Visionary's flow. If we're caught in the Organizer's overriding need to get it right, the Collaborator gently shakes us out of our rut. If we're unreliably veering curb to curb in excess Collaborator, or drifting off in Visionary meandering, the Organizer can ground us in a more stable place. And when all else fails, the determined Driver fires us up. "Bring it on!"

Practice brings you access to your whole and balanced team. Now, what can stop you? For every barrier, there is a way to break through! Now that you can call upon any pattern, you're able to do excellent things with greater ease. Let's look at some ways to apply your whole team to moving your life and leadership to its greatest.

CHAPTER EIGHT

Lead in Ways Others Can Follow

THE MESSY WORLD OF RELATIONSHIPS

"Your new job is not all the tasks you've just told me about," I said to John, one of my coaching clients who had just been awarded a promotion. He'd been telling me about the dollars, deals, and difficulties he now had to "get his arms around," and I could see the task list growing endlessly in his Organized Driver mind. I work with so many leaders who think of their jobs in terms of the numbers they have to make, the products they have to deliver, or the duties they have to perform. What they miss in their focus on the deliverables is the human interconnection that makes it all possible. "The numbers are the clean part," I told him. "Your real job is in the messy world of relationships."

People will forget what you said, people will forget what you did, but people will never forget how you made them feel.

—Maya Angelou

Near the outset of our journey, I borrowed Kevin Cashman's definition of leadership, "authentic self expression that creates value," and stressed that leadership could happen at any level. But the flip side is that if no one is following, even if you're at the top of an organization, you're not truly leading. Now that organizations are becoming flatter, more matrixed, and partnered with other companies, leading with chain-of-command directives is becoming less relevant to the way things get done. That's not to say it doesn't have a place—it certainly does—and it will achieve a compliant level of performance. But to move to greatness calls for influence and inspiration, qualities that stir others from inside out to their own best performance and get them moving with you.

Spotlight: Kevin Johnson

President of Windows services, former head of sales and marketing, Microsoft

Quote: *"I love business. I love technology, I love customers, and I love people."*

What *Fortune* magazine says: *"A hard-headed operator with Gatesian shrewdness—and Oprah-like personal skills."*

Expressed Profile: Easy in all the patterns and a great Collaborator.

Communication that starts in the others' shoes . . . To launch a new customer-service initiative at a large sales meeting, Kevin opened with a video he'd made of respected, frustrated employees handling customer complaints. "You could see the pain on their faces," Kevin said. People so deeply identified with the problem that they went wild over Kevin's "Make It Right" solution, and made it a big hit.

Every day, we subtly choose who we'll follow. Who gets our extra effort? Who gets ignored? Even if you run your own one-person company, you rely on many people for services, products, clients, advertising, technology, and so on. You can achieve a compliant level of support through conventional transactions—this much money for that much work. But where you get extraordinary support is where you have real relationships. In those cases, others are choosing to follow your energy (i.e., respond to your request) with extra effort and energy of their own.

It is the same in organizations. The most effective, powerful leaders in today's flatter organizations are not those sitting in a particular "box" in the organization chart. They are those who have the best relationships, those who inspire the extra effort and can mobilize the right people to make big things happen. They are leaders who communicate in ways others can hear, and lead in ways others choose to follow.

Now that you know how to expand your freedom of authentic self-expression into any pattern, you have the versatility to get more people moving with you than ever before. Let's look at how you can communicate in ways others can hear and navigate the messy world of relationships to even greater effect in the world around you.

A MASTER COMMUNICATOR

Let's watch a master communicator in action, Microsoft's Kevin Johnson. He knows how to get huge numbers of people moving with him, as when he launched a customer service initiative in 2002. At that time, Microsoft's customer service ratings were at an all-time low and, with the spread of viruses, many people were losing confidence in the company's products. Kevin didn't expect outright opposition to his customer service initiative from the Sales and Marketing teams, but when they gathered in New Orleans for an annual meeting, he wanted to inspire enough enthusiasm to ensure its success.

If Johnson had been reading the research on how to inspire people toward change, he couldn't have tuned his communication any better. In the words of one such study, people need a "change of heart"[55] to get on board if they're not already sold. A change of heart is an emotional shift—a valence swap from negative (or neutral) to positive—and it requires actual emotion. Here's how Kevin brought that about at the New Orleans meeting.[56] He started by stepping into the shoes of people in this very audience: frustrated Microsoft employees. He'd had a video made of several well-respected employees handling customer complaints. "You could just see the pain on their faces," Kevin recalled. "One person said, 'Sometimes I get exhausted representing this company.'" The huge auditorium, packed with people, was dead silent. Some people were crying. "Maybe I brought them down too far," Kevin was thinking to himself up on the stage. Then he announced his new initiative: a "Make It Right Fund" that would give salespeople unlimited resources to solve customer problems. "The place went wild," he said. The initiative worked beautifully; customer satisfaction ratings soared to all-time highs. Moreover, the funds invested to "make it right" turned out to be less than a percent of the increased sales brought in by the reinvigorated team.

"Everybody looks up to him," said a Microsoft marketing manager of Kevin Johnson. *That* is a leader others are choosing to follow, and to extraordinary results.

BECOME THE OTHER PERSON AND GO FROM THERE

Stepping into someone else's shoes is a great start to any communication, but especially if your goal is to influence. Sometimes when I'm teaching a module on influence in a leadership program, I ask for a volunteer from the audience to model this physically. They know I was an aikido instructor, so I assure them that no one is going to get hurt. This

An Aikido Approach to Influence

We face each other . . .

I push. He pushes. I push harder. He pushes harder. We hold each other in place.

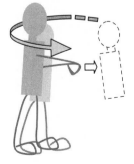

I move around to look and lead in his direction.

demo works best when a really big guy, someone maybe 6 foot 2 inches, steps up to face all 5 foot 3 inches of me. "Clearly, I can't lead by overpowering this guy," I tell the group. I'll have to do the aikido equivalent of the lateral leadership they're being asked to show in organizations when they don't have position power.

We hold out our hands as if to shake, but instead I ask him to grab my wrist. I push on him. He pushes back. I push harder. He pushes harder. "This is the wrong way to go about influence," I tell them. "Many people think that if they just push their point harder, eventually they'll get it across. But it doesn't work that way"; they can see the standoff between the two of us. The harder we push, the more we hold each other in place, and the more invested each of us becomes in not giving in.

"So what are you looking at?" I ask my six-foot-two push-partner as I move around, stepping nearly into his shoes, seeing what he sees, pointing the same way he was pointing. We look a little bit like we're ready to tango; now it's easy to lead my partner in the direction most natural for him to follow, which is where he was already pointing. Once he's moving, it's possible to lead him in new directions. This move is so basic in aikido, students learn it in their very first class. Yet it captures the essence of what makes influence work. As Tanouye Rotaishi said: "Become the other person and go from there." If you completely step into the other's point of view, even if you struggle to find the right words, you're already off on the right foot, because you're starting from a place of empathy.

Many of us don't normally start there. How about you? When you start speaking to someone, who are you thinking about? Are you thinking about yourself and what you want to say? Or are you thinking about the other person? Where she's at right now, how she views what you want to talk about, whether she's present and listening. Without thinking much about it, most of us launch into our mini-monologues with only our own agenda in mind. If the other person reacts in body language horror, we might pause to consider our approach. But generally we don't attend to the thoughts, feelings, fear, and needs of the other person when we're asking them for a spreadsheet. We just want the darn spreadsheet! For basic tasks given to people who work for us, this one-way approach works well enough, and for task-oriented Drivers, it may be the only way they know.

But people-oriented Collaborators (and that Collaborative capacity in you) know how to juggle their own point of

The Dance of the Collaborator

view with the other's perspective, which means they can get many more people than their direct reports moving with them. They start by empathizing with the other—"Is this a good time?"—and launch in only if there is an opening. They keep reading the other's subtle signals of pro or con and checking in: "Does this make sense? Can you get on board with this?" By being able to move back and forth between the other person's and their own agenda, they improvise a way to bring the two together. They find out what's important to the other, whether some horse trading is called for, and what it will take to win the other person over. Listening and seeding the dialogue with good questions, they draw out the other, and once the other is drawn out—here comes classic aikido—their energy can be more easily led.

So whether you're a Collaborator by nature or by practice, you can use its strength in seeing both sides to move your communication and influence to greatness. "Become the other person and go from there."

That's not to say that Collaborator is the only energy you'll need in good communication or influence. The Organizer's good listening skills help draw out the other. The Visionary's imagination, ability to connect the dots, and knack for seeing the essential talents of others (even hidden ones) will help you find new ways to move forward together. And the Driver will help you stay focused on your target, get the point, and move to action. Moreover, once you've "become the other person," where you go from there depends on what you find. If you're dealing with a Driver, better make your point quickly. If this person is a Visionary, you'll need to paint a picture, giving the context surrounding your idea. If the person is an Organizer, make room for questions. So the Collaborator is, by no means, the only pattern needed for good communication. But its ability to engage with empathy is the gateway to knowing whatever else you need.

READING AND SPEAKING TO THE PATTERNS IN OTHERS

So you've engaged with empathy; you've stepped into another's point of view. How can you read which pattern he's functioning in? What are the best ways to approach a person in each pattern? Fortunately, the patterns are easy to read once you know what to look for, and they're easy to approach once you understand the patterns in yourself.

You know the Driver is the functioning pattern when you sense criticism, pushback, or an assertive edge. Drivers are generally in a hurry and don't want you wasting their time. Get to the point, but don't get in their face. Just show them how your idea is in their interest, and have some hard data to back up your case.

You can recognize Organizers by the number of questions they ask. While Organizers are generally composed and proper, you may sense their frustration at being interrupted (you weren't on their list). And their first re-action may seem cautious or resistant. Was something broken? Did it need fixing? But if you catch them at a good time, you'll get a good hearing, and you should be prepared with plenty of specifics. Explain why your idea is the right and responsible thing to do, and give them time to think about it. A rushed answer from an Organizer is usually "no."

You often hear people functioning in the Collaborator even before you see them; they love to talk. Friendly and frequently dramatic, they love a good story, so give your idea a beginning, a middle, and a happy ending. Allow time for their story too (remember, they love to talk). If your idea stands a chance with them, they'll want to play with it, look at it from a few angles, and see how it applies practically to people.

The first thing you'll notice about Visionaries is that they never stop mov-ing. Their eyes might drift off into space as your idea reminds them of 14 other possibilities. They're not disagreeing with you when they start brainstorm-ing ideas on your idea; in fact, it's a good sign that you've captured their in-terest. They're going to want to know the context around your idea and get to the essence of what problem your idea solves. Be prepared to wander a bit; after discussing it with a Visionary, your idea may never be the same. . . .

Table 8-1 summarizes what you can look for and how you can effectively influence people in any of the patterns. Since you can literally see the move-ment of the patterns, you can tell what pattern a person is functioning in. Ei-ther ahead of time or in real time, you can metaphorically "become the other," sense the person's pattern, and adjust your approach accordingly. To write it out this way or to read it written out this way may seem like a lot of work. But this is energy you're sensing and it happens almost instanta-neously once your pattern sensors are tuned and paying attention. It becomes as reflexive as noticing the temperature in a room and adjusting your cloth-ing. Moreover, adjusting your approach is not a foreign script you have to contrive ahead of time. It can come right out from the voice of the appropri-ate pattern in you. Such is the authentic beauty of being able to access all four patterns.

Now that you appreciate the differences in how each pattern likes to be approached, how do you effectively approach a group?

COMMUNICATING TO GROUPS

In some sense, the four patterns are always in the room, even when we're talking with one person. We will influence someone best through the lens of their dominant pattern, but we have to touch all four pattern bases in our communication if we're going to win over the whole person.

Likewise with a group, our communication needs to cover all four sets of needs. But in what order? What do we use as the "lens" for a group? Your inner Collaborator already knows the answer: tell a story! Storytelling is the best way to connect all of these needs, plus inject that heart-changing passion you need to get people moving with you.

Emotion Matters

People remember what they learn with emotion. The more emotion, the better they remember it. If you flash back to your earliest childhood memories, you might notice that each is accompanied by strong emotion: joy, fear, excitement! This emotional link has been studied at many levels:[57] nervous system connections are made stronger in the presence of emotion-mediating molecules. Rats learn mazes faster when cheese (joy) or electric shocks (fear) are involved. Advertising messages are stickier, in other words, more memorable, when they elicit emotion. Even political parties in the United States have figured out that they get more attention (and money) when they generate more emotional heat, which is partly behind their virulent partisanship.

"Emotion is the electrical current of leadership communication," say Boyd Clarke and Ron Crossland in *The Leader's Voice*.[58] The prime carrier of emotion, they've found, is storytelling. It's what links everything together and is mandatory to leadership communication. So how can we best tell our stories to an audience with diverse needs? Let's turn to our pattern panel, starting with the master storyteller, the Collaborator.

TELL A STORY

COLLABORATOR: Stories are best with a beginning, middle, and end. Show tension and then resolve it. We have learned in this rhythm since we were children.

DRIVER: I don't know that I'd call it a story in business—more like a case—but I like a beginning, middle, and end, too. So long as the point is clear early on.

TABLE 8-1   How to Read and Approach Each Pattern

	Driver	Organizer
What to Look for (to read the pattern functioning in the moment)	Pushback (especially if you're pushing)	Self-control composure, placed
	Direct, clear statements	Asks many detailed questions
	Criticism, finding the flaw in your argument	Cautious response, concern with risk
	Sense of distrust, testing you	Reserved, skeptical
	Alert, strong	Gives impression of being interrupted or waiting for you
	Rapid speech	
	Impatience, hurriedness	Steady, measured speech
	Steely eyes	Being "all ears"
	Oriented to tasks and goals	Oriented to plans and processes
How to Approach	Make eye contact	Make sure they have time
	If standing, face from a diagonal—not square in their face	Give them time to get settled; face them directly
	Make your point fast	Give them a framework for what you're going to tell them
	Have your facts and numbers straight	Speak in steps or numbered points; explain why this is right
	Be clear and precise about what you want	Invite questions and be prepared with answers
	Be strong under fire—don't cave	Give them undivided attention
	If pushed, look for win-win	Don't overstay your welcome; they're busy
	When you're done, get out	Give them time to think about it

Collaborator	Visionary
Bobs head, waves hands	Leans, moves around in a flow
Friendliness	
Talkativeness, enthusiasm	Drifting attention
Weighs what you're saying, interactive	Connects your idea to others
Asks a few, practical questions	Sees your talents
	Gets off the subject
Dramatic speech, laughter	Open-ended speech
Multitasks	Sees possibilities, but nothing specific, brainstorms
Oriented to people and what's practical	
	Eyes look out into space
	Oriented to problem-solving and the future
Engage them first before jumping into task	Get them present with you first; match their energy
If possible, be roughly shoulder-to-shoulder	Start with the big picture or an overview of the problem
Tell a story, make it exciting	Get to the essence interactively with them
Be prepared for tangents	
Use humor and emotion	Show what's possible
Emphasize what's practical for people	Engage their imagination, build on their ideas
Give them time to talk, enjoy being with them	Expect to brainstorm
Let them play with your idea	Nail down as little as possible, leave open as much as possible
Give them lead time, but do check back	Watch your time

VISIONARY: Yes, the point can go near the beginning, but it's best if you start with some context, otherwise the point comes out of the blue for most of your audience. The context can be brief, but it has to paint an overall picture: what's the situation? Why should we care? You're not limited to using only words. You can also use symbols or pictures; earlier we saw that Kevin Johnson used video clips to set up the context, and to great emotion.

DRIVER: And then, *boom*! here's the point. Your idea, solution, initiative, or request. If you're lucky, the place goes wild with acceptance. But you're not done yet.

ORGANIZER: Because my fellow Organizers in your audience are already thinking of questions. So now you need to tell people how this thing is going to work, or why they should agree with you. Give them some specifics or prove your case with facts. If you're laying out a change, give them the steps or explain what it means for their daily work. Emotion is important here in the middle, too, though you're generally settling doubts more than raising hopes. The raising hopes part is better at the end. In this middle part, you want to let people know what's not going to change, to settle their fears about what is changing. Let them know what to expect and in what timeframe, to reduce their worry about what will happen to them. Let them know why your answer is best, and remove their doubts with the data to prove it.

COLLABORATOR: Now we're coming to my part, the spirit-lifting, energy-raising, action-priming end of the story. Here you give people ways to get totally engaged with what you've told them: a way to play with it, take action on it, test it out, socialize it, improve it, whatever applies. Can they do it?! Are they with you!? That down the road they may proudly strip their sleeves. . . .

ORGANIZER: We don't always require that level of grandeur in our communications. What we do require is a good emotional connection to our audience and a good story with a beginning, middle, and end, where each of us does our part.

DRIVER: I remember things visually, and I've been drawing a structure for what we've been talking about.

VISIONARY: Excellent! And I've created a symbol and flow for it: a baseball diamond, so people will remember to touch all four patterns in whatever story they want to tell.

The Bases to Cover When Communicating with a Group

Add Specifics
Organizer

middle

Engage Others
Collaborator

Make Your Point
Driver

end   beginning

Set the Context
Visionary

USE YOUR STRENGTHS

Now that you have the method, apply it best using your natural strengths. For example, use humor if it comes easily to you (Collaborators, are you listening?). Strong Visionaries might want to put audience participation into their stories. Betsy was once telling a story about how we all affect one another, and she passed a rope through the audience. At the appropriate point in the story she had everyone start pulling on it. She made the audience part of the story, and created the emotion of felt learning. Drivers, who are drawn to the visual, could make their points through pictures flashed on a screen at exactly the right moment. Organizers might find their story sticks better with a leave-behind card for each person, summarizing their story's main points and call to action. Use your natural talent as you cover the bases.

SHEDDING THE LIGHT ON LEARNING

Even once we know the formula for great communication, following it is not always easy. Sometimes we have to do some serious digging to find the weak pattern in ourselves that we need to improve how we lead, teach, or talk to others.

As a teacher of dance, movement, and learning styles, communication was always a big part of Betsy's work. "I use the lightbulb theory of learning," Betsy once told me, in her typically Visionary way. In response to my puzzled expression, she explained, "Shed light on the whole essence and the parts become clear." That style of whole-to-part learning and communicating works great for Visionaries, and before she knew about the patterns, Betsy figured it worked great for everybody.

But she didn't always get through to people. "Before I started applying the patterns to my own teaching, I'd just bowl my audience over by insisting that they see the whole picture," Betsy told me, "I thought everybody could do it. Why couldn't they just use their intuition to interpret my train of thought? In those early years of teaching, my classes were a lot more difficult than they had to be."

As she learned about the patterns, a number of lightbulbs clicked on for Betsy as well. Especially as she discovered the Organizer, her most buried pattern, by far. "So that's what my writing professors were trying to get me to do in my papers, with their insistence on outlines and order," she put together. "And maybe that's what some of my students need from my lectures." But the Organizer's way of learning, which is to focus on the parts and eventually build

Betsy's Visionary approach to learning

The lightbulb goes on and everything's clear . . .

a whole picture, felt completely foreign to her. She decided to find her own Organizer from inside out. While she much preferred modern dance, Betsy disciplined herself to take Organized ballet classes daily for a year (This would be pretty extreme medicine for a typical leader, but Betsy led a dance troupe). "Wouldn't you know, I started being able to find my keys," she laughed.

Even more importantly, she started outlining her presentations and filling in details that would help Organizers follow her lead. She still loves "lightbulb learning" but she no longer assumes everyone knows where the switch is, and she's much better at checking in with people to make sure they're following her. She also pays extra attention to body language, which she's good at reading. "Whenever I get that 'held in check' look, which means an Organizer has a question they're not asking, I review in my mind what detail I missed and fill it in, or just pause and invite their question."

LEADING THROUGH LISTENING

Whether we're reading body language, inviting questions, or hearing other's words, learning to listen well is as important a part of leading and communicating as the speaking side. Listening is highly underrated. It doesn't make the splash of speaking. I don't think there's ever been a Toastmasters set up for honing listening skills. And yet, everything I've read around the influence process emphasizes the critical role of listening. People's minds are most open to new ideas—including ours—when they're doing the talking and we're listening. If we're doing all the talking, we may be unwittingly pushing them into close-minded resistance, equivalent to the standoff I had with Mr. Six-foot-two.

Even if we're not trying to influence someone, listening is critical anytime we want to help them learn or develop. When we're listening, we're holding a space for the other person to fill. The deeper we listen, the bigger the space. I've been struck by this since becoming a coach (and wish I had known it when I was a manager). I've learned to listen with every pore in my body, and the deeper I listen, the deeper the other person digs, the more they put together, and the smarter they become. It makes sense that we'd be the kind of leader others want to follow if they feel smarter in our presence. When we listen deeply, we make people feel deeply respected.

The quiet power of listening . . .

- Communicates respect

- Opens the other's mind

- Reveals the other's patterns, intention, and thought process

- Creates a space for the other to fill

- Draws out the other's wisdom

How to Listen Deeply

So what does it mean to listen deeply? And how can we use our inner team of patterns to do it? Our inner expert in listening is the calm, composed Organizer. It's verbally oriented, learns by listening, asks questions freely, and knows how to be quiet. Indeed, the quieter we can be on the inside, the more we can concentrate on what is being said on the outside.

While our Organizer is the consummate listener, it does best with help from the other patterns. Our inner Collaborator is a natural at reading facial expressions and emotions, empathizing, and picking just the right moment to feed in a suggestion. Our inner Visionary is best at sensing the essence of the other person and understanding the whole context in which she's speaking. Ideas may start popping up as our Visionary connects what we're hearing to other things we know—the CEO's latest comments, an article in last month's *Economist*. Who knows how we make these connections? As long as our steady Organizer follows the thread, one of these ideas may help the other person triangulate on her point or approach. This is also where our Driver comes in, to push for clarity or to move the person to action, if that's what's called for. If you want to become a better listener (Drivers, are you listening?) quiet down, focus on the other person, and let your Organizer take the lead, with a little help from its friends.

Understanding the Other's Meaning

Another aspect of being a better listener is to become smarter about what people mean in the various pattern voices. When people speak to us, depending on what pattern they're coming from, even if they use the same words, they don't all mean the same thing. This has been pointed out for years in cross-cultural studies, where "yes," for example, doesn't always mean "Yes, I agree with you." (Cross-cultural studies are a great way to see how the patterns play out around the world, and much more work could be done here.) A simple statement like, "I'll have that report to you tomorrow by 10:00 A.M.," may have very different meanings, depending on who's saying it.

If it's a Driver speaking, it means the person will work as fast as necessary to pull the report together and have it to you at 9:59 A.M. It might have a few errors in it, but you'll have your report on time.

You'll also get your report on time from an Organizer, but it will be a high-quality report, even if the person had to stay up half the night working on it, shut the office door, miss an important meeting, and ignore the phone.

If a Collaborator says "I'll have that report to you tomorrow by 10:00 A.M.," he means you'll probably get your report sometime tomorrow. It's in

**What do they *really*
mean when they say . . .**

*"I'll have that report to you
tomorrow by 10:00 A.M."?*

Driver: You'll have a
good-enough report at
9:59.

Organizer: You'll have a
high-quality report at
10:00 A.M. and I'll have
stayed up half the night.

Collaborator: I'll juggle it
in and you'll probably get
your report tomorrow.

Visionary: I'll intend to
have your report by
10:00, but other events
may arise.

the queue of all the things he's juggling, and it will get done around 10:00 A.M. if everything goes well.

The Visionary means that she intends to have the report to you around 10:00, but of course she will be at that meeting the Organizer missed and if something of vital importance came up, surely you'll trust her judgment to take care of what's most essential.

Same words, radically different meanings. Does this mean you have to keep translating in your own mind—"Gee, if this person is speaking in Driver and I'm listening in Organizer we must be in Belgium. . . ." It's not that complicated. Again, this is energy you're sensing; it starts happening automatically with a bit of practice. Once you can "become the other person," you need only to consult that same voice in yourself to understand their meaning. But you have to get practiced in knowing and hearing each of the patterns in yourself. If you have a weak member on your inner team, that's where you're likely to misunderstand others. And misunderstandings can lead to conflict, which is where we turn our attention next.

THE PATTERNS IN CONFLICT

Becoming a leader others want to follow means navigating the messy world of relationships. One of the ways you can become a leader others want to follow is to use the patterns to handle the really messy parts of relationships: the conflicts.

This is a notoriously underdeveloped leadership skill. When we give 360-degree feedback during leadership programs, behaviors around handling conflict always end up with the lowest scores in groups overall. Even if you work for yourself or have never had feedback on how you handle conflict, you know it can be tough. It dredges up conflicted feelings in the best of us.

The patterns don't make conflict go away, and we wouldn't want them to. Conflict is one of the great generative forces of the universe; not even a single atom would hang together without conflicting forces at work. Attraction and repulsion, feminine and masculine, even the patterns themselves represent conflicting, counterbalancing forces. For this very reason, the patterns make conflict much easier to navigate.

Let's start with understanding what upsets each of the patterns and how they each respond. And remember, we're not just talking about people out there, but also the patterns in you. Reading through these triggers and reactions, you may recognize what's true for you most often. But the whole truth is: you're host to the whole party.

Drivers Hate to Lose

No pattern is more conflict-prone than the Driver. Drivers sometimes seem like they're spoiling for a fight. They tend to be critical of others, impatient, aggressive, and often push other people's buttons. Nothing personal, but they're in a game of win and lose, and nothing upsets them more than losing. They don't want to lose power, security, control over a situation, and they especially don't want to lose face. Their reaction to conflict is to push harder, even to run over people. It's my way or the highway!

Organizers Can't Be Wrong

Get-it-right Organizers, on the other hand, are most upset by the fear of getting it wrong, not being good enough, or losing self control. It also bothers them when they do something right and nobody notices. In conflicts, they may work mightily to hold themselves together and stay calm, but that doesn't mean they're not upset. At first, they may try to make things right or explain their actions. But if the conflict keeps escalating, it's as if anxiety jams their circuits, and they freeze, withdraw, or get very quiet.

Collaborators Fear Rejection

The Collaborator is the most moody and dramatic of patterns and, in seeing both sides of an issue, can even have an argument with itself. But being people-oriented, Collaborators are most upset by fears of rejection or betrayal, such as being thrown out of the in-group. They also get upset when people aren't cooperating. But push them too much and they, too, will dig in their heels. Collaborators become loud and dramatic in conflict, and often make it personal. They'll insult your pride, profession, and entire family, and later say they didn't really mean it. They did, but they didn't, you know, it was just the heat of the moment. Collaborators in conflict should not be taken too literally.

Visionaries Want Harmony

The Visionary, by contrast, may not say anything in conflict. Their more likely response is to go away, mentally, emotionally, or altogether. They don't like to be locked into battle any more than they want to be pinned down on details. Visionaries dislike any conflict that disrupts the "wa" (i.e., harmony) or seemingly goes against the natural way of things. They are particularly troubled when people don't treat each other fairly. Visionaries much prefer to leverage differences constructively, not fight about them.

As Visionaries know, the seeds of conflict in our world start with conflict among our inner "selves." The deeper we understand our patterns and their conflicting needs, the more genuine compassion we can have with the people around us. The more we respect the patterns in ourselves, the more we honor them in others. We don't have to be "spoiling for a fight" on the outside if we're fundamentally at peace on the inside.

Armed with this map of the patterns in conflict, summarized in Table 8-2, let's see how to put it to use in a real conflict you're facing.

A PATTERN APPROACH TO HANDLING CONFLICT

Reflect for a moment on your work and the sort of conflicts you get into or see around you every day. Someone's not performing well, or is upset, or is resisting a necessary change. Someone let you down, didn't deliver, or sold your project down the river. Or maybe you just disagree with someone on a matter of values, a future direction for a project, or a technical point. How can your knowledge of the patterns (and your own inner team) help you handle these situations with wisdom, to make conflict the constructive, creative force it can be?

Know Yourself

Know your own "hot buttons" and your most common reactions to having them pushed. In the heat of the moment, it's hard to have the same level of self-awareness you have right now, reading this book. So you might want to review Table 8-2, consult your own inner team, and jot down the things that typically upset you and your reactions to them. (All of these questions are collected on a worksheet you can download from our website: http://www .movetogreatness.com).

- What upsets you? What are your hot buttons?
- What are your most typical reactions to conflict?

The other side of knowing yourself is knowing how you push other people's buttons. Like many Organizers, for example, I push other people's buttons when I have to be right (and they don't agree) or have to do things *my* way (and they have another way).

- What is it that you do that sometimes triggers conflict or makes it hard to work with you?

Know the Other

"Become the other person and go from there," applies to conflict as much as it does to influence and other forms of communication. But just as we lose self-awareness, we lose the ability to "become the other" when we're in an agitated state. So, in the relative cool of this moment, think about someone with whom you've been in conflict. This exercise works best if you picture an actual person, not just a type of person or a department at work, but an individual with whom you've been in conflict frequently or intensely.

- Write down the person's name.
- Thinking about the person's likely patterns, what is upsetting to them in this situation? What is the person's worst fear in this situation?
- How is the person reacting to the conflict?

If you're not sure, look over the reactions to conflict in Table 8-2 and pick out those that seem closest to your case. Sometimes it's easiest to start with the other person's reaction, connect it to a pattern, and then work backwards to what's most upsetting to people in that pattern. Or quiet down for a moment (let out a lo-o-o-ng, slo-o-ow exhale), and imagine looking through the person's eyes back at you and the conflict situation. From that perspective, what is the person's worst fear about this situation?

Choose Your Timing

Not all conflicts can be handled at the moment they erupt. Indeed, that's often the worst time to make real progress, because every upset pattern is operating in its least functional state! Moreover, if you consider our natural timing, thoughts change quickly, muscle tone changes slowly, and emotions are somewhere in between.[59] Once the adrenaline of a good battle is dumped into our bloodstream, it's going to take maybe 20 minutes for it to clear, and it will have set off other stress responses that need to play out. A "cooling off period" is a great idea, when one is possible, to let the patterns return to their well-functioning selves. "Let's sleep on this and come back to it tomorrow," you might say. Or, "Time for a break; we'll regroup in an hour."

TABLE 8-2   The Patterns in Conflict and Ways to Handle It

	Driver	*Organizer*
Causes of Conflict (Hot buttons)	Losing (power, face, the "game") or even the chance of losing Faults they find in others Not achieving their goals Things not happening fast enough Not being allowed to compete or confront "It's out of line"	Being wrong or improper Being rushed Not knowing how to get it right or what to do Unethical situations Being pushed around Not being recognized Being ridiculed Not being allowed to ask questions "It's not right"
Deep Fears	That they won't come out on top or be victorious Loss of power, face	That they're not right or good enough Loss of self-control, self-respect
Reactions to Conflict	Pushes harder Gets abrasive, even abusive Runs over people	Low level: explains, justifies High level: freezes, gets quiet
Needs to Move Forward	A way to save face and win at something A sense of honor	A way to feel good about themselves again, a way to be right A sense of recognition

Collaborator	Visionary
Rejection, being left out, ignored, out of the spotlight	Conflict itself, lack of harmony, disruption in the flow
Lack of teamwork or interaction	Being hemmed in or pinned down on details
Not having enough fun or variety	Having no chance to be imaginative or spontaneous
Disloyalty	
Not being allowed to wander off task	Lack of risk or adventure
Questioning the authority they stand on	Being isolated
"It's not cooperating"	"It's not fair"
That they're not loved, others don't want them around	That they won't serve the greater purpose, others won't deal with what's essential
Loss of relationship	Loss of peace
Gets overly dramatic, loud	Goes away, wanders around
Personally attacks and partly means it; negative teasing	Emotionally withdraws, even if still physically present
Digs in heels	
A way to get involved or interacting again	A way to re-establish harmony, get things flowing again
A sense of loyalty	A sense of fairness

A break is not only useful for cooling off, but real work often needs to be done on the inside before the conflict can be resolved on the outside. Drivers, for example, may have to do some major rearranging of the way they look at things to fit a new, conflicting idea into their internal "structure." Organizers may need time to better understand or ask questions.

But don't wait too long, when wounds may have festered or the conflict will have escalated by a worsening situation or the actions of others. Your inner Collaborator (once it cools down) and your Visionary (once it comes back) are your best judges of rhythm and timing. You can consult them to know when it's possible to move forward productively with this person.

Move Forward

The aikido move described when we were talking about influence (see page 162) also applies to conflict: see what the other sees, point where the other is pointing, and move forward from there. It's easiest to work something out with people when they're moving (as opposed to stuck). And it's easiest to get people moving toward something they want. Ways to move people in any pattern forward are summarized in Table 8-2, as are the hot buttons you'd do well to avoid. Combined with insight on how to approach people in any of the patterns (Table 8-1), you can adopt an approach that's most likely to work.

Without knowing the specifics of your conflict, for example, I can tell you that if you're clashing with a Driver, a good way to move forward would be to get to the point quickly, and find a way for the Driver to win at something and not lose face. If your conflict is with an Organizer, the best move might be a way to let him get settled with what you're saying, be right about something, and be recognized for it. Thinking about a conflict at this meta-level of the patterns makes it less personal and specific.

A way forward for each of the patterns . . .

Driver: Give them a way to win at something and not lose face.

Organizer: Give them a way to be right about something and recognized for it.

Collaborator: Give them a way to be involved or on the team and don't abandon them.

Visionary: Give them a way to use their imagination and return to harmony.

- Given the pattern your partner-in-conflict exhibits, what would be a way forward for someone in that pattern?
- Thinking of your person in particular and the specifics of your conflict, how can you bring about that forward movement?

Knowing the patterns in yourself, you're able to use them as a diagnostic tool for others. For every way the patterns can trip over one another and push each other's buttons, there is a way to move forward, a way to move with others to greatness.

PUSH WITHOUT PUSHING

"I know I shouldn't push so hard," admitted Neil, a fiery, passionate marketing director of a financial services company. And everyone around him agreed. "Neil pushes too much," several colleagues told me in interviews, "he's always coming at us with new ideas, and it's just too much." "He's comes at you like a fire hose" said another. "He doesn't listen."

"It's just so hard to get anybody's attention," Neil offered by way of explaining his pushy approach.

"What do you do if somebody pushes their ideas on you?" I asked him. I had him stand up with me and do the wrist grab and pushing exercise I showed you earlier. I pushed on him and of course he pushed back. "What, you're not listening," I said in a louder voice and pushed harder. He pushed back harder. "I'm not getting your attention!" I nearly yelled and pushed harder. And he started laughing. A good-natured Driver–Collaborator, of course he recognized himself in this scene.

A high-energy extrovert, Neil was simply overwhelming people and was responding to their lack of response by turning up the volume. "It won't work," I told him. "You might be able to push the people who work for you. But you'll never make your best ideas happen through all these other departments by pushing harder. You need to learn to push without pushing."

"Ah, like Tai Chi," he said. He went on to fondly relate his experience taking Tai Chi classes years earlier, where he came to appreciate that great feeling of effortless effort. "Our teacher would say 'Do this arm lifting move without lifting your arm,' and at first we were totally confused what she was talking about. But eventually we got the hang of pressing a foot into the floor and almost pneumatically the arm would pop up. Yes, that was really something. I don't know how I can do Tai Chi at work, but . . ."

"That's exactly what you can figure out," I finished for him.

Neil was up for the experiment and, since he enjoyed Tai Chi, it wasn't too tough of an assignment. I encouraged him to find a class where he would learn not only Tai Chi forms, but also the partner work (where Tai Chi becomes more of a martial art) that starts with "pushing hands." He was also going to play with bringing that same effortlessness and spaciousness into his work conversations.

Building Sensitivity

Pushing hands was his first "Aha." He learned in class that if he pushed too hard, he lost all sensitivity to how his partner was pushing. He kept dialing down his push and sensing more until, as he put it, "I knew where people were going before they did." *This* he could apply. He applied it to a conversation with the IT director, Jane. He'd been in repeated conflict with Jane around when an overhaul and update of the customer database would take place. "Usually, she gives me some sorry excuse for why dates are slipping and pretty much clams up." Her reaction was evidence of an Organizer pattern, he could now see. "I think I used to intimidate her. But last week I just listened. I asked Jane what she saw as the problem, and the more she talked, the more I could see where she was going. She was trying to get a new outsourcing contract in place, and only then would my projects, along with others, get on a realistic timetable. My first instinct was to jump down her throat about why I hadn't heard of this contract before, but I held back. 'Tai Chi' I kept telling myself, 'Find out where she's going and how you can use that . . .' I don't know that I did that well, but for the first time we had a real conversation and I got real information from her." His next move, in addition to continuing Tai Chi, was to figure out ways to help Organized Jane move forward toward meeting his goals, as well as hers.

The next breakthrough came a few weeks later. Neil had been in a meeting with the COO where Jane was also present. "I admit, I was initially being somewhat manipulative," he said. "Remembering how much Organizers like to be right, I made it a point to tell Jane she was right about something in this meeting. Instantly her posture straightened a bit and her face brightened. I thought, 'My God, if that little comment made such a difference, she's really felt beaten down by all of us.' Suddenly I wanted to help her succeed."

Changing the Relationship

When they talked after the meeting, Neil was genuine in asking how he could help her get a number of projects on track. And he listened. The outsourcing contract was getting hung up in the legal and finance departments. He offered to join her in approaching them to speed things along. He listened more. Another problem was unclear priorities from his department. He agreed to hold a meeting where every marketing IT project would be reviewed and reprioritized. Jane must have felt the shift in his approach; people can feel when we're fundamentally for them. Rather than being defensive, she shifted to being helpful, something Organizers love to be when they're not backed up onto their heels. Rather than being his most conflicted relationship at work, Jane became a great supporter.

Neil was ecstatic, or at least that's how I interpreted his animated retelling of this tale. In the subtle refinement of Tai Chi, he had learned that when we change how we are in relation to others, they change how they are in relation to us. Neil continued to play with the technique of "inviting some emptiness" into his leadership conversations. And sure enough, he found it gave others more room to fill. Neil was still his high-energy, Driver–Collaborator self and he still pushed a good many initiatives. But by adding more of the Visionary's openness and the Organizer's listening, he cast a wider net around his leadership. His agenda broadened to the point that others could find their goals in it as well, and when he pushed, others were pushing with him.

Being a leader others want to follow moves our greatness to new capacity in the world. But it brings out new capacities in us as well: communicating in ways others can hear, influencing by listening, becoming the other person, and moving forward out of conflict. Fortunately you have your own inner team of pattern experts to help you find this versatility. The more deeply you understand the patterns in yourself, the more other people will recognize that you understand *them*. More than anything, what makes you a leader others want to follow is when you bring out the greatness in others. Wouldn't you want to follow a person who did that for you?

CHAPTER NINE

Move Teams and Organizations to Greatness

A LEADER WHO MOVED A TEAM TOWARD BALANCE

For the next stop on our journey, let's go to Sweden.

Sweden has shown up in cross-cultural studies as the most collaborative country on earth. It's fitting, as we now turn to how the patterns can help you better lead teams and organizations, to visit a country where teamwork abounds.

If you were to combine a Collaborative, team approach with the Visionary's orientation toward learning, you'd get the creative business approach called "action reflection learning," pioneered by Sweden's MiL Institute. In their work, MiL consultants typically get task-oriented, Organizer–Driver companies to regroup, reflect, and rethink ways of working that solve big problems. Being interested in learning themselves, people at the MiL Institute asked Mark (my Collaborator husband who felt right at home in Sweden) and me to do some programs for their consultants using the FEBI.

One part of the FEBI report that we especially like to use with teams sorts 24 important work behaviors from most preferred to least preferred for the group. It also maps those behaviors to their most natural patterns; for example, "think outside the box" would be associated with the Visionary. As soon as we put up the slide showing the rolled-up responses from the MiL consultants, the room burst into laughter: the entire top half of most preferred behaviors all belonged to the Collaborator and Visionary. Every one of the Driver and Organizer behaviors were relatively weak in the organization. Even Mark and I had never seen such a stark pattern split in a group report, though being in the most collaborative country in the world, perhaps we shouldn't have been surprised.

MiL's leaders were also surprised by the extremes of the report, though the findings resonated with them. "This confirms the necessity of the direction we've already started to move toward intuitively," President Lennart Rohlin observed. "When we first started we didn't have competitors, but now we do, and we need more of the Driver to compete effectively. We need more of the Organizer to develop our proposals. Now we have names for what we've been missing. Now we have a map to get there."

The "map" he was referring to, and what you'll learn in this chapter, are ways to diagnose and strengthen the patterns in teams and organizations, so they can move to greatness. In some cases, they need greater focus on their strongest patterns. In other cases, as with the MiL Institute, they need to strengthen weak patterns for greater balance.

Lennart recognized that he had to personally move more into the Driver's seat and bring more discipline to the organization. He started pushing his management team to greater focus and accountability, and added a new member to the executive team. "Guess with what kind of Home pattern!" he joked later. Within one year, he and his newly focused team were able to reverse what had been declining profits and drive revenue up 20 percent. In ways both practical and symbolic—identifying top priorities, setting measurable goals, starting and stopping meetings on time—Lennart is leading the MiL Institute toward enough wholeness and balance to continue being a leader in what it does best.

DIAGNOSING THE PATTERNS OF A TEAM

"The team is the primary unit of performance in most organizations," concluded Katzenbach and Smith in their definitive 1993 work, *The Wisdom of Teams*, and, if anything, that's even more the case now. Teams are how organizations scale down to do greater things than they could do operating through the formal organization. Teams are how individuals scale up to do greater things than they could do by themselves. This in-between level of teams is the next place where your newfound pattern knowledge can do a world of good. And it's a good well worth doing given how important teams are to creating value. Whether you're formally the team leader, exerting lateral leadership among colleagues, or pulling together a loose confederation of independent contractors to get something done, moving teams to greatness moves your own leadership to a new level.

Given that our behaviors are expressed in the four energy patterns, when we come together on teams, dominant players and patterns of behavior emerge in what could be called the team's energy or climate. Climate expresses what it feels like to be on that team, from processes and norms ("we start and stop on time") to the level of trust and quality of relationships. What might we look for to discern the dominant patterns in the teams we're a part of?

Driver Teams Keep Score

You can tell when teams are dominated by Driver energy because they don't waste time. They get very clear on goals, put real measures in place, divide up the work, and get to it. Since Drivers prefer working independently, short, infrequent meetings suit them well. The real strength of Driver teams is that they are results oriented and keep score. They can be unforgiving of subpar performance from a team member, being quicker to criticize than they are to support. Above all, Driver teams want to win—as quickly as possible!

Organizer Teams Keep Track

No team manages its time, agenda, processes, or projects as well as one dominated by Organizer energy. The strength of Organizer teams is in laying out how people will work together and keeping track of commitments and progress. They're also teams that listen well, take notes, publish minutes, and may even follow *Roberts Rules of Order*. Logic dominates in Organizer teams, as they make solid, fact-based decisions and try to do the right thing for all stakeholders.

Collaborator Teams Build Trust

Did you hear the one about the Collaborator team meeting that ended early? Of course not, because it would never happen. Teams dominated by Collaborator energy are lively, engaged, supportive, and long on spending time together. Their greatest strength is their ability to build trust, which is the foundation of all successful teams. They're also great at understanding customers, empathizing with employees,

Team meetings are a different experience in each pattern . . .

The Driver Team:
Meetings are fast and few; they're a time to sync up so individuals can go off and get things done

The Organizer Team:
Meetings are orderly and on time; they're a time to coordinate activities, make decisions, and identify next steps

The Collaborator Team:
Meetings are engaged and frequent, often running over; they're a time to connect and share stories and views on practical ways to proceed

The Visionary Team:
Meetings are imaginative and hard to follow; they're a time to brainstorm possibilities and generate ideas

finding practical solutions, and getting buy-in. Being well connected, they sometimes pull off the seemingly impossible. And celebrate wildly.

Visionary Teams Hatch Ideas

Don't expect much order in teams dominated by Visionary energy; they tend to leap all over the place. Meetings are characterized by open dialogue, open time on the agenda, and open-ended questions like, "What would it take to disrupt this market?" Visionary teams are best at getting to the essence of problems, leaping to creative solutions, and finding the future.

The Best Teams Are a Mix

In truth, all of the patterns need a seat at the table for a team to move to greatness. As with individual leaders, teams get into problems in the absence or overuse of any of these patterns. Table 9-1 (see page 188) gives you a way to diagnose the patterns dominating a team, and provides some warning signs that a team may be using a pattern too much or too little. Being able to read the energy of a team is part of what we need to know to move it to greatness. We also have to consider what the team is trying to accomplish and where it is in its lifecycle, which we turn to next.

KNOWING WHERE A TEAM NEEDS TO MOVE

Teams, like the individuals in them, have lifecycles. The lifecycle of teams has been described in various models, but probably the most poetic version—and it will certainly do for our purposes—is forming, storming, norming, and performing.[60] While all of the patterns have a role to play at every stage, some of the patterns are called upon more than others in the early stages.

FORMING, STORMING, AND NORMING

When a team is first forming, Collaborator energy is especially important to build the foundation of trust and respect. The team still needs to have an overall purpose (Visionary), goals (Driver), and enough process to move forward (Organizer), but getting to know one another enough for trust to sprout is the key outcome of the forming stage.

The Driver comes to the fore in storming, where matters of Who's In Charge Here get settled. Even if overall team leadership has been determined, all team members still need to sort out where they fit, what they can be in charge of, what they have to relinquish to play well on this team, and how much they can direct it. In many ways, a good, challenging storming phase makes a team stronger, like metal forged by fire. But without sincere efforts to harmonize (Visionary), cooperate (Collaborator), and work through the issues (Organizer), teams can destroy themselves at this stage (though they rarely disband; more often they stagger on dysfunctionally).

The norming stage is where the Organizer comes front and center to sort out how the team will work. How often will it meet? How does it keep track of actions and progress? How will members act with one another? Will a Web-based tool be used for virtual meetings? Are Blackberries on or off? These sorts of norms get settled at this stage, and are best settled with a view to the big picture (Visionary), a sense of urgency and clarity on goals (Driver), and plenty of pragmatism and give and take (Collaborator).

THE ESSENTIAL OIL

As teams move through these stages, the Visionary serves an additional, crucial function as something of a lubricant that keeps the team moving toward its essential role. Betsy once tried to advise a team that was guiding a women's college through the thorny process of going coed and this crucial quality was lacking. The team operated like an unwieldy, clunky machine: "We need to go coed for financial reasons," came the edict, clunk, with no broader sense of purpose. Lacking a vision, the team was not clear on what they were trying to sell to others, but clunked their way through perfunctory actions and deadlines nonetheless.

If you've ever been part of a team like this, you know how clumsy and ineffective it can be. Without the Visionary's pull toward a purposeful future and its open-minded oil for meshing the gears of differing thought, teams can get stuck trying to clunk their way through a pointless plan.

PERFORMING IN ALL PATTERNS

Avoiding that trap, teams can make it to the performing stage where they really start rocking. At this stage, the team needs all of the patterns to function

---

The patterns most needed at different stages in a team's lifecycle

Visionary is needed, to "oil" the movement between all of the stages for best performance.

Forming: Collaborator is needed, to get members to know one another, build trust.

Storming: Driver is needed, to focus on a clear on direction, sort out power issues.

Norming: Organizer is needed, to figure out how the team will work.

Performing: Whatever pattern best matches the team's purpose; however, all patterns are needed in some measure.

TABLE 9-1   The Patterns in Teams and Ways to Strengthen Them

	Driver	Organizer
A teams dominated by this pattern . . .	Stay on point; keep focus Push for results Measure progress Provide clear direction	Meets and work in orderly ways Manages their progress and actions with accountability Instills quality Listens well Breaks large tasks down into small
Warning signs that a team has too much . . .	Lacks trust; team members compete more than cooperate Breaks too many rules; moves too fast Burns people out	Gets stuck in process; follows too many rules Moves too slowly Gets stuck in the way things have been Thinks too small
Warning signs that a team has too little . . .	Lacks focus, edge, urgency, speed or measures Gets lost in too many initiatives or ideas, too much drama or process Not honorable	Lacks process, quality or accountability Moves so fast or sloppily that important matters are missed Not respectful
Ways to build this pattern on a team . . .	Set clear goals Identify top 3 priorities Challenge people's thinking; be direct Measure the critical Cut processes in half Hold fast meetings (e.g., standing up) Use visuals to convey important performance measures	Keep action lists Organize a project plan; track commitments Hold regular, timely meetings Establish clear roles and responsibilities Define coordinating processes, norms Prepare for meetings with prework; give people a chance to pull their thoughts together

Collaborator	Visionary
Keeps things fun	Keeps opening up possibilities
Weighs matters in human terms and for their practicality	Makes new connections
	Focuses on the future
Builds empathy, trust, and team spirit	Gets to the essence of issues
Readily engages stakeholders	
Spends too much time spent socializing, runs late	Too many ideas, too little follow through
Doesn't deliver, lacks accountability	Too focused on what can be and not practical with what is
Gets too political or dramatic, runs hot and cold	Overly impulsive
Lacks trust, warmth, and ability to see multiple points of view	Lacks imagination, thinks too small
	Misses the essence
Gets so focused on task that people are forgotten	Lack of flow ("oil") and purpose in the team process
Not loyal	Not Fair
Get to know each other better	Hold brainstorming sessions
Get together away from work, have fun	Open up incremental thinking ("what would it take . . .")
Give people a way to get involved, get passionate	Have unscheduled time on agenda
Practice changing points of view	Foster informal communication
Proactively engage stakeholders	Explore forces to harness
Celebrate! Include quirky milestones and mock awards	Hold meetings in creative venues

well. The team's climate will have likely stabilized and, like most individuals, it will have a pattern profile with a dominant Home pattern. Ideally, the dominant pattern of the team matches its purpose. For example, if a team were charged with developing a market-disrupting, blue-ocean strategy, Visionary would be the best dominant pattern. On the other hand, if its purpose were to halve the time required to assemble a computer, you'd want Driver to dominate, with a strong assist from the process-oriented Organizer. If it were focused on customer-service issues, you'd want plenty of Collaborator energy.

While it might be nice if the energy of a team matched its purpose, often it doesn't. But our pattern knowledge does give us a way to diagnose the mismatch and correct, or at least reduce, it. We can't move all teams to greatness, but at least we can nudge them out of dysfunction!

The questions below give you a way to apply your pattern knowledge to move a team you're part of to greater effectiveness. You might want to answer these questions yourself, make them a part of a team-building exercise, or both. You may already have a clear idea of the pattern(s) most needed on the team, but when that becomes shared understanding, the power to move the team is greatly multiplied. Visit our website at movetogreatness.com if you'd like to download a worksheet of this process.

- Which pattern(s) currently dominate(s) on your team? (see Table 9-1 on page 188)
- Which pattern is weak?
- What life-cycle stage is your team in? (forming, storming, norming, performing
- What is the purpose of your team?
- Which pattern best matches that purpose?
- What does your team do poorly or less well? What problems does it keep running into?
- Which pattern best addresses those weaknesses or problems?
- Based on the above, which one or two patterns most need strengthening on your team?
- What one or two things could you do to strengthen the pattern(s)? (see Table 9-1 on page 188)

What do you do if multiple patterns turn up as needing attention? In my experience, you can work on strengthening up to two patterns at a time, such as the Driver and Organizer in MiL's case. Since any two patterns form a style, it's easy enough to hold the idea of strengthening that style on a team. But more than two is tough, as it doesn't represent much of a focus anymore. My suggestion, if you see that three or even all four patterns need strengthening, is to consider the team's priorities or lifecycle and take it one pattern or style at a time.

TEAM-BUILDING IN THE PATTERNS

The activities that have been classically considered team-building—all those rocks and ropes and soft, fuzzy stuff—are Collaborator ways to help teams build trust. And for good reason. In study after study of what makes teams work, trust emerges as a must.[61] Patrick Lencioni, in his *5 Dysfunctions of a Team*, puts trust and respect at the foundation: a lack of trust is the primal dysfunction that dooms a team to superficial niceties and, at best, grudgingly compliant performance.

Trust and Realistic Expectations

Even teams that you might expect to be well past the forming stage (based on how long they've been intact), can suffer from a lack of trust. This is especially true of executive teams, which often comprise more than their share of highly ambitious Drivers, complete with their competitiveness and fault-finding distrust of others. As a collection of individuals Driving their respective parts of the organization, the team may function reasonably well as "cabinet" to the "president" of the group. But if it has to do anything new or big—from revising its strategy to rebalancing its budget—without trust and teamwork, the exercise is doomed to mediocrity at best, failure at worst.

Some people, and you can see it in their patterns, enter a relationship trusting until otherwise notified (Collaborators and Visionaries), while others trust cautiously (Organizers) or only with proof that it's in their interest (Drivers). Teams, where people express all of these patterns, simply won't gel without people getting comfortable with one another. Trust develops only when people know what to expect from one another. Patterns other than the Collaborator certainly contribute to trust—the consistency of the Organizer matters, as does situational competence. But getting to know each other is a prerequisite for setting realistic expectations. Some people have a good deal of empathy and can make this connection almost instantly. Others take time and shared experience. On a team, you'll have both, and if you don't give it time, trust has little chance to build.

Building Trust

If you're dealing with a team that is just forming, or perhaps formed some time ago but never developed enough trust for the tasks it now faces, what can you do to bring out the Collaborator?

Play a little. Think about little kids and how they figure out how to get along by playing together. If we're engaged in a game, we interact more with each other, we play in the give and take. I've taken teams out bowling—it's especially fun when no one bowls well—and by the end, everyone is cheering and giving each other high fives. Or you can cook a meal together. You'll find that getting everyone engaged in the process of cooking gets them engaged more naturally with one another. Wine helps, too!

Or get them laughing. Any time a bunch of people are laughing, the Collaborator comes to the fore. Take the team to a comedy club. Or better yet, bring someone in to teach them improvisational comedy and make them the show. We trust people more after we've seen them outside their normal work personas, after we've let our hair down and shared a good laugh with them. People who regard one another as friends or "buddies" give each other the benefit of the doubt, and that's what you want on a team.

A Day That Changed the Life of a Team

I once knew a team that built more trust in one day than most teams do in their lifetime. And the team started out badly, combining two warring factions in a highly fractured organization. These were people who had been at each other's throats in meeting after meeting. "Your numbers don't make sense!" one would holler. "Your schedules are padded!" another would counter. Yet this team was charged with integrating all the budgets and schedules across the organization and then cutting 20 percent of the cost out. They were called, somewhat ironically, the Reconciliation Task Force, but the first challenge they faced was reconciling their own differences.

People on this team were ready to hate each other from the start. They went off-site for a day, not to jump into number-crunching tasks but with the one aim of getting to know one another. They spent the morning cooking breakfast in a homeless shelter, which reminded them that, tough as the team's job was, it was still a high-class problem. Just the process of cooking together, serving people, and being in that environment brought out sides of people no one had seen before. Who knew that obnoxious Don could flip two pancakes at once?

In the afternoon, they went for some fun. Being on the coast, they hired a company that takes teams out on old America's Cup–class sailboats and builds them into a racing team. No one knew much about sailing, but everyone was given a job to do and pretty soon they were getting the hang of moving together. Ready about! Hard a lee! Who knew Jane could grind a winch so fast?

Late in the afternoon, they gathered in a private room at a local restaurant where they could really talk. Over cocktails and dinner, their one task was to tell their stories. Not just "I'm Carol from Finance and I've been with the company for three years," but their real stories. Each person spent half an hour interviewing a partner and being interviewed, then told the partner's story to the group. Emotions ran high, and tended mostly to laughter, but there were some touching moments, too. Who knew that one of Carol's greatest fears as a child was that her family would lose their home and she'd end up in a homeless shelter? She'd almost come undone at the shelter that morning, and confided that the only thing that got her through it was watching her colleagues and knowing that she belonged with them. You could have heard a pin drop after *that* story. "To Reconciliation!" Jane thundered, happily grounding the tension. "Of the past, present, and future!"

"Hear, hear!" followed the sounds of raised voices and glasses.

The team was never the same. After that day, they came to *mean* something to one another and went on to do great work, far beyond what anyone in the organization had thought possible. I often wonder how many teams waste time, in the name of time efficiency, launching into task mode without ever getting to know the human beings in the room.

You don't have to let your teams fall into that trap. There are countless ways to get people playing together; whole books have been written about it.[62] To all these suggestions, you can now add what you know physically about the Collaborator: it develops through back and forth movements, rocking up and down on waves, swing-like dancing, belly laughter, seeing both sides, and engaging in play. Trying to grow teams without the Collaborator's vital energy is like trying to grow grapes without sun.

PATTERN-BUILDING ON TEAMS

Besides being essential to bringing a team together, sometimes the Collaborator is also what's needed to help a team get its job done. This was the case for a team I worked with at a major computer company; this team was charged with improving customer service. They needed Collaborator energy not only to come together—a challenge in itself, the team leader, Jean, had warned me—but also to see through their customer's eyes if they were ever going to improve service.

An Over-Driven Team That Learned to Collaborate

Not surprisingly, Collaborator energy was weak in the company overall, which was a big part of their customer-service problem. They weren't oriented to customers, and had let service and maintenance problems fester to the point where the CEO was getting hundreds of phone calls a day. He had personally chartered this team, and gave it authority to work across the organization.

The team gathered at its first meeting like uneasy delegates from warring nations. Drivers are quick to find fault in others, and this team had plenty of Drivers—and plenty of faults to find: "How did we get in this mess?"; "Well, if your system was more reliable . . ."; "If the call center didn't keep people on hold forever . . ." Several people pushed on each other, while others simply disengaged. Jean did her best to bring the team back to its mission and goals, but there was a lot of anger in the room. The team was storming before it had even formed.

Halfway through the first meeting day, we stopped and had the team assess how it was doing. Not well.

"We're not listening to each other," one said.

"We're not cooperating."

"We're not trying to solve the real problem."

We changed gears and brought out the patterns. We got people moving and laughing in each of the patterns, and gave them their FEBI reports, as well as a roll-up report for the group.

"No wonder we're not listening!" aha'd one of them, looking at the high percentage of Drivers in the room, "it's a miracle we haven't killed each other." Not one person had Collaborator as a Home pattern.

"Well, that's kind of an omission for a customer service team, don't you think?" Jean observed. "Maybe we should go out and find one." While that might be a good idea, I told them, it was even more important for every one of them to find that Collaborator energy in themselves and bring it out in this team.

Having the patterns to point to made it easier for people to quit pointing at each other. Even the conflicts of the morning started being talked about in a more patterned, less personal, light. Knowing they had to focus on the Collaborator and the Visionary, which was also weak, gave them places to look for solutions. Seeing through the eyes of the customer and thinking outside the box became themes for the rest of the meeting. Jean led them through brainstorming ways of getting the customer's perspective, and every one of them took "empathy assignments," from sitting in a call center to visiting customers to joining the CEO for an unpleasant hour of disgruntled phone calls.

As their work continued over the months, Jean kept challenging the team to think outside the boundaries of the current organization. "If we were a start-up," she'd ask, "how would we solve this problem?" The team came up with some successful quick wins as well as longer-term recommendations to address deep roots of the problem. Jean did not have to find new members to move her team to greatness. She simply had to get everyone understanding where to go and be willing to move there.

Teams Weak in Driver

The Collaborator and Visionary are by no means the only patterns a team may need to build. I've worked with a number of teams that were weak in the Driver pattern. These teams got bogged down in details and missed the point, or failed to measure their progress and hold one another accountable. Sometimes what a team needs most is the simplifying energy of the Driver to cut through all that they could do to focus on the vital few things they must do. Teams like this need to agree on their goal, then set a few clear, measurable objectives against which they track their progress. At the Collaborator-rich game company Cranium, the meeting rooms have no chairs, which creates an environment for crisp, focused meetings. People stand, which keeps things brief, in a room with a carpet featuring big red dots to help people stay on point.

Dis-Organized Teams

Sometimes the Organizer is exactly what a team needs to move it forward; in fact that's often when I get called in, as sort of Organizer-on-wheels. Teams lacking Organizer energy often struggle with the basic blocking and tackling of team process: moving through a well-planned agenda, hearing all voices, following the thread of dialogue to conclusions and next steps, tracking actions, and bootstrapping to goals. Sometimes companies assign Organized project managers to their vital cross-functional teams, which is great for bringing discipline to the team. But often what happens is that everyone else abdicates their Organizer role and the poor project manager can't carry it alone. To build more Organizer discipline into team meetings, Boeing used to have a numbered checklist (what else?) on the walls of its meeting rooms with Tips for Teams. If you're on a team that is too loose to make progress during a meeting or from one meeting to the next, bringing in some of the Organizer's structure is the perfect antidote.

Table 9-1 captures numerous ways you can build any of the patterns into the teams you're a part of. Sometimes a team needs the soft, fuzzy stuff and other times it needs more edge. Sometimes it needs more order and other times less. With the patterns, you have a way to diagnose what a team *does* need and dial in the right prescription to move it to greatness.

THE PATTERNS OF AN ORGANIZATION

Let's scale up. The patterns provide their insights at every level, including the level of companies and the culture of organizations. Google, for example, in the business of searching the chaotic, Visionary Internet, has a suitably chaotic, Visionary culture to match. Shona Brown, who literally wrote the book on how to use chaos as a strategy,[63] is Google's senior vice president of business operations. Among other things, she oversees ten or so projects that disrupt one part of the company or restructure another, trying to tease out how little management Google can get away with and then backing it off some. "If I ever come into the office and I feel comfortable," she says, "if I don't feel a little nervous about some crazy stuff going on, then we've taken it too far."[64]

IBM: A Company That Had to Change Its Patterns

Contrast Google's approach with the formality and structure of more traditional companies, such as the old-time IBM, and you can see how business cultures overall are shifting from Driver–Organizer hierarchies (where everyone could find their box on the org chart and had one boss) to faster, more innovative Driver–Visionary cultures (where people now report in several directions, do most of their work laterally, and often don't bother to update the org chart!). IBM is itself a good example of a company that had to make that shift if it was going to survive. Back in the 1970s and early 80s, when mainframes ruled, IBM was Driven, ambitious, and formal. The company was known for its unyielding procedures and strict dress code: business suits and white shirts only, thank you. When quirky, innovative Apple came along and introduced the personal computer, IBM's initial reaction was dismissive—who needs a computer on his desk?—exactly what you'd expect from a company with a single-minded belief in the business it had structured.

IBM was wrong, of course, and it soon recognized that and started playing catch up. The company realized that not only did its products have to change, but its people did, as well. IBM did exactly what the patterns would prescribe to add more Visionary and Collaborator to its culture. It shifted, for example, to a more casual dress code, created workspaces where people could meet informally, and reorganized the business to be more team-based and less hierarchical. This was not an easy transition to lead a company through; Lou Gerstner, IBM's CEO through much of the 90s, likened it to teaching an elephant to dance.[65] But in leading IBM out of the formal bureaucracy it had become, Gerstner breathed new life into this aging giant and made it young again.

The Lifecycle of Organizations

Companies, like people and teams, also have lifecycles. Just as different patterns come to the fore at different stages of individual and team development, so do they come into prominence at different stages in a company's lifecycle. Healthy, growing companies need all four essential energies.

Ichak Adizes has done some great work chronicling corporate lifecycles. He makes a distinction between young, growing companies and old, aging companies—not as a function of years so much as in the tension between how flexible they are (Visionary) versus how controlled (Organizer). The early stages—start-up, infancy, adolescence—are characterized by rapid, flexible growth, but without enough Organized controls to hold a company together, it flies apart (e.g., it doesn't build solid infrastructure, fails to deliver, etc.). With a healthy tension between flexibility and control, a company can hang out in a mature growth phase that Adizes calls the "prime" of its life. As soon as it quits growing, or when the spirit of Visionary entrepreneurship falls off, it enters an inflection point between growing and aging.

This inflection point, a stage Adizes calls "stable" is a dangerous stage for a company—it's the stage Shona Brown insists on avoiding at Google by backing off management (i.e., controls) wherever possible. For this stable stage is deceptive; at the surface, it still looks like things are humming along. But unless the pump of growth is reprimed, this is the start of a vicious cycle through the stages of decline—aristocracy and increasing bureaucracy—as cost cuts become increasingly radical, controls tighten, and people hang on for dear life to whatever power or job they have left.

Prime Organizations Need Whole and Balanced Leadership

Interestingly, while Adizes didn't start with an understanding of the patterns, he ended up there. He saw that four leadership qualities were essential for a company to enjoy the "prime" of its life: performance (Driver), entrepreneurship (Visionary), administration (Organizer), and integration (Collaborator). Every dysfunction of a young company and every stage of a company in decline is the result of too little of one of these patterns. For example, early on, if a company shows too little Drive for performance it won't get going. As the company grows, too little of the Collaborator's integration means it won't work effectively across silos. A healthy company needs leaders listening for and creating a healthy balance among all four patterns.

DIAGNOSING THE PATTERNS OF AN ORGANIZATION

Managing the energy patterns of an organization is a job for leadership because, like people, companies have their favorite Home patterns, too. On the upside, we might call this their brand image, and a strong, clear brand can be a tremendous advantage. Yet left to their own unconscious devices, companies can overdo their strengths to the point of letting their virtues becoming weaknesses, just as unaware people can. Good leaders can spot imbalances and apply the same approach to companies that is so successful for individuals: know and win on your strengths but bring in enough of the other patterns to stay out of trouble.

So how do we diagnose the patterns of an organization and where it might be getting in trouble? Here, and summarized in Table 9-2, are some clear signs to look for.

You know you're dealing with a company dominated by Driver energy by the numbers; it's first, fast, and financially astute. People in the company know their priorities, have clear, measurable goals, and absolutely keep score. Driver companies are focused on beating the competition. As Jack Welch once described the Driving GE he created, "Every day people come to work knowing they can WIN!"

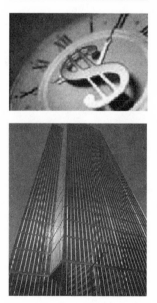

The Driver Company: Pushes Limits, at Times Too Far

But when that energy becomes a focus on winning at all costs, you have the meltdown of an Enron. Driver companies run the risk of sacrificing quality for speed or ethics for advantage. On the other hand, with too little Driver energy companies get bogged down in too many priorities or too much politics or bureaucracy.

Organizer companies build their brand around trust, quality, and dependability—think of companies in health care, insurance, or manufacturing. The dutiful ring of a mission statement (as opposed to a Vision statement) is itself a sign of an Organizer company. Merck, for example, has a mission statement that reads like a list of good deeds. Organizer companies tend to be process-rich, proper, perfectionistic, and polite.

Too much Organizer energy and the organization slows down and costs rise. That, plus its predictability, can make it a sitting duck for competitors to attack. On the other hand, too little Organizer energy and the company lacks the stability, quality, and integrity that people count on when they do business with it.

You find fewer companies dominated by Collaborator energy compared with other patterns, but you can bet they have a lot more fun. Collaborator companies are practical, too, and are truly oriented to people—especially to customers—not as lip service, but as a brand (think Avon, the Company for Women). Collaborator companies know that the key to happy customers is happy employees, and they go the extra mile for their people as well.

Where Collaborator companies stumble is in creating a country club atmosphere that tolerates poor performance or gets bogged down in politics. Or they may try juggling too many things without the discipline or processes to pull it off. But what's far more common are companies with too little of the Collaborator's fun, practicality, or way with people.

Visionary companies know their essential purpose, which generally orients everybody in a broad, flexible sense, as in Google's mantra, "Do no evil." Light on controls and heavy on innovation, Visionary companies are about disrupting markets, uncovering unmet needs, and creating the future.

The Organizer Company: Does the Right Thing—Slowly

In the extreme, Visionary companies fail to execute, or they find a future that has no following. But too little Visionary energy and companies age quickly, draining themselves by protecting the past or futiley defending their markets.

PATTERN-BUILDING THAT MOVES AN ORGANIZATION

What can you do as a leader to move an organization in the direction of one of these patterns? First, you need to do the same analysis for the organization as we did earlier for teams: recognize where it is and where it needs to go (you can use the same worksheet, too; just treat the entire organization as your "team."). Once you know which pattern you want to move toward, the levers are countless, since the patterns operate at every level. From the work environment to processes, policies, rewards, training, special events, brand building, employee benefits, recruiting practices, logos, slogans, and much more, any of these can be done in the spirit of a particular pattern to bring out more of that energy in the organization.

Some companies, like some leaders, don't have a strong Home pattern that translates into a clear brand identity. AT&T comes to mind, in the post-divestiture years, when it was casting about for what it wanted to become.

Other companies portray one image to the public ("We're all about innovation"), but struggle to live it on the inside (where they're bogged down by too many controls). These companies do well to move toward the pattern that strengthens what they're trying to be good at.

Companies that already have a strong brand culture—for example, a strong Home pattern or primary style—are generally well-aligned internally with the same brand-pattern they project externally: Dell (Driver), Merck (Organizer), Southwest (Collaborator), and Google (Visionary) are all examples we've talked about. These sorts of organizations more often need "tweaking" of a weaker pattern for better balance.

For example, we worked with the CEO of an organization whose brand was built around Driver and already had plenty of it; he wanted to bring out more of the Collaborator spirit among his leaders. As part of an overall leadership development program, he took his executives out to a race car track, where they alternately drove fast and served on a pit crew (a great example of using a strength to approach a weakness at an organizational level). Another leader of a fast-moving company where people were burning a little too hot wanted to foster the Visionary spirit and the quiet composure of the Organizer. She had a room for meditation put into the building where people could go any time of day. She also brought in a yoga instructor for optional morning classes.

You'll find that being able to move yourself physically into any pattern—

and to consult your own inner team of pattern experts—becomes a boundless source of inspiration for creating similar movement in the "body" of an organization. Table 9-2 gives you numerous ways to both read the patterns operating in an organization, and to "right" them. Whether your organization needs more alignment or better balance, more heat or more light, you'll find countless ways to get it moving to a new level of greatness.

The Collaborator Company: Passion, People, and Perhaps Overextension

THE MAGIC OF HIGH-PERFORMING TEAMS AND ORGANIZATIONS

Every so often, magic happens. An organization moves from good to great and sustains its success for years. A team overcomes enormous barriers and outperforms expectations, and every person on it never forgets the thrilling experience. What accounts for this magic? As you might guess, a good many people have studied it—among the thought leaders are Katzenbach and Smith for teams, and Jim Collins and Ichak Adizes for organizations. While magic defies a simple formula, their findings do point to some common elements in what makes a team or organization good and what moves to it great.

The basic formula for "good"—that is a well-functioning team or a healthy, growing organization—is an appropriate balance among the patterns. That doesn't mean every pattern is used equally. As we've seen, "good" gets even better when the team or organization wins on its pattern strengths (which match what it's trying to do), but brings in enough of its weaker patterns to stay out of trouble. But all four energies are as essential to teams and organizations as they are to leaders themselves.

This much can be prescribed. The magic of greatness is something extra that comes out of deep, human caring. A team shifts into high-performing gear when its members come to care deeply about one another's success.[66] Almost instinctively, with natural ease, they begin operating as a whole rather than as a collection of individual parts. Leaders who move companies from good to great are those who embody what Collins calls "willful humility," a dogged determination and deep caring about the company, its customers, and its people, putting the interests of the whole ahead of one's own. This deep caring— are we allowed to call it love in a leadership book?—creates a phase shift, where the diverse energies of the team or organization start functioning fundamentally for one another rather than against one another or only for themselves. Greatness emerges when the differences represented by each pattern are not only tolerated, but celebrated; when they're not only a functional tension (which is still a far cry better than a dysfunctional one), but a powerful, generative force.

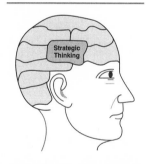

The possibility of this greatness exists for every team and organization you're a part of. But to create it in the world, you must experience this profound synergy among the patterns in yourself. Which brings us back, not full circle, but more full-spiral, to you and your journey to greatness.

The Visionary Company: Possibilities Abound— Does Enough Get Done?

TABLE 9-2   The Patterns in Organizations

You can use this table both as a diagnostic description of how the patterns show up in organizations and as a proactive prescription for bringing out any pattern you want more of.

	Driver	*Organizer*
Organizations dominated by this pattern emphasize . . .	Action and results; outcomes and the bottom line Winning	Orderly processes, quality, reliability, doing what we say we will do Correctness
Buildings are . . .	Bold, jutting skyscrapers, no frill warehouses	Quiet campuses where everything has its place
Workplaces have . . .	Striking contrast, (e.g., black, white, and red), sparse furnishing, no frills	Orderly offices, logical layouts, plenty of storage, quiet places to think
Processes are . . .	Minimal and focused on outcomes	Step-by-step, unambiguous
Rewards employees who . . .	Win, achieve numbers	Deliver without fail, are solid contributors
Rewards with . . .	Variable, outcome-based bonus, status perks (e.g., parking place, better office)	A raise, more responsibility, formal public recognition
Hiring Practices	Hire from the best schools	Establish criteria, competency models, put people through a disciplined selection process
Example Logo	Lightning bolt	Red Cross
Typical Slogans	"Just do it" "Be Your Own Action Figure"	"Solid as a Rock" "We Deliver"

Collaborator	Visionary
People and passion; serving customers, developing employees and having fun	Future possibilities, harmonizing with the flow, thinking outside the box, multiple paths
People	Insight
Colorful, fun, with a jumbled sense of abundance	Futuristic, harmonized with nature
Warm colors, common places to gather, overstuffed furniture, toys	Places to network or be alone, open space, people can work in or out of an office
Practical, oriented to the ways people really work	Adjustable to different needs or situations
Are team players, work across boundaries	Have great ideas, solve big problems, find the future
Quirky, fun public recognition with monetary awards; gift certificates, a day off with family, team perks, more support	More freedom, a piece of the future they've created
"Who do you know who's good and will fit in around here?"	Ask unusual questions during interviews, screen for smart, imaginative people
Heart	Rainbow
"The LUV airline" "The Company for Women"	"Invent . . ." "Do no evil"

CHAPTER TEN

Engage as a Whole and Balanced Leader

GETTING THE BAND BACK TOGETHER

DRIVER: Who called this meeting?

VISIONARY: I did. I've been thinking . . . all this talk of teams . . . all that we just covered about strengthening teams and what makes them high performing . . .

DRIVER: What's your point?

VISIONARY: Not only does it apply to teams on the outside—it applies to us, as well.

COLLABORATOR: I see where you're going. We can become a whole and balanced, high-performing, inner team!

ORGANIZER: You're right! How we function as patterns inside and outside are logically symmetric. Not only does our inner work improve the outward effectiveness of whole leaders, but applying what we know about outside teams, we can improve our internal process.

COLLABORATOR: It's not just process. It's how we trust and respect each other. It's how we support one another. It's that deep caring for each other that makes us really function as a whole.

DRIVER: This is just navel gazing! Where are we going with this?

ORGANIZER: You're right, too, Driver. We don't want to spend all day in here. But don't you see the point? Thoughts form in language and, whether we speak them aloud or keep them to ourselves, those thoughts are in the voice of one of us. Before we met one another, we couldn't discern who was speaking, and it was probably the same one or two voices most of the time anyway. When the weakest among us tried to speak, the rest often didn't listen. Just like teams on the outside!

> *Be really whole*
> *And all things will come*
> *to you.* —Lao-Tzu

205

COLLABORATOR: That's true. We haven't always been cooperating.

VISIONARY: The purpose I see to coming together as a high-performing team is that, fundamentally, this is who we are! What would be possible for us if everything we did was fundamentally for one another and the whole that we create?

DRIVER: We still want to field our strongest players, but I see what you're saying: now we have players for all positions. We'll win for sure!

ORGANIZER: We'll certainly be the best we can be.

COLLABORATOR: We'll have a way around every obstacle, a way to play with everything life throws at us and have a good time while we're at it.

Can you imagine such a conversation among the pattern players in you? Would your players be ready to make peace with each other? Or move beyond tolerance to the depth of respect and mutual support that characterizes truly high performing teams? If you recall in chapter 2, when you were first learning about the patterns, I encouraged you to recognize whether you had some attitude about one or more of them, such as disrespect, irritation, or uneasiness. If you did, perhaps it's too soon for respect to have bloomed; it's only been a few chapters for you and, truthfully, getting comfy and appreciative of my inner Collaborator has been a journey of years for me. Whether or not you experience it as an inner conversation, this imaginary bonding of your own inner team is exactly the way to wholeness and extraordinary effectiveness.

You've already taken several steps along this journey in recognizing the patterns in you and around you, and in seeing the limitations of patterns misapplied. You've made a further, critical leap if you've designed a practice for increasing your freedom of movement in a pattern you'd like more of. You've now seen some valuable ways to apply the patterns where you work—in improving communication, influencing others, handling conflict, leading teams, and tweaking or transforming organizations. Now, here you are in the final chapter of this book and, far from being over, your pattern journey is really ready to take off. Let's explore how you might continue it.

WATCH YOUR LIFE

"The patterns have given us a map," MiL Institute president Lennart Rohlin observed when we were working with his organization. He's right, and it's a map of ourselves as much as it is a map of the teams, the organizations, and the world around us. If you think about what a road map does for you when you're traveling in a car, it shows where you are in a broader context. Maps don't care if you've traveled down this road before or if you're a visitor, they'll take all of your experience—the familiar and unfamiliar—and show it in the same broad context. This is a wonderful thing about maps: even when you're in familiar territory, they tell you more about home, and when you're in new territory they keep you from getting totally lost.

Now you have a map of the patterns, a whimsical version of which is offered below, but any table in this book could be part of that map. You have a pretty good idea where Home is, where you're more and less comfortable. Now take that map and watch your life. Watch what's familiar with map in hand and you'll see it in a richer, fuller context. "So that's why I have such a hard time listening when I'm racing through my day. I'm in full-blown Driver mode and the Driver is a lousy listener," you might recognize. Or, "*That was a pretty Visionary meeting. It might have been a waste of time, or perhaps an important seed was planted. Let's see what develops.*"

A *pattern map* . . . *puts the familiar and unfamiliar into context.*

Watch for the Patterns and Their Side Effects

Watch your life. In watching mine, I saw something new just the other day. As I was hurriedly packing for a trip, I realized why, when I rush, I always forget something. Aha! The Driver has single-point focus and the point is to get out the door at a specific time; everything else fades to gray. No wonder I forgot my toothbrush. So now I know anytime I rush (which brings on the Driver) I risk missing something, and it may be much more important than a toothbrush.

Mark tells a funny story of being in an airport when he became very impatient and angry (signs of the Driver!) as he was standing at the ticket counter hearing about some interminable flight delay. He left his computer bag on the counter. "Now I know whenever I get angry," he says, "to stop, take a breath, and ask, 'What am I forgetting?'" This is watching your life.

Become More Familiar with Home

If your pattern scores on the FEBI survey were close—so close that you may not be clear about where Home is—this is another place where watching your life will clarify matters. You may find your true Home is a buried treasure, not the pattern you've been laboring in the most.

Holly, for example, knew she was artistic and surmised that Visionary was Home for her. But as she watched her life using the patterns, she noticed that her favorite art was playwriting, that her teaching was passionate and filled with stories, and that she influenced people so easily she took it for granted. "*Wow!*" she concluded, "I'm a natural Collaborator after all." She could also see why she had buried this playful pattern in the past. But it's buried no more! Now it flows out of her like sunshine.

Watch your life. The FEBI wasn't around, of course, when I was learning about the patterns, but if it had been, my scores early on would have been completely untrustworthy. Initially, my pattern prejudice was so strong I was wishing for anything-but-Organizer as my Home pattern. The more I watched my life, the more obvious the truth became: "So that's why I take to meditation so readily, but can get stuck in the form . . . So that's why I find project management so easy . . . that's why I'm always explaining myself . . . and there's me making another list!" Once I could see these things, and see them on the map of all pattern possibilities, I felt positively freed! I could do these things or not do them. I could embrace and use the strengths of Organizer, but not fall prey to its excesses. Now I can take my Organizer for granted because I know it's Home. I can relax into it—let things get much more messed up than I used to—because I know I can sort them out later.

As you watch your life and as Home becomes more familiar, you learn to use your natural strengths with natural ease.

Notice What's Missing

Watching your life, you might also learn that you use some aspects of a pattern quite easily, but other aspects hardly at all. This was a revelation for my colleague, Sarah, a highly imaginative leader who had recently been promoted but was still doing her previous job as well. Watching her life, she could see where she already had easy access to the big-picture thinking of the Visionary, but not such easy access to its letting go qualities. With the map of the patterns, she could see how to use more of what the Visionary pattern had to offer and how it could help her let go of the past.

As you watch your life, and get to know your Home and all that's familiar in the context of the patterns, you, too, will uncover treasures and freedom. You'll find what you can count on—that you can Drive toward goals with one hand tied behind your back, for example, or leap to new Visionary ideas at the drop of a hat. You'll see where and why you get into trouble, trying to negotiate, for example, from the Driver's single-minded point of view or communicating in broad, Visionary concepts while your audience is struggling to find the point. In every case, you'll see where another pattern player could come to your rescue, where moving to another place on the map would help. Watch your life with the map of the patterns, and its familiar contours will reveal tremendous, new insights.

"PATTERNIZE" AND ENERGIZE ALL THAT YOU LEARN

You can also apply the pattern map to new territory. Leadership development and business in general are rich with new things to learn; new books, articles, models, and methods are popping up all the time. Now, with your map of the energy patterns, you'll be able to see the pattern underpinnings to any new material. Say, for example, you want to implement the good advice of Blue Ocean Strategy,[67] which is all about disrupting markets and changing paradigms. You'll know this is Visionary thinking. More to the point, you'll know ways to move yourself, your teams, or your organization into the Visionary mindset that does it best. Without a pattern map, you can read a book like this again and again, but if you tried to put it into practice using an Organizer's mindset, the result would still be too cautious and incremental.

The Patterns of Situational Leadership

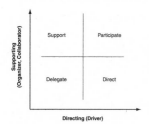

The amount of Driver is traded off against the more supportive patterns of Organizer and Collaborator in the model of situational leadership.

As another example, say you just learned about Situational Leadership, based on the work of Ken Blanchard and Paul Hersey, who observed that there is no one right way to lead. Sometimes you have to be direct and tell people what to do; other times you have to invite more participation, support others in reaching decisions, or delegate altogether. And they're absolutely right. What they couldn't tell you—because they didn't have a pattern map back then—was how you could move from being a diehard, directing Driver to being a supportive Collaborator when the situation called for it. They said, in effect, "this is what a supportive leader does; do this." But with energy patterns that connect how outward doing relates to inward being, you know that if you want to be a supportive, Collaborative leader in your behaviors, you'll do it best if you access the Collaborator on the inside. Sure, you could try play-acting the role of a supportive leader in your direct Driver mode, but it wouldn't be an effective, authentic expression of a whole leader. It would be a surface act, and people would see right through it.

By seeing the patterns in—i.e., "patternizing"—all that you learn, you energize your engagement with new material, have a way to put it into context, and make it your own. You can do this with anything: take any book off your shelf right now. What patterns are suggested by its title or subject matter? What would you guess are the patterns of its author(s) or the nature of their advice?

The beauty of seeing the patterns in what you learn is that once you know where the authors or teachers are coming from, you can put their advice into context ("Okay, this is Jack-Welch-the-Driver talking, of course it was possible for him to fire 11 of his 13 direct reports when he first came to GE; he's a tough guy"). You also know where *you* need to move if you want to put their good advice to work in the most effective way ("If I'm going to push Welch-like changes through my organization, I'll need a lot of Driver energy").

You can also select topics or authors of a specific pattern to bring out that energy in yourself. If you shout into the strings of a grand piano, the strings that match frequencies in your voice start to vibrate. By the same principle of resonance, when you throw a good Collaborator tale toward the "strings" of your inner team, if you really enjoy the read (this doesn't work if you dismiss it as nonsense), your inner Collaborator metaphorically "vibrates" or gains strength. This can be yet another way to develop specific patterns in yourself.

"PATTERNIZE" NEW SITUATIONS YOU FACE

Of course, most of the new learning and unfamiliar territory in life is not confined to comfortable books, blogs, or classrooms. Rather, it happens on-the-job, one wave of change after another, in new situations you face all the time. But here, too, "patternizing" helps. It gives you a way to read the energy of a new situation and the people in it, and then figure out which patterns will work best.

For example, when Ursula was promoted from a group of peers to become their new boss, she struggled with how to establish a new relationship with each of them, especially since several of them had also wanted the job. Once she identified their patterns, she could speak with each person in ways they could hear and respect. I then encouraged her to step back and look at the whole situation—new boss, somewhat resistant group—what patterns did she think suited the whole situation?

"Well, the Collaborator for sure," Ursula said without hesitation. "And I suppose the Organizer's good listening skills. We need to set a clear direction, but the only way I'm going to get buy-in is if they feel a part of the process."

Locating this new situation on her pattern map took Ursula less than a minute but provided useful navigation for months of good work. When you use your pattern map to chart new learning and unfamiliar territory, you are never lost. Almost instantly, the situation will feel more familiar and easier to learn; eventually it becomes just another way to use the right players on your inner team to move to greatness.

REVIEW AND REVITALIZE YOUR PRACTICE

Perhaps the best way to further your pattern journey is to take to your practice like a bold explorer. Become intensely curious: What's working? What's not? What's important now? Where you need to make adjustments? By reviewing and revitalizing your practice, you keep it relevant to your outer life, and keep deepening its ability to integrate your inner team.

If you went through the process of designing your own best practice in chapter 7, you already have a great starting point. Try your plan for a couple of months, and take note of which behaviors, attitudes, and responses change and which stay the same. And remember, it's good to involve others in your plan; it's important to have a set of eyes other than your own giving you feedback on whether your good intentions are showing up in your actions. It takes something in the range of three to six weeks to "rewire" the

Keep a journal . . .

Serious explorers are never without a log of their travels.

People often forget how difficult a pattern was for them at the start of their practice. You may find more joy and motivation in your work with the patterns if you keep a record.

You might jot down . . .

- The small victories . . . and large ones!

- The barriers you encountered

- How you changed your practice

- What you discovered

- The first time you found freedom over a bad habit

- The first time you didn't get locked up in a habitual tension (i.e., override)

- What you want to remind yourself of over and over.

body for a new activity, so give yourself a bit of time before judging the comfort or effectiveness of a new practice.

Discomfort Is a Good Sign

In fact, if you're uncomfortable when you first begin working on your plan and even less effective than before, that's a really good sign. It means you're letting go of the tried and true and plunging into new territory. Mini warm-up exercises before you engage new behaviors will certainly ease your discomfort and support your effectiveness sooner, but some difficulty is par for the course. Whenever you're learning something new, performance slips a bit before it can get leaps and bounds better. The great golfer Tiger Woods comes to mind, with his incredible courage to keep reinventing his game. He goes through a lull for a few months as he works out a new swing, with every less-than-stellar performance broadcast to the world. And then he comes back, *bam, bam, bam*, and wins one tournament after another. So if part of your practice includes, say, holding Visionary brainstorming sessions with your team and the first one made you feel out of your element, that's a good sign. Keep going!

Practice Is Conscious Competence

The cycle of learning has sometimes been expressed as a movement from unconscious incompetence (before you knew how to access the Visionary, for example) to conscious incompetence ("I need more Visionary to be effective") to conscious competence, which is practice ("I'll make a practice of holding brainstorming sessions and taking Tai Chi classes"), to, finally, unconscious competence, when the practice has done its work (the Visionary pattern, in this example, is functioning freely). At this point, you don't need the same practice. You may still choose to continue holding brainstorming sessions or taking Tai chi classes, but they don't require the same kind of conscious attention. The eye of practice is free to focus on something new.

You can recycle the process (and the handy Organized worksheet!) of chapter 7 again and again as your life or leadership changes and as you develop in your practice. The process started with the Visionary exploration identifying an opportunity or challenge facing you right now. Whenever that changes in a big way, it's a good time to reflect on implications for your practice.

EXPLORE THE MACRO

Explore, focus, plan, and engage: each of the patterns played a role in the process we used in chapter 7 for designing a practice. Another way to use this process—and this may especially appeal to your inner Collaborator and Visionary—is to be less systematic, but more systemic in how you apply it. So rather than starting from an exploration of discrete opportunities or challenges facing you, you might ask a much bigger question, such as: What is the purpose of my life? Who am I?

You may have engaged some of this macro-level thinking when you started teasing out what would be possible for you if you met the opportunity or challenge and what that would do for you. But you can explore questions as large as your life. And then you can "patternize" your answers, and focus, plan, and engage around this systemic, purposeful orientation.

To see how this might work for you, take a look at the questions below and pick one that intrigues you and one that maybe irritates you—that's where your energy is! Jot down your answers to both. These questions are also available on the movetogreatness.com website, if you'd rather download them. Remember to call up your Visionary voice as you reflect on them.

- What is the purpose of your life?
- Who are you (when you're not doing anything)?
- What do you want to be remembered for at your funeral?
- What is the greatest good you could offer to the world?
- What ultimate mission do you want to accomplish in your lifetime?
- What really matters and how do you live that?

When Maria, a deeply committed, seemingly tireless chief operating officer for a nonprofit educational institute looked at these questions, she chose two to answer:

- What ultimate mission do you want to accomplish in your lifetime?
  That through my work, more children are staying in school, learning more, and are better equipped for this fast-moving world. Personally, that I have been the wife and mother my family needed, and that they are happy.
- What is the greatest good you could offer to the world?
  Being the best I can be.

**Systemic Practice at the
Macro Level**

Explore: What is my
purpose? Who am I?
What is my greatest
good?

Focus: Given this, what's
most important right
now?

Plan: What patterns
would help? What can I
do?

Engage: Who can help?
(make it fun, hold me
accountable)

FOCUS, PLAN, ENGAGE

In the next phase, the focusing phase, we bring in the Driver to ask, "Given this big picture, what's most important right now?" When Maria was pushed with this question, her statement—"Being the best I can be"—made her pause. "I have to take better care of myself," she concluded. "I'm going to get emotional here," she continued haltingly, as if warning were required, "I guess I hadn't realized how hard I've been pushing." Her first answer also reminded her how much it mattered to her to be present for her family. In this brief, focused reflection, two important commitments popped out.

In the planning phase—and this can take just a few mind cycles and a matter of moments—Maria looked at the patterns at work in her life. What patterns would help her take better care of herself and be more present for her family? "Well, I need to return to my long-abandoned exercise program," she admitted. Being a strong Organizer, she didn't lack for discipline; what she needed was more of the Visionary's ability to let go of the small stuff (or innovate around it), so she could tend to this larger picture. Since she already wanted to return to an exercise program, she looked at how she could bring more Visionary spirit into it. She also committed to using her Organizer strength to block time for her family on weekends and hold it sacred. The final phase—the engage part—was easy; her family loved her "plan" (and appreciated her for making it); they were happy to hold her accountable.

These last few phases—focus, plan, and engage—can be done again and again using the same purposeful starting point. Another time, Maria might look at these same answers and decide that what's most important right now is to develop better measures of educational effectiveness and, with Driver clarity, could initiate a project to get better numbers. Many leaders post answers to macro questions like these in some visible place in their office to keep informing their day-by-day decisions.

Whenever you want to run your macro answers through the next few phases, here are the questions to answer.

- Given this big picture, what's most important right now?
- What patterns would help you move in this direction? What can you do?
- Who can help? (make it fun, hold you accountable)

EXPLORE THE MICRO

You can also make your practice more systemic by working in the micro direction, where you apply a microsecond process in the small moments, continually exploring what patterns are operating. Ask yourself: "How can I approach this most effectively?" Some leaders exude this competence, whether they consciously developed it or intuited their way there.

Systemic Practice at the Micro Level

Moment-by-moment, ask

- What patterns are operating?

- How can I approach this most effectively? How can I move there?

Captain Johnny, an exemplary cruise ship captain, is such a leader. "He's the captain of the future," his boss says of him. "He knows where we're going as a company and how to steer the ships there." (Visionary and Driver coming to the fore.) Aboard his ship, this affable fellow is hailed by dozens of passengers. "We're going to have a blast," he shouts to a large Harley Davidson contingent onboard, "My Harley's in the hull!" (playing Collaborator). Continuing his tour around the ship, he greets passing staff, pausing to lean toward the ear of a bartender. "How's business?" he asks, taking the financial pulse on his way to brief safety procedures to a new crew coming onboard (Driver and Organizer). Johnny makes the transitions look effortless. Moment-by-moment, he adjusts his authentic pattern expression to the situation at hand.

To build this competence, if you don't already have it, takes conscious attention, i.e., practice. The practice, in this case, is not a chunk of dedicated time, but rather a dedication to asking "patternizing" questions again and again (What patterns are operating? How can I approach this situation most effectively?) and then moving yourself momentarily into the best pattern for the situation. If you find that you can't quite move into one of the patterns— it's not a fully onboard member of your team yet—apply a more dedicated practice to get that pattern limbered up. Any pattern you can get a good feel for in your body (and a good feeling about!), you have access to at a moment's notice. For a while, this micro-patternizing process takes conscious effort. But eventually it becomes an unconscious competence that is woven through the fabric of your perfectly whole life.

INTEGRATE INSIDE

Many people find even greater insight by scanning inside for the patterns operating in the moment. A simple way to do an inner scan is given on page 219. At first it may seem a bit self-indulgent, especially to the Driver in you. But the payoff is tremendous: nothing will open up the potential of your life more than finding and releasing what holds you back on the inside. It's something every great athlete, martial artist, performer, yogi, and meditator knows: that outer progress, however it's defined, comes through inner work.

The first time you do a scan, you may not see much. Don't be discouraged; like any other sense, it gets more refined with use. Think of the first time you tasted wine (or whatever you've developed a fine taste for). At first, maybe all you could tell was red or white, dry or sweet. You weren't picking up black-berry undertones or whether this wine goes better with fish or beef. But if you keep tasting wine, especially if you take an interest in it—if you go to wine tast-ings or order the crisp white wine suggested on a menu to complement your pear salad and appreciate that it really does go together—you start noticing more. I was once talking with a leader who got so good at wine tasting he started entering contests. He could discern not only the blackberry undertones and other such winespeak, but pick out a cabernet grape from a particular vineyard in South Bordeaux harvested in 1991! Now that's a refined palette.

Can you imagine having the same level of inner insight? Maybe the first time you look, all you sense is gray and a stiff neck. But a few scans later, you might notice that if you soften your ribs, you can feel the Collaborator center down in your belly. Sometime later you'll notice that if you feel for the Collaborator's rhythm inside, your neck loosens just a bit. And maybe it's not so gray anymore, but more defined: This is how Driver moves through me— like a zipper, getting me aligned and focused from the bottom up.

If you take an active interest in gaining inside knowledge—akin to going to wine tastings—you might build a mini-break into your day using the integrative exercises at the end of this chapter. We call these "integra-tive" because they're designed to start you in one pattern and lead you mindfully through the other three. In one minute, you can experience all four energies easily functioning within you. You might start with a quick scan and then do the integrative exercise for your Home pattern. Or do the exercise for a pattern you want more of. Or splurge: take a full five minutes and do all four!

THE INNER JOURNEY IS THE OUTER JOURNEY

Focus on your inner team for the simple reason that it matters: the inner jour-ney and outer journey are the same. Coming to appreciate and leverage your different pattern players on the inside is also coming to appreciate and lever-age diversity on the outside in the people around you. Internally accessing  each of these energy patterns lets you externally express a whole set of leadership behaviors in the most effective way. Pulling together as a whole and balanced team on the inside is engaging in the most excellent and efficient way on the outside.

That's not to say that finding and making peace with each of these patterns in you is as simple as a fanciful four way conversation (though that's not a bad place to start). In my experience, it has been a journey of many years, an onion of many layers. I've so appreciated the patterns for helping me play my best game. But I appreciate them even more for helping me see through the game itself.

Ending the Endless Lawsuit

In my pattern journey, I started with not even recognizing Home! The frivolous Collaborator also made me uncomfortable. Making peace with these patterns came in fits and starts. For example, whenever I'd relax my must-get-everything-done pace to play a little, some inner agitation kept pushing me back into action: must be productive, must be productive. I could finally ask myself more deeply, "Why? What's the point of all this productivity? Sure, the world rewards productive people, but sometimes those rewards have nothing to do with what's essential in my life, so why do I keep leaping into action?"

Digging more deeply and coming to know the competing forces of these patterns in me, I eventually saw the underlying fear of an Organizer intent on building her case for being "good enough." And since this case is never won once and for all—"You're only as good as your last gig"—that inner Organizer was stuck in an endless, futile loop, piling on evidence. Meanwhile, my Collaborator was shut down, with no time for play. I read a book once that aptly called this inner battle the Great Lawsuit,[68] the thing we're always trying to prove. It made me feel marginally better to know that this was a common experience. If we don't resolve this lawsuit on the inside, we end up projecting it into our outside world and fighting our battles there. Often, we don't see that's what we're doing, but as I watched my life closely (meditation is good for that) I saw that was exactly what I was doing. No wonder I resented overdone Organizers and dismissed Collaborators. I was doing the same thing on the inside!

Seeing these tendencies didn't make them vanish instantly, believe me. But they didn't get all of me anymore. I was no longer enslaved by them. My Organizer side has finally learned how to move beyond the lawsuit by serving the whole picture, not focusing on itself. And Collaborator has finally been allowed to come out and play. These inner changes have most assuredly affected how I show up in the world. As I look back on my driving, disciplined ways, I can see where, as a leader, I just wore people

There is one thing that, when cultivated and regularly practiced, leads
to deep spiritual intention, to peace, to mindfulness and clear comprehension, to vision and knowledge, to a happy life here and now, and to the culmination of wisdom and awakening. And what is that one thing? It is mindfulness centered on the body.
—Gautama Buddha

out. Only after relaxing into more of the Collaborator's joyful spirit did I notice that others were drawn more to my joy than they ever were to my discipline!

Making the Patterns Your Own

The only way to really move toward the greatness of a whole leader is to remain whole in the process, to change both inside and out. The work we do on the inside is not so much a change of personality as it is a reclaiming of more of our natural, true being. Making peace with all of the pattern players in ourselves is making them our own; they're not roles that we borrowed from our parents or behaviors that were forced on us when we were young, but authentic aspects of who we are right now.

This is a most worthwhile undertaking for, like it or not, we're stuck with all the patterns as aspects of our character. Our only choice is whether we make them complementary or conflicting. To make them complementary, we have to allow them on our team and let each find its authentic voice. If we don't, they go underground, fail to deliver their goods, or cause trouble. For example, if we reject our Driver voice because it reminds us of the screeching commands of a childhood bully, we never find the true Driver in us who could provide essential edge to our every endeavor. Moreover if our inner team isn't getting along, much of our energy is drained by inner conflict, and all the ways it permeates our relationships with others.

Finding our own authentic expression of these patterns is making deep peace with ourselves. And there is something positively contagious about a leader who knows, from inside out, how to reconcile the tensions of being human. Whole and balanced, you become the leader others naturally want to follow. Reclaiming your ease and agility in any of the patterns and being able to act with freedom in the moment, not because of compulsions from the past, you will dance in the dynamic balance that is your leadership at its best, your life at its fullest. Ultimately, the greatness you move to is the wholeness of who you are.

INTEGRATIVE EXERCISES

You can use these exercises in a mini-break to feel the integrated functioning of all four patterns in you. Start with a scan and then move into the integrative exercise for your Home pattern or for a weak pattern. Better yet, do all four in the order that follows. If you make a practice of these exercises, you'll increasingly find the Visionary's flow and ease, the Driver's power, the Collaborator's resilience, and the Organizer's composure in every step.

The Inner Scan

1. Let out a sigh of relief.
2. For the next minute or so, scan what's going on in you at this moment. Close your eyes and listen or feel for the patterns in you:
   - Feel, with the slightest pushing, the Driver center firing in your lower abdomen.
   - Feel, with the slightest rocking, the Collaborator center in your belly.
   - Feel the sense of Organized composure and upright character centered at your solar plexus.
   - Feel the Visionary's ever-extending energy through your entire body and out the top of your head.
3. Explore with the intent to find the patterns, feel their movement or readiness for movement, and release any tension in the way.

Visionary: Integrative Roll

1. Stand with **feet hip-width** apart at **parallel to each other**, eyes toward the horizon.
2. Bend your knees, keeping them over your feet, as you roll your head forward and down toward the floor. Let your **head hang** freely as your fingers near (or touch) the floor.
3. **Rock** a bit from side to side, forward and back, until you feel your weight fall **equally through the arches** of both feet.
4. As if **pushing the floor away** through your arches, slowly come up, **unrolling** your spine from the bottom, one vertebra at a time. Feel for the Driver, Collaborator, and Organizer centers as you unroll past them.
5. Unroll your shoulders and neck, looking to the horizon. Feel a sense of weight through your arches and energy out the top of your head. Do five times. Try to keep the weight falling into your arches each time.

Driver: Integrative Zipper

1. Stand with **feet hip-width** apart, feet **parallel**, eyes to the horizon. Hold a sill or countertop as needed to keep your balance in this exercise.
2. **Bend your knees**, keeping them over your feet. Let your **hips drop** straight down and keep your **head straight**.
3. Keeping your upper body still, **roll your heels off the floor** and notice the Driver center firing. Imagine slotting a zipper together at the base of your spine.
4. **Press down through your toes** to push your upper body straight up as you straighten your legs. Feel a **zipper action from the base** of your spine up, sequentially firing the Driver, Collaborator, and Organizer centers.
5. **Lower your heels** to the floor. Feel an extension down through the floor, up through your spine, and out the top of your head. Do five times. When you're done, walk around and notice how easily you push into the floor as you walk.

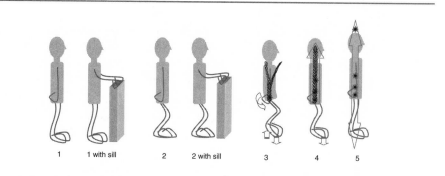

1   1 with sill   2   2 with sill   3   4   5

Collaborator: Integrative Swing

1. Stand with **feet a bit wider** than your hips and **parallel** to **each** other, eyes toward the horizon.
2. **Bend your knees. Push your left foot down and twist to the right**, keeping your upper body straight. Bend your knees again, **push down the right foot and twist to the left**. Keep swinging left and right, your arms loose like spaghetti and your hands freely hitting your body before you reverse direction. Feel the movement come from your feet and Collaborator center.
3. Repeat 10 twists. As you twist, feel how the Collaborator center (belly) interacts at the base with the Driver center and in the torso with the Organizer center. Feel the flow of the Visionary fling out the arms.
4. Reduce the motion by half and half again until the swinging damps out and your body feels weighted and aligned. Walk around and feel the weight falling into your feet.

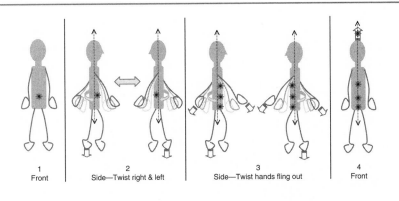

1	2	3	4
Front	Side—Twist right & left	Side—Twist hands fling out	Front

Organizer: Integrative Composure

1. Stand with **feet hip-width** apart **parallel** to each other, eyes toward the horizon.
2. Place **palms together**, with the heels of your hands at your solar plexus, **elbows out to the side**. Notice that the Organizer center turns on.
3. **Press** your palms slightly together and feel the firing of the Driver center. Back off the pressure until you can just barely feel the Driver center activated.
4. **Bend your knees slightly**, dropping your hips straight down. Let your **tailbone relax** and drop slightly, using the image of slotting a zipper at its base.
5. Slowly **straighten your legs**, feeling the **zipper action** up your spine, engaging every center all the way up. Let your hands come up so you're looking at your thumbs and **tilt your head back**. Feel the zipper extend out through the top of your head. **Return your eyes to the horizon**.
6. Do five times. When you're done, walk around and notice a subtle lift to your walk.

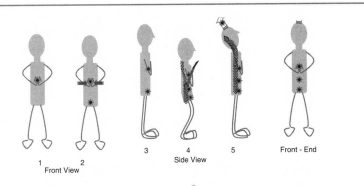

1	2	3	4	5	Front - End
Front View			Side View		

FEBI Validation and Connection to Other Models

The unique feature of the patterns and FEBI is that they link mind and body. However the patterns do have similarities to other temperament models, and the FEBI has been put through the rigors of validation common to the best psychometric instruments. While our research into the patterns and FEBI continues, here is a summary of what we know so far.

VALIDATION AND FACTOR ANALYSIS

In our initial validation study on the FEBI, we had a number of people (n = 120) take both the FEBI and another psychological instrument, the NEO, and compared their answers. We found that the FEBI measured what we wanted it to measure, and correlated predictably with the NEO.

We also did a factor analysis on the FEBI to discern whether the traits associated with each pattern would mathematically factor into distinct and irreducible clusters. This is an important criterion for psychological assessments because it says the instrument is measuring something fundamental, akin to primary colors making up our multicolored personalities. For the past several decades, factor analysis has been used to discern the number and composition of the primary factors in human personality. The models vary, but a number of them converge around four, and show strong correlations to the energy patterns. Even in the so-called five-factor personality model, which is something of a "gold standard" in the business, four of the factors show up much more clearly in factor analysis than does the fifth.

> Fundamental factors of personality are like primary colors; each one is essential and they're not made up from one another.
>
> The energy patterns have this mathematical quality.

Our FEBI factor analysis showed that the energy patterns factored into four clusters. Other models, such as the NEO and HBDI factor into four similar chunks, and we see strong correlation between the FEBI and these instruments.

We're continuing our research on a broader data base, and doing FEBI comparisons to 360 data, as well as to other instruments. We're also taking advantage of the mind-body connectedness of the patterns in studies comparing electromyographic (EMG) recordings of people's patterns with how they answered the FEBI. To our knowledge, this will be the first time a psychometric instrument has been validated using EMG data.

For those of you who know your "type" in terms of some of these other instruments, here are a number of ways that the FEBI results compare and connect.

MBTI

FEBI and MBTI

Similarities:

Driver → Extroversion on task

Collaborator → Extroversion with people

Organizer → Judging (J)

Visionary → Intuitive Perceiving (NP)

Differences:

FEBI emphasizes that we have all patterns and a preference order.

The MBTI[69] measures one's preferences along four scales related to how one gets energy, takes in information, makes decisions, and generally organizes life. Based on where you land on a scale, you're declared to be an ISTJ (i.e., Introvert-Sensing-Thinking-Judger), an ENFP (Extrovert-Intuitive-Feeling-Perceiver), or any of 14 other combinations in between. The MBTI is a wildly popular instrument, more than 60 years old now, and has been more recently refined to tease apart five subscales within each of these scales. A number of these subscales correlate with the four energy patterns, though they're intermixed in the scales of the MBTI. For example, within the scale of Extrovert–

Introvert, different subscales show two distinct ways to be an extrovert: one can be highly initiating on task, which is the energy of the Driver, or one can be highly social and gregarious, which is Collaborator energy.[70] Most of the subscales within the Judger–Perceiver scale trade off Organizer energy with Visionary energy. We've seen that most people landing on the Judger side of that scale are also strong in the Organizer pattern. And people combining big picture thinking with a preference for Perceiver ("NP" types in the MBTI) show up strongly in the Visionary pattern.

Like the MBTI, the FEBI shows preferences, though we focus more on the order among the four fundamental energies (MBTI doesn't compare the relative strengths of its four different scales), and pay particular attention to what's at the bottom. Even if you have strong preferences for some of the patterns, what I hope you always keep in mind is that you have all four, and that if your current preferences aren't working for you, you have freedom of movement.

DISC

FEBI and DISC

Similarities:

Driver → D Scale

Collaborator → mostly I Scale

Organizer and Visionary → some traits in common with S and C scales

Differences:

FEBI is based on four factors, whereas DISC is based on high and low combinations of two scales. As a result, some aspects of the Visionary and Organizer are not well-measured in the DISC.

Like the energy patterns, the DISC[71] model uses four scales on which one can measure low to high. The four DISC scales were derived from the work of William Marston, based on four combinations of two basic factors: whether we're more challenging or submitting and whether we're more active or passive. As you might imagine, an active challenger, what's called the D scale in DISC, lines up quite nicely with the energy of the Driver. While Marston did not explicitly include the body, he described this scale as "pushing toward," which is the same movement essence as the Driver. The I-scale (the active submitter) mostly correlates with the Collaborator, with a few Visionary traits thrown in. Here again, we see two different ways to be "active" correlating with the Driver and Collaborator types of energy. The more passive scales of S and C represent a blend of traits we associate with the Organizer and Visionary. The DISC scales aren't really set up, however, to detect the drifting, leaping imagination of the Visionary or the step-by-step linearity of the Organizer.

A number of popular and important "spinoffs" have come from the DISC, including social styles and the situational leadership model. These related models similarly line up with the FEBI in having something like a Driver pattern, as well as a more user-friendly (i.e., less pushy) way to be extroverted, which maps closely to the Collaborator. The Organizer and Visionary traits are partly split or missing among their other scales.

HBDI

FEBI and HBDI

Similarities:

Driver → mostly Blue

Organizer → mostly Green

Collaborator → mostly Red

Visionary → mostly Yellow

Differences:

FEBI based on movement in the body, whereas HBDI is based on a metaphorical model of the brain.

The Herrmann Brain Dominance Indicator (HBDI)[72] is another four-factor model in which one can score low to very high in four ways of thinking. Developed by Ned Herrmann, this model started from brain physiology and what was known about the more analytical "left-brain" versus the more artistic "right brain." He also distinguished the more conceptual, frontal cortex kind of thinking from the more emotional, midbrain sort of thinking, although he was the first to admit that the model was more metaphorical than physical; the brain is not so neatly compartmentalized in its functioning. The so-called left-brain modes, given the colors Blue and Green in the HBDI, correlate strongly with the energy of the Driver and Organizer, respectively. In some cases, HBDI associates a trait with the Green quadrant that we regard as a Driver characteristic (i.e., more like Blue), but peeling back a layer, this arises from the fact that a word can mean different things to different people. For example the HBDI maps an orientation toward "security" to the Green quadrant. From an energy pattern perspective, "security" is indeed a concern to Green-like Organizers, who find security in knowing which rules to follow. But it's also of big concern to Blue-like Drivers who will structure situations and exert control in order to feel secure.

Likewise, the two right-brain quadrants, given the colors Red and Yellow, closely correlate with the patterns of the Collaborator and Visionary, respectively. Again, we might argue about whether some traits are really confined to just one quadrant on the right-brain side. But the two models agree entirely in the traits mapped to left- and right-brain halves. It's significant that that the HBDI quadrants match the four energy patterns so closely, even though the two models were derived quite differently: the HBDI came from brain functioning, the patterns came from how nerves act on muscles. Their similarities again suggest some common underpinning to brawn, brain, and behavior. The two models are also philosophically aligned in the value of wholeness. Ned Herrmann, the consummate whole and balanced leader, had phenomenal capabilities in both left-brain engineering and right-brain arts, and did much to establish the value of using the "whole brain" in business.

The HBDI has been in use for decades and hundreds of thousands of people have taken it. While more long-term research remains to be done on the FEBI, much of what we've learned from HBDI studies allows us to make some predictions for the energy patterns as well. For example, HBDI data shows that in a large, random sample of people, all four quadrants are equally represented.[73] Among specific professions, however, biases do emerge. For example, a higher percentage of philosophers and psychologists favor the Yellow quadrant (Visionary), whereas mechanical engineers and accountants favor the Green (Organizer). HBDI studies have also looked at the differences between men and women and find no gender bias in the Yellow or Green quadrants. However men are somewhat more represented (55 percent) in the Blue quadrant (akin to our Driver) and the inverse is true of women in the Red quadrant (i.e., Collaborator). While this difference is significant, and we would predict a similar difference for the patterns, there are certainly plenty of Driver women and Collaborator men.

NEO

FEBI and NEO

Similarities:

Driver → subscales for Extroversion on task, achievement striving

Organizer → mostly Conscientiousness

Collaborator → subscales for Agreeableness, positive emotions

Visionary → mostly Openness

Differences:

Several NEO subscales do not correlate to a particular energy pattern.

The NEO[74] is one of the more popular instruments based on the five-factor personality model. The five factors—Neuroticism, Extroversion, Openness, Agreeableness, and Conscientiousness—are each divided into six subscales. It is at the subscale level that we see the clearest correlations to the FEBI[75]. For example, four of the six subscales of Conscientiousness correlate strongly with the Organizer; one of them (Achievement striving) correlates with the Driver. The sixth subscale, Competence, shows little correlation, nor did we think there'd be one; it's possible to be competent in any pattern. The NEO subscales do measure all four patterns, and also have a few scales (like Competence) that don't particularly correlate with any pattern. We even found a surprise bonus in the data showing one correlation we hadn't predicted. One of the Extroversion subscales is Positive Emotions, and I initially thought one could be positive or optimistic in any pattern. But the correlation data showed that Collaborators really are more optimistic, reminding me of a quote my husband often uses: "Optimists and pessimists agree on one thing: Optimists have better lives."

Additional Resources

Visit www.movetogreatness.com for more information and resources, where you can:

- Download worksheets to design a practice (chapter 7), handle conflict (chapter 8), diagnose a team or organization (chapter 9), or deepen your practice (chapter 10);
- Learn how you can take the FEBI online or set up the FEBI for your group or organization;
- Find out about FEBI-based programs, products, and services;
- See the schedule of *Move to Greatness* workshops and public events;
- Learn how, if you're a coach or trainer, you can become certified in the FEBI.

Visit www.moves4greatness.com for more information on the Coordination Patterns™, where you can:

- Find out more about Coordination Pattern training or how to become a registered Coordination Pattern trainer;
- Learn about other applied uses of the patterns and additional pattern exercises.

Endnotes

CHAPTER 1

1. Miller, Jody. 2005. "Get a Life," *FORTUNE*, November 28.
2. Useem, Jerry. 2006. "Secrets of Greatness," *FORTUNE*, March 20.
3. Yerkes, R.M. & Dodson, J.D. 1909. " The relation of strength of stimulus to rapidity of habit-formation." *Journal of Comparative Neurology and Psychology*, 18, 459–482.
4. Loehr, J. and Schwartz, T. 2003. *The Power of Full Engagement*. NY, Simon & Schuster.
5. Wood, John. 2006. *Leaving Microsoft to Change the World*. NY, Collins.
6. The quality of letting go, openness and entering a flow condition is the aspect of yoga that exercises the Visionary pattern. You'll see that yoga is also good for developing the Organizer in its quiet composure and holding of postures.
7. This is similar to the pattern of pushing against identified by Karen Horney and later incorporated as the Directive, Dominance or "D" style of the "DiSC" temperament model. See Martson, William. 1928. *Emotions of Normal People*. (Taylor and Francis, Ltd.) and Geier, John. 1992. *DiSC Personal Profile System* (Geier Learning Systems). Geier, John. 1992. Coordination Patterns calls this the pattern of Thrust. Rathbone's original term for this pattern was Resistor, as it arises from the firing of the antagonist muscle first followed by the agonist, which can be thought of as applying the brakes and then gunning the engine. The effect in passive movement, such as Rathbone's arm rotation test for these patterns, is one of constant resistance.
8. Shape is the name given to this pattern in the Coordination Patterns schema. Rathbone originally called this pattern the "Posturor."
9. McCoy, Kevin. 2006. "Merck CEO Sets Sights on Change." *USA Today*, February 27.
10. "Perceverator was the name Rathbone initially gave to this pattern, as it arose from the back-and-forth firing of the agonist/antagonist muscle pair. See Rathbone, Josephine. 1936. *Residual Neuromuscular Hypertension*.

NY, Bureau of Publication, Columbia University. In Coordination Pattern terms, this is the pattern of Swing.

11. Rathbone originally termed this pattern the "Assistor" as it arises from the firing of the agonist first—i.e., the "engine" muscle. Moving without the initial resistance of antagonist muscle firing (e.g., the "brake") creates a quality of effortlessness in active movement, or a sense of assisting the motion in passive movement. In Coordination Pattern terminology, this is the pattern of Hang.

12. A blue ocean strategy creates uncontested new markets, in contrast to competing in the shark infested waters—i.e., "red" oceans—of the existing paradigm. See Kim. W. C. and Mauborgne, R. 2005. *Blue Ocean Strategy*. Boston: HBS Press.

CHAPTER 2

13. Rathbone, Josephine. 1936. *Residual Neuromuscular Hypertension*. NY, Bureau of Publication, Columbia University.

14. Rathbone used different names for the patterns. She called them: Resistor (Driver), Posturor (Organizer), Perceverator (Collaborator) and Assistor (Visionary).

15. Hunt, Valerie and Weber, Mary. 1964. "Validation of the Rathbone Manual Tension Test for Muscular Activity," *Archives of Physical Medicine and Rehabilitation*. 45:525–529.

16. See, for example, Hebb, D. O. 1949. *The Organization of Behavior*. NY: Wiley, and Edelman, Gerald. 1987. *Neural Darwinism*. NY: Basic Books.

17. Kestenberg, Judith and Sossin, Mark. 1977. *Role of Movement Patterns in Development*. NY: Dance Notation Bureau.

18. The ages here are typical, but approximate, and align with the research of Piaget, Rogers and others. See, for example, Gruber, H. and Voneche, J. eds. 1977. *The Essential Piaget*. New York: Basic Books; Rogers, C. 1961. *On Becoming a Person*. Boston: Houghton Miflin.

19. Focus Energy Balance Indicator and FEBI are trademarks of Focus Leadership, LLC.

20. Some people find it easier or more useful to assign a range to some of the mini FEBI questions, rather than a single answer. If you'd like to answer with a range, go ahead.

21. Some researchers distinguish "temperament," referring to our intrinsic nature, from "personality," which speaks more broadly to how we behave on the outside. Since this distinction is not necessary for our pur-

poses—we're more interested in the integration of inside and out—I'm using the two words interchangeably.

22. See, for example, *The Future of The Body*, by Michael Murphy (CA: Tarcher, 1992) for a compendium of research around mind and body interconnectedness.

CHAPTER 3

23. This pushing posture to the world was also identified by Karen Horney as one of the fundamental neuroses in human personality and by William Martson as a fundamental temperament factor in the DISC.

24. Dell, Michael with Fredman, Catherine. 1999. *Direct from Dell*. NY, HarperBusiness.

25. Interview (2007), "Profile: Michael Dell." *PQR*, Spring.

26. Breen, B. (2004), "Living in Dell Time." *Fast Company*, Issue 88, November.

27. Serwer, A. 2006. "The Education of Michael Dell." *FORTUNE*, March 7.

28. Elkind, Peter. 2005. "Satan or Savior." *FORTUNE*, November 26.

29. Kramer, Rod. 2006. "The Great Intimidators." *Harvard Business Review*, February.

30. Seller, P. 2006. "Star Power." *FORTUNE*, February 6.

31. Loehr, Jim and Schwartz, Tony. 2003. *The Power of Full Engagement*. NY: Simon & Schuster.

32. Kramer, Rod, op. cit.

CHAPTER 4

33. He later added "Safety first and foremost," lest he be misunderstood as suggesting that NASA should compromise safety. Despite tragic and ultra-memorable accidents, safety is ground into every part of NASA's culture. But similar to how it manages missions and programs, NASA can get a lot of small stuff right and still lose some big ones.

34. See Cameron, J. 1992. *The Artist's Way*. New York: Tarcher/Putnam.

35. Vickers, M. *"The Prince of Citi."* *FORTUNE*, March 2.

36. "Making the Trains Run on Time." 2006. *The Economist*, February 18.

37. Collins, Jim. 2001. *Good to Great*. NY: HarperCollins.

38. Shaw, Robert Bruce. 1997. *Trust in the Balance*. San Francisco: Jossey Bass.

39. McGinn, Daniel. 2006. "How She Does It." *Fast Company*, April.

40. Useem, Jerry. 2006. "Secrets of Greatness." *FORTUNE*, March 20.

41. Meditation is not a purely Organizer practice by any means. But it develops and uses the Organizer's calm shape as something of a container for the internal combustion of the ego.

CHAPTER 5

42. Harris, John. 2006. *The Survivor: Bill Clinton in the White House*. NY: Random House.
43. As part of our FEBI validation research, we had a number of people take the FEBI, as well as another psychological instrument, the NEO-PI-R, which has a subscale for positive emotions. People who scored highly in the positive emotion category also scored highly in the Collaborator pattern. There was no significant correlation between positive emotions and the other three patterns.
44. Sarasohn, Lisa. 2006. *The Woman's Belly Book*. Novato, CA: New World Library.
45. Serwer, Andy. 2004. "The Hottest Thing in the Sky." *FORTUNE*, March 8.
46. Ibid.
47. Schlender, Brent. 2006. "Pixar's Magic Man." *FORTUNE*, May 29.
48. Craig, Susan and Kelly, Kate. 2004. "NYSE Chief Has Balancing Act." *The Wall Street Journal*, February 3.
49. Thiagarajan, Sivasailan and Parker, Glenn. 1999. *Teamwork and Teamplay*. San Francisco, CA: Jossey-Bass/Pfeiffer.

CHAPTER 6

50. Useem, Jerry. 2006. "Making Your Work Work For You." *FORTUNE*, March 20.
51. Heifetz, Ronald. 1994. *Leadership without Easy Answers*. Boston: Harvard University Press.

CHAPTER 7

52. Goldsmith, M. and Morgan, H. 2004. "Leadership is a Contact Sport." *Strategy+Business*, Fall, pp. 70–79.
53. Deep bodywork merits an entire book of its own, and I cannot praise it highly enough. If you'd like to know more, see *Bodytherapy* by William

Leigh (Vancouver, Water Margin, 1989) or check out the website of a master practitioner at www.integralbodywork.com.

54. Coordination Pattern training is also a great approach to deepening your work with the body. For more information, see Betsy's website at www.moves4greatness.com.

CHAPTER 8

55. See, for example, Kotter, J. and Cohen, D. 2002. *The Heart of Change*. Boston: Harvard Business School Press.

56. Kirpatrick, David. 2006. "Rising Star: Kevin Johnson, Microsoft." *FORTUNE*, January 24.

57. See, for example, Pert, Candace. 1997. *Molecules of Emotion*. New York: Simon & Schuster, or Hebb, D.O. 1949. *Organization of Behavior*. New York: Wiley.

58. Clarke, B. and Crossland, R. 2002. *The Leader's Voice*. New York: Select Books.

59. Pert, Candace, op.cit.

CHAPTER 9

60. This life cycle was first coined by Bruce Tuckman in 1965. He later added a 5th stage of adjourning and transforming.

61. See, for example, Katzenbach and Smith, op.cit., Katzenbach, J. 1998. *Teams at the Top*. Boston: Harvard Business School Press, Lencioni, P. 2002. *5 Dysfunctions of a Team*. San Francisco: Jossey Bass.

62. See, for example, Thiagarajan, S. and Parker, G. 1999. Teamwork and Teamplay. San Francisco: Jossey Bass.

63. Brown, S and Eisenhardt, K 1998. *Competing on the Edge: Strategy as Structured Chaos*. Boston: Harvard Business School Press.

64. Lashinsky, Adam. 2006. "Chaos by Design." *FORTUNE*, October 2.

65. Gerstner, L., Jr. 2003. *Who Says Elephants Can't Dance?* NY: Collins.

66. Katzenbach and Smith, op.cit.

CHAPTER 10

67. Kim, W. C., and Mauborgne, R. 2005. *Blue Ocean Strategy*. Boston, Harvard Business School Publishing.

68. Benoit, Hubert. 1990. *Zen and the Psychology of Transformation.* Rochester, VT: Inner Traditions International.

APPENDICES

69. Briggs Myers, Isabel. 1998. *Introduction to Type.* Consulting Psychologists Press, 6th Edition.
70. Indeed, these two ways to be an extrovert are identified by separate subscales in the more refined version of MBTI Step 2.
71. Marston, William. 1928. *Emotions of Normal People.* Taylor and Francis, Ltd., Geier, John. 1992. *DiSC Personal Profile System.* Geier Learning Systems.
72. Herrmann, Ned. 1989. *The Creative Brain.* Lake Lure, NC:The Ned Herrmann Group.
73. Herrmann, Ned. 1996. *The Whole Brain Business Book* NY: McGraw-Hill.
74. Costa, Paul. and McRae, Robert. 1985. *The NEO Personality Inventory.* Odessa, FL: Psychological Assessment Resources.
75. We asked a number of people (n = 120) to take both the FEBI and the NEO and compared their answers. We found clear and significant (> .4) correlations between the energy patterns and every one of the subscales we predicted they'd correlate with.

About the Authors

When **Ginny Whitelaw** was in seventh grade, she wrote to the National Aeronautics and Space Administration (NASA) asking what courses she should take in school to best prepare for becoming an astronaut. Sixteen years later she was working at NASA, though her path led to senior management rather than space. She ended up leading the overhaul in the way the International Space Station was developed and managed, eventually becoming Deputy Manager for Integration of the Space Station Program, and receiving NASA's Exceptional Service Medal for her efforts.

Ginny now runs her own company, Focus Leadership, LLC, focusing on the development of whole and balanced leaders. A biophysicist by training, she combines a rich scientific background with her own senior leadership experience, as well as 30 years of training in Zen and martial arts. For many years she has been an executive coach, faculty member, and program director with Oliver Wyman's Delta Executive Learning Center. She has also served as adjunct faculty to Columbia University's senior executive program.

Dr. Whitelaw has taught and coached leaders in some of the world's top companies, including Merck, Avon, Dell, XL Capital, Sprint, Cemex, EMC, Novartis, Medtronic, Marsh, and Bank of America. She also has small and non-profit organization leadership experience, having founded and run four companies, including two major training centers for Zen and Aikido. She is a Zen priest, a fifth-degree black belt in Aikido, and teaches Zen meditation alongside her work as a management educator and executive coach.

Ginny is a frequent speaker at professional conferences and events with such groups as the American Society for Training and Development and the Professional Coaches and Mentors Association. Together with Mark Kiefaber, she developed the Focus Energy Balance Indicator™ (FEBI™), a unique personality assessment interlinking mind, body, and behavior. She holds a Ph.D. in biophysics from the University of Chicago, as well as a B.S. in physics and a B.A. in philosophy from Michigan State University.

 **Betsy Wetzig**, dancer, choreographer, and teacher, is the originator and director of Coordination Pattern™ training, which has conducted workshops throughout the United States, Europe, and Australia for more than 30 years. Betsy also developed applications of the Coordination Patterns to Full Potential Movement and (with Dr. Patricia Pinciotti) Full Potential Learning™.

Betsy's professional training included a variety of modem dance, ballet, and improvisational techniques, including a three-year scholarship with Martha Graham's Company Class, and performances with such notables as Jose Limone, Helen McGehee, Ruth Currier, and Art Bauman. She taught with Art Bauman at the Dance Theater Workshop in New York City and the American Dance Festival. Betsy was awarded a fellowship from the National Endowment for the Arts in choreography and has also received a number of other state and private foundation grants. Always interested in choreography and the essence of dance, she directed the Wetzig Dance Company from 1971-82, and before that, Sound Shapes, an improvisational group of dancers and musicians. Both endeavors were strongly influenced by her research into the Coordination Patterns.

She is currently a principle presenter at the Twin Ponds Integrative Health Center in Pennsylvania, where she also teaches Coordination Pattern Trainer certification courses. For many years, she taught movement, dance, and education courses at Cedar Crest College, PA and, before that, Upsala College, NJ. She was a founding member of the Mind-Body Collaborative Partnership, through which her workshops are presented to such groups as the American Massage Therapy Association, Congress on Research in Dance, American Dance Therapy Association, and International Alliance for Learning, as well as to individual businesses, educational institutes, school districts, and developmental groups.

Betsy graduated with a B.A. in Dance from Randolph-Macon Women's College in Virginia.

Index